T0361759

"Having served more than forty years with the Department of State, I experienced firsthand the discovery of clandestine listening devices in Moscow, the armoring of cars, and installing protective devices and barriers to keep our diplomats and secrets safe. During every step of that journey, I was accompanied by U.S. Navy Seabees. *Detachment November* immediately brought me back to relive the incredible history between the Foreign Service Officers and Seabees of the Diplomatic Security Service that continues today."

—**John Bainbridge,** former Director of the Office of Security Technology, Bureau of Diplomatic Security

"The history of the Diplomatic Security Service is not complete without the dynamic involvement of the U.S. Navy Seabees since 1964. Through captivating storytelling of adventures in the far reaches of the world, *Detachment November* does justice to the unheralded men and women of the Diplomatic Security Service that advance U.S. foreign policy, safeguard national security interests, and further diplomacy around the world."

—**Ambassador Eric Boswell,** former Assistant Secretary of State for Diplomatic Security, 1996-1998 and 2008-2012

"Throughout my career, it was the norm that when we visited an overseas post, U.S. embassy workers were unanimous in exclaiming: "Yay! The Seabees are here!" I am extremely pleased that Timothy Dahms has finally put this story to print. From Cold War drama to more recent security challenges, Timothy Dahms's well-written and extensively researched review of this partnership for national security comprehensively memorializes the stories and successes that, until now, have been limited to lore, war stories related between colleagues, and a disparate smattering of official documents."

—**John Fitzsimmons,** former Deputy Assistant Secretary of State and Assistant Director, Countermeasures Directorate, Bureau of Diplomatic Security

"The U.S. Navy Civil Engineer Corps (CEC) and Seabees have a history of superlative commissioned and non-commissioned officers that have defined our legacy. *Detachment November* illustrates the true character of our community by shining light on a less visible mission essential to our nation's stature and global leadership. The fine men and women of the Department of State Naval Support Unit have spread the CEC and Seabee legacy worldwide for more than half a century. And only now, through extensive research and personal experience, Timothy Dahms leads us through the complete story of U.S. Navy Seabees in Diplomatic Security!"

—**RADM Bret Muilenburg,** CEC, USN, (ret.) 44th Commander of Naval Facilities Engineering Systems Command and Chief of Civil Engineers

"George Washington said, 'Discipline . . . makes small numbers formidable; it procures success to the weak and esteem to all;' U.S. Navy Seabees attached to the Naval Support Unit, State Department, are the epitome of this sentiment, performing well beyond expectations and what their numbers would suggest possible. Their ubiquitous support to a worldwide mission ensures some of the most sensitive diplomatic missions are provided with the requisite security to keep our secrets and our personnel safe. From my own firsthand knowledge working with Seabees while assigned to the U.S. Embassy in Moscow, Russia, I can unequivocally say that *Detachment November* provides a rare and compelling look into an operational area that is often overlooked but indispensable to the United States' interests and objectives around the globe."

—**MCPON Russell Smith,** USN, (ret.) 15th Master Chief Petty Officer of the Navy

"A Chief's Mess cannot be tighter than when scattered to all corners of the world. The Seabees of Naval Support Unit, State Department, have the privilege to lead and impact the lives of others in parts of the world that others may never see. I would challenge any Seabee to seek out special duty assignments to grow and develop in unfamiliar territory to lead and represent amongst the many communities of our great Navy. Bringing this diverse experience back to the Naval Construction Force better prepares us all to build and fight!"

—**FORCM Percy Trent,** USN, (ret.) 17th Force Master Chief of the Seabees

DETACHMENT
NOVEMBER

www.amplifypublishinggroup.com

Detachment November: The Unclassified Story of U.S. Navy Seabees in Diplomatic Security

For more information, please contact:
Amplify Publishing, an imprint of Amplify Publishing Group
620 Herndon Parkway, Suite 220
Herndon, VA 20170
info@amplifypublishing.com

Library of Congress Control Number: 2024918318

CPSIA Code: PRV0225A

ISBN-13: 979-8-89138-406-4

Printed in the United States

For the thousands of men and women serving
behind the scenes in Naval Support Unit and the
Diplomatic Security Service who courageously keep
Americans safe well beyond our shores.

DETACHMENT NOVEMBER

The Unclassified Story of U.S. Navy Seabees in Diplomatic Security

TIMOTHY DAHMS

an imprint of Amplify Publishing Group

Contents

List of Figures xiii

Acronyms xv

Preface xxiii

PART I. SETTING A FOUNDATION

1 | The Department of State,
Office of Security Technology 3

2 | The United States Navy Seabees 15

3 | The Cold War and Espionage 23

4 | A Partnership Begins 33

PART II. BUILDING A LEGACY

5 | The Naval Support Unit 39

6 | A Particular Set of Skills 53

7 | The Early Years (1964-1982) 63

8 | A Changing Environment (1983-2000) 79

9 | A New Age (2001-Present) 109

PART III. DIPLOMACY AT WORK

10 Officer In Charge and
    Assistant Officer In Charge 135

11 Global Leadership 147

12 Western Hemisphere Affairs 165

13 Europe 175

14 Southern Europe 191

15 Near East Affairs 199

16 Africa 217

17 South Central Asia 229

18 East Asia Pacific 239

19 A Global Pandemic 249

20 Havana Syndrome 255

Conclusion........................... 259
Acknowledgments...................... 261
History of Unit Commendations....... 263
List of OICs......................... 264
List of AOICs........................ 265
Endnotes............................. 267
Index................................ 281
About the Author..................... 291

List of Figures

1. Admiral Ben Moreell, "Father of the U.S. Navy Seabees." Photo courtesy of Naval History and Heritage Command. 17

2. The NAVFAC Organizational Chart for Echelon II and III commands per the Standard Navy Distribution List. 40

3. History of NSU personnel allowance. 42

4. NSU Seabees unpacking materials brought to recover from the Dar es Salaam embassy bombing. Photo courtesy of Steve Fox. 104

5. SECSTATE Madeleine Albright meets NSU team in Dar es Salaam, Tanzania. Photo courtesy of Carmelo Melendez. 105

6. DS team overseeing Antonov AH-124-100 loading for delivery to Kabul. Photo courtesy of Diplomatic Security. 112

7. CE2 Chris Beck attempting to keep an impala away on the Presidential Compound. Photo courtesy of Diplomatic Security. 113

8. DS team photographed with President Karzai. Photo courtesy of Diplomatic Security. 114

9. The U.S. Navy DOS badge. Photo courtesy of the author. 140

Acronyms

ABHC	Aviation Boatswain's Mate Aircraft Handler Chief
AO	Area of Operations
AOIC	Assistant Officer in Charge
AQI	Air Quality Index
ASEAN	Association of Southeast Asian Nations
AU	African Union
AWOL	Absent Without Leave
BU1	Builder First Class Petty Officer
BUPERS	Bureau of Naval Personnel
CAA	Controlled Access Areas
CBMU	Construction Battalion Maintenance Unit
CBO	Seabee Office
CCIR	Commander's Critical Information Request
CDC	Centers for Disease Control and Prevention
CEC	Civil Engineer Corps
CG	Consular General
CIA	Central Intelligence Agency
CINCPAC	Commander in Chief, U.S. Pacific Command

CMC	Command Master Chief
CMP	Countermeasures Program
CMR	Chief of Mission Residence
CO	Commanding Officer
CONSEC	Construction Security Surveillance
CPA	Coalition Provisional Authority
CPOIC	Chief Petty Officer In Charge
CTS	Cyber and Technology Security
DATT	Defense Attache
DCM	Deputy Chief of Mission
DEA	Drug Enforcement Administration
DFOW	Definable Feature of Work
DHS	Department of Homeland Security
DK	Disbursing Clerk
DNI	Director of National Intelligence
DOD	Department of Defense
DON	Department of the Navy
DOS	Department of State
DS	Diplomatic Security
DSS	Diplomatic Security Service
EA	Engineering Aide
EBO	Embassy Branch Office
EOD	Explosive Ordnance Disposal
ESC	Engineering Services Center
ESO	Engineering Services Offices
ETRI	Expanded Threat Reduction Initiative
EU	European Union

EXWC	Naval Facilities Engineering and Expeditionary Warfare Center
FBI	Federal Bureau of Investigation
FBO	Foreign Building Operations
FE/BR	Force Entry/ Ballistic Resistant
FEMA	Federal Emergency Management Agency
FITREP	Fitness Report
FRC	Florida Regional Center
FSB	Federal Security Service (translated)
FSE	Facility Services Engineering
GFM	Global Force Management
GTMO	Guantanamo Bay, Cuba
HA/DR	Humanitarian Assistance/Disaster Relief
HDSVS	High-Definition Secure Video Systems
IED	Improvised Explosive Device
IMF	International Monetary Fund
INDOPACOM	Indo-Pacific Command
ISIC	Immediate Superior in Command
ISIL	Islamic State of Iraq and the Levant
ISIS	Islamic State of Iraq and Syria
KGB	Committee for State Security (translated)
LAA	Limited Access Areas
LAV	Light Armoring Vehicle
LPO	Leading Petty Officer
LT	Lieutenant
LCDR	Lieutenant Commander

LTJG	Lieutenant Junior Grade
MCESG	Marine Corps Embassy Security Group
MCMAP	Marine Corps Martial Arts Program
MEBCO	Moscow Embassy Building Control Office
MNF-I	Multi-National Force-Iraq
MOA	Memorandum of Agreement
MRE	Meals Ready to Eat
MUSE	Mobile Utilities Support Equipment
NATO	North Atlantic Treaty Organization
NAVFAC	Naval Facilities Engineering Systems Command
NBG	Naval Beach Group
NCC	Navy Crane Center
NCG	Naval Construction Group
NEC	Navy Enlisted Classification
NECC	Navy Expeditionary Combat Command
NGA	National Geospatial-Intelligence Agency
NMCB	Naval Mobile Construction Battalion
NOB	New Office Buildings
NRO	National Reconnaissance Office
NSA	National Security Agency
NSU	Naval Support Unit
NUC	Navy Unit Commendation
NWU	Navy Working Uniform
OBO	Overseas Building Operations
OIC	Officer in Charge
OPS	Operations Officer

OSB	Overseas Support Branch
OSD	Office of the Secretary of Defense
OSPB	Overseas Security Policy Board
PACOM	Pacific Command
PCC	Post Communication Center
POE	Principal Operating Environments
PME	Project Management Execution
Prime BEEF	Prime Base Engineer Emergency Force
PWD	Public Works Department
QAL	Quality Assurance and Liaison Branch
RCSO	Regional Cybersecurity Officer
RDSE	Regional Director for Security Engineering
RED HORSE	Rapid Engineer Deployable Heavy Operations Repair Squadron Engineer
ROC	Required Operational Capabilities
RSO	Regional Security Officer
RTO	Regional Technical Office
SCIF	Sensitive Compartmented Information Facility
SDA	State Department Apartments
SEAL	Sea, Air, and Land
SECDEF	Secretary of Defense
SECNAV	Secretary of the Navy
SECSTATE	Secretary of State
SEL	Senior Enlisted Leader
SEO	Security Engineering Officer

SES	Security Engineering Services
SIM	Systems Integration Monitoring
SMA	Senior Military Advisor
SME	Subject Matter Expert
SSI	Security Systems Integration
ST	Office of Security Technology
STO	Security Technology Operations
STS	Security Technical Specialist
SY	Office of Security
TDY	Temporary Duty
TMF	Temporary Mission Facility
TNC	Transitional National Council
TSA	Transportation Security Administration
TSC	Transitional National Council
TSO	Technical Security Office
TSS	Technical Security System
TS-SCI	Top Secret Sensitive Compartmented Information
TSU	Technical Security Upgrade
UA	Unauthorized Absence
UAS	Unmanned Aerial Systems
UCT	Underwater Construction Team
UN	United Nations
UNVIE	United States Mission to International Organizations in Vienna
UPS	Uninterrupted Power Supply
USAID	United States Agency for International Development

USDA	United States Department of Agriculture
USO	United Service Organizations
USSR	Union of Soviet Socialist Republics
WHA	Western Hemisphere Affairs
WHMO	White House Military Office

Preface

The Naval Support Unit (NSU) of the Department of State (DOS) has often been given the moniker "the Navy's best kept secret" by those in the unit. This is both a badge of honor as well as testament to the men and women of the U.S. Navy Seabees who have served in the NSU for decades. Today, the Seabee force stands at approximately 10,000 enlisted and 1,800 officers, both active and reserve duty. This small force has nearly as many active-duty assignments in special programs as it does in regular assignments. The Seabees have been revered and respected for their capabilities and "Can Do" attitude since their inception in 1942, as the following quotes indicate.

"The only trouble with your Seabees is I don't have enough of them!" This was General Douglas MacArthur's response to Admiral Ben Moreell when asked how the Seabees were performing during the Pacific-island hopping campaign during WWII.

"The difficult we do at once; the impossible takes a little bit longer." Anonymous quote capturing the essence of the Seabees "Can Do" mentality.

"So, when we reach the 'Isle of Japan' with our caps at a jaunty tilt, we'll enter the city of Tokyo on the roads the Seabees built." A sign

posted by the 3rd Marine Division, 2nd Raiders Battalion on Bougainville Island, Papua New Guinea during World War II (WWII). U.S. Marines recognized early on in WWII that without the Seabees paving airfields and laying roads across the many captured Pacific Islands, the United States would have never been able to attack Japan's islands and bring an end to the war.

Since March 5, 1942, the Seabees have been the force of choice for expeditionary construction. They have continuously built upon this legacy, forged in war, to become the hard-nosed but soft-hearted Seabees of today. However, today, it's more difficult to call up the Seabees, as a result of the modern Global Force Management (GFM) system used by the Department of Defense (DOD). This system enables forces from any branch that holds the Required Operational Capabilities (ROC) for the Projected Operational Environment (POE) to be tasked to meet mission-support requests.

As the former Officer in Charge of NSU from 2018 to 2021, in this book, I will tell the story of the Seabees, who have been attached to the DOS since the mid-1960s and whose motivation and dedication had an immediate impact on every mission. In addition to its demonstrable values, i.e., their skills, as exemplified with the Seabee's mission at Camp David, NSU and the Seabees have owned the construction security surveillance mission for decades, and senior DOS officials have never shown any intent to relieve them of this significant responsibility.

The unit's internal view that it's the best-kept secret in the navy is because very few people know NSU exists. For example, in 2018, Admiral Harry Harris, the former Commander of U.S. Pacific Command (PACOM), now known as the U.S. Indonesia Pacific Command (INDOPACOM), learned he had a U.S. Navy Seabee at an embassy within his Area of Operations (AO) only shortly before he retired with forty years of service. Knowing that if there is one Seabee, there's probably more, he became curious about how many more were in his AO.

He inquired with Rear Admiral John Korka, Commander for Naval Facilities Engineering Systems Command (NAVFAC) for the Pacific and the U.S. Pacific Fleet Civil Engineer. He wanted to know how many Seabees were located at embassies in PACOM. This led to an inquiry to Lieutenant Adam Gerlach, NSU Officer In Charge (OIC) at the time, who was asked to provide the number of NSU Seabees in the Pacific. Admiral Harris later served as the U.S. Ambassador to South Korea in Seoul, and although currently no Seabees are stationed in Seoul, NSU does service the post regularly.

When I have spoken to civilians within our Immediate Superior in Command (ISIC), they seldom have a full comprehension of what NSU does, or even know that we fall under the NAVFAC organization. NSU comes in and out of the picture quickly to accomplish its mission, leaving again before anyone knows they were there. The Navy has SEALs, Explosive Ordnance Disposal (EOD) technicians, Coastal Riverine Groups (CRG), among others, that you may have learned about in the media or via heroic portrayals by Hollywood. The Seabees, however, have moved through history less visibly, appearing in the background of every major engagement since WWII, and witnessing many major historical events at embassies and consulates throughout the world since 1964.

There was one movie about the shadowy force. Starring John Wayne, the picture was titled *The Fighting Seabees* (1944), and it dramatized the story of the creation of the Seabees and their vital role in WWII. Since then, the Seabees have only been written about sparingly. In 2017, retired Rear Admiral Michael Giorgione published *Inside Camp David*, which gave a firsthand account of the Seabees at the presidential retreat, Camp David. And in 2019, *The Battalion Artist* was published, which is a collection of sketches by a Seabee drawn during his deployment across the Pacific in WWII. Finally, there is an overlooked self-published book called *Navy Seabees: Mission Tanzania* by former Utilitiesman First Class Petty Officer (UT1) James Renken, which is about the terrorist attacks at the U.S. Embassies in Tanzania and Kenya and the following NSU response. The occasional article in a news magazine or newspaper will highlight what the Seabees have accomplished, but it is often relegated to the back pages.

I've always been interested in history. I read a lot of biographies and was inspired by David McCullough to document everything from the most mundane moments of my life to major decisions and events that were to determine where I would end up. On my thirtieth birthday, I began a daily journal on the off chance that I might someday participate in something worth writing about. It would capture many incredible stories and events I experienced while serving as the OIC for NSU beginning in 2018.

Admiral Ben Moreell, the "Father of the Seabees" and Civil Engineer Corps Officer, had no patience for those who waited for work to come to them and once told a friend, "If you can't find enough work to keep busy, you can always write a book."[9] In that spirit, I began writing this book in the middle of the COVID-19 pandemic, in June 2020, when I had hours of free time on my hands during lockdown. I did not set out to write a book about the unit in the beginning of my tour. However, with access to historical documents and the people with stories and experiences to share, the book seemed to come together effortlessly from the day I sat down and started writing. Once I had gotten past a certain point and started telling friends, family, and coworkers what I had started, I knew I had to finish.

I intend to tell the story of the NSU Seabees and how this unit, which I had the privilege of leading for three years, was the most rewarding and challenging personal and professional experience of my life. Now it is my honor to share the history and achievements of these "Professionals Around the World," and show more people that the NSU Seabees are some of the finest Sailors in the U.S. Navy. The best kept secret is out!

PART I

Setting a Foundation

1

The Department of State,

Office of Security Technology

The Department of State (DOS) is one of the oldest departments in the executive branch of the U.S. government, established in 1789 as the Department of Foreign Affairs. DOS's first Secretary of State was Thomas Jefferson, who served from 1790–1793. He was appointed after serving as the Minister to France. Succeeding him as Secretary of State was a veritable "who's-who" of Americans: Timothy Pickering, John Marshall, James Madison, James Monroe, John Quincy Adams, and many more. The ability of these first diplomats to promote American independence and secure loans to fight the British in the Revolutionary War, and later the War of 1812, was critical for the survival of the United States of America's mission to defend life, liberty, and the pursuit of happiness.

Throughout most of the nineteenth century, most Americans seldom traveled abroad. The risk of crossing the Atlantic was substantial. Not until after the Industrial Revolution and the growth of steam power did Americans set out to the far corners of the world in greater numbers. However, even before that time, American ships regularly carried goods back and forth from European ports, so U.S.

consulates had been established in cities where trade with American ships was occurring. The consul officers were directed to record the number of American ships entering the local port, report political and commercial developments within the city, as well as any preparations for war by the host nation. Appointed consuls and vice consuls drew their income from private trade and official services. As the amount of trade and responsibility grew in each port city, additional consular agents were appointed to reside in other large cities inside the respective countries.

In addition to facilitating trade, consuls communicated any hazards to arriving Americans regarding their safety and the security of their goods or ships at the ports. At first, consuls mostly dealt with stranded American sailors or ships needing return passage.[1] However, this role expanded into the security role that consulates continue to hold today, providing refuge, protection, and support for Americans abroad in times of need, as well as visa and passport assistance for those traveling to the United States.

The broad use of visas did not become mainstream until the Immigration Act of 1924 (Johnson-Reed Act or Asian Exclusion Act). This legislation, following the global upheaval of World War I, limited the number of immigrants to the United States and led to the creation of U.S. Border Control. Furthermore, the act required immigrants to have a visa issued by a U.S. consulate overseas. The advancement of photographs and printing technologies improved the design and processing of these documents to prevent counterfeiting.

The first embassies of the United States were simply large homes that consuls worked from. As the demand grew to provide more services to Americans living or traveling abroad, the consular facilities quickly became insufficient. The original locations often became Chief of Mission Residences (CMR), and office buildings were erected or purchased nearby. The Chief of Mission holds the rank of Ambassador, which is the role filled by the most senior U.S. official in a foreign country. Notable Chiefs of Mission, located in places like France, the United Kingdom, and the Netherlands, include Benjamin Franklin, Robert Livingston, John Adams, and Thomas Pinckney to name a few.[1] These days, approximately 40 percent of U.S. Ambassadors are political appointees, and the remainder are personnel from the ranks of the U.S. Foreign Service.[2] The "mission" in this context refers to the particular work done in each country. Sometimes there are multiple missions in one country, requiring multiple Ambassadors. However, there is only one Chief of Mission for each country where the United States maintains diplomatic relations.

As the years went by, staff and missions grew. Other organizations and agencies within the federal government began seeking space in the embassies to perform their overseas work. Some of these entities include United States Agency for International Development (USAID); the U.S. Department of Agriculture (USDA); DOD; Department of Justice, represented by the offices of the Drug Enforcement Administration (DEA) and the Federal Bureau of Investigation (FBI); Department of the Treasury; Department of Homeland Security (DHS), to include the Transportation Security Administration (TSA); and the Centers for Disease Control and Prevention (CDC). This growth often coincided with significant historical events in each of the locations, such as wars, famine, disease outbreaks, or natural disasters.

The size of the DOS footprint and diplomatic presence in countries across the world correlates to the strength of the relationship between the United States and those countries, the number of missions in a country, and how many ex-patriots live there. Places such as Germany, Japan, Thailand, Mexico, Switzerland, and Austria are a few of these countries where the United States has posted large numbers of personnel. Some of the other missions that are at embassies include the United Nations (UN), European Union (EU), North Atlantic

Treaty Organization (NATO), Association of Southeast Asian Nations (ASEAN), African Union (AU), International Monetary Fund (IMF), and the World Bank. As an example, the U.S. Mission to International Organizations in Vienna (UNVIE) participates in or is a member of the following organizations with the UN: International Atomic Energy Agency; the UN Office on Drugs and Crime; the Preparatory Commission of the Comprehensive Nuclear-Test-Ban Treaty Organization; the UN Office of Outer Space Affairs; the UN Commission on International Trade Law; the International Narcotics Control Board; and the UN Industrial Development Organization.[3]

As a result of a growing presence overseas and the unfortunate reality of state failures and war, facilities had to become more secure. The security of an embassy and its personnel serving abroad is the overall responsibility of the Chief of Mission. Today, the Regional Security Officer (RSO) is the Foreign Service Officer who carries out the daily burden of making that security a reality. However, it was not until 1916, during WWI, that the first iteration of the Diplomatic Security Service originated.[4] Prior to WWI, most DOS work overseas was for building trade relationships, work that was carried out by small staffs of often less than twenty-five. Personal security and the containment of sensitive information was the individual's responsibility.

The content of official communications, messages, and cables were the most sensitive information that officials needed to protect. Diplomatic couriers have their origins in ancient Greece and Rome, and this is where the modern saying, "Don't shoot the messenger" comes from. Throughout history, each country's recognition of couriers has been a symbol of respect on the international stage, and couriers should be allowed unhindered passage through the country, even if it is considered hostile territory. Oftentimes, the messages carried by the couriers from the front lines to the decision makers have helped prevent additional bloodshed.

It was on April 4, 1916, that Secretary of State Robert Lansing created the Secret Intelligence Bureau. WWI marked the exponential growth of espionage, counterintelligence, clandestine operations, and, eventually, terrorism. The special agents of the Secret Intelligence Bureau were the first iteration of Diplomatic Security Service Special Agents, as they are known today, and they were the first professionals dedicated to the safety and security of the American representatives abroad, protecting their work and carrying out investigations into fraud and espionage.

The years in between WWI and WWII saw a substantial cut in funding for the bureau, but the work it was tasked to do carried on and, in fact, grew. Slowly, the bureau rebuilt itself until it boomed again leading up to WWII. As the United States tried to remain neutral, passport fraud was rampant in Germany and Russia, as its citizens attempted to cross borders using neutral-country credentials. It was also the intelligence gathering done by the bureau in Europe that fed information back to Washington, D.C., for the U.S. president to gauge when a tipping point may occur. Unfortunately, even with the network established, no one was able to prevent or better prepare for the attack on Pearl Harbor.

Following the conclusion of WWII, the world changed significantly and continued to change rapidly. Communism was at the forefront, and significant leaks of classified information were occurring from the Department of State. DOS responded by creating the Office of Security (SY) in 1945, which focused on three facets of security: physical, personnel, and overseas.[4]

Prior to the formal establishment of the SY, the only concern was the physical security of its building. As you may imagine, this was done by locks, barricades, fences, and gates. As threats became more sophisticated, the need to provide technical security, such as alarms, camera systems, and other wired devices grew. As a result, the need for a new group of Subject Matter Experts (SMEs) was also evident. Those SMEs were called Technical Security Engineers, but they were also referred to as Technical Security Officers within the newly established Security Office.[5]

A pivotal moment in 1952 caused a cataclysmic shift within SY, which proved to be only the tip of the iceberg. A listening device was hidden in a replica seal of the United States that was gifted to the U.S. Ambassador to Russia and affixed in his residence, and he unknowingly fed sensitive information to the Russians. Throughout the 1950s, the Technical Security Officers, serving as Audio Countermeasures Experts, succeeded in finding and removing more than 100 wired microphone systems in various countries behind the so-called Iron Curtain (collectively known as the Eastern Bloc). At the time, the United States did not realize the importance of limiting access by foreign nationals to restricted areas at overseas facilities, nor were they particularly careful to supervise the reconstruction work being done by foreign national contractors in restricted areas. It wasn't until the 1960s that this information was made public.

After the downing of an American U2 spy plane in 1960, accusations flew back and forth between Russia and the United States, and an escalation of mutual spying ensued. In 1962, with the public and U.S. Congress in shock over the latest developments, Congress quickly approved funds to double the amount of Technical Security Officers and reorganize the Office of Security. The reorganization led to the creation of the Division of Technical Services – the precursor to today's Office of Security Technology (ST).[5] The Technical Security Officers who worked throughout the Eastern Bloc countries suggested to headquarters personnel that access control and surveillance of non-Americans was of primary importance in preventing the repeated installation of clandestine listening devices. As a result of those suggestions, secure conference rooms and communication centers were developed, which led to the request for U.S. Navy Seabees and ultimately led to this very book.

Due to changes in policy and procedures, no planted wired micro-phone systems were discovered within existing facilities since 1964. This may be a good indication that the presence of knowledgeable Seabees at construction sites, as well as improved procedures for admitting visiting foreign nationals into buildings, prevented further installa-tions. However, this does not mean radio and other devices were not discovered in adjacent or adjoining facilities.[5]

Many changes took place in the early 1960s, but it was the rise of terrorism in the second half of 1960 and throughout the 1970s that expanded the Office of Security's responsibilities and visibility. The number of diplomatic posts was also rapidly growing as the decolo-nization of Africa took place and many other countries gained their independence.

From 1940 to 1978, the United States increased its overseas posts from 48 to 117.[5] This required a diplomatic presence in these new nations and exposure to more dynamic security environments. After multiple kidnappings and killings of U.S. Ambassadors, the first in 1968, an initiative to armor cars was taken up by SY and the Seabees. After the Israeli team killings during the 1972 Munich Olympics and the storming of the U.S. Embassy in Tehran in 1979, the SY saw its next significant increase in mission and scale.

Until 1973, the Foreign Operations Division provided operational guidance and support to the security and counterterrorism programs of the Foreign Service outposts abroad. After the inception of the counterterrorism program in 1973, the number of Regional Security Officers grew drastically. Today, there is at least one RSO at each U.S. embassy around the world, including multiple assistant RSOs at most large facilities.

Despite the growth in mission, funds were slow to follow. Improved security requirements implemented in the 1970s were not realized for many years. At the time, the new terrorist threat was not widely acknowledged by appropriations committees, so limited funds were available for overseas posts, and only a fraction of the work required to bring all facilities up to the appropriate security standards was done. Due to this lapse in funding, the use of comparatively cheap Seabees' labor became more prevalent in order to maximize the restricted funds. It was at this time that the Seabees' Naval Support Unit saw a significant increase in personnel numbers to help address the needs of DOS.

After multiple bombings and attacks on American diplomatic facilities and diplomats, culminating in a large truck bomb in Beirut in 1983, U.S. Secretary of State George Shultz convened the Advisory Panel on Overseas Security, led by former National Security Agency Director Bobby Inman. Later known as the Inman Panel, it recommended the reorganization of the security programs into the Bureau of Diplomatic Security (DS) and the Diplomatic Security Service (DSS). The reorganization, in conjunction with the Foreign Relations Authorization Act of 1986, formally established the DSS as a United States law enforcement agency with criminal investigative authority and ability to arrest suspects and execute warrants in every country around the world with an U.S. diplomatic presence.[4] RSOs, Couriers, and Security Engineering Officers (SEOs) are all part of the DSS. With the establishment of the Bureau, it renamed the Division of Technical Security to the Office of Security Technology.

SEOs, formerly known as Technical Security Officers, have various engineering or physics backgrounds and come from industry, other agencies, the military, or they join straight out of college. They are all Foreign Service Officers and spend approximately two thirds or more of their careers serving overseas with their families.

Up until the year 2000, the organizational hierarchy of the Office of Security Technology only consisted of one Senior Foreign Service position, the Director. For a short period, there were two, including the Countermeasures Program Chief, but that position was downgraded to FS-01. Retired ST Office Director John Bainbridge, following the creation of the Security Technical Specialist (STS) skill code in 1998–1999, was asked if he had a "plan for improving (the) Office's management hierarchy."[6] Based on precedence within the DSS Special Agents hierarchy, he proposed creating new Regional Director for Security Engineering positions at the major regional technical centers overseas. The plan was approved. It grew the number of Senior Foreign Service positions from one to eight in order to stop "the most seasoned and valuable SEOs from leaving the Foreign Service at the peak of their careers."[6]

Today, in a few nondescript buildings in downtown Rosslyn, Virginia, the leadership of approximately 200 SEOs and nearly as many STSs, who keep Americans safe while abroad, work tirelessly to ensure United States diplomacy has secure facilities to operate from in nearly every country in the world.

The Office of Security Technology falls under the Countermeasures Directorate within the Bureau of Diplomatic Security. The bureau is led by an Assistant Secretary who reports to the Undersecretary for Management and, under certain circumstances, directly to the Secretary of State.

The Countermeasures Directorate manages the development and implementation of all physical and technical countermeasures security standards and policies that apply to DOS facilities domestically and overseas; securely transports classified diplomatic materials across international borders; and provides defensive equipment to protect the lives of government personnel, classified information, and property. The Countermeasures Directorate is comprised of three offices: Office of Security Technology, Office of Physical Security Programs, and Office of Diplomatic Courier Service. The mission of the Office of Security Technology, Bureau of Diplomatic Security, is to assist in providing a safe and secure environment for the DOS's conduct of diplomacy through the application and use of appropriate technical security countermeasures. The Office of Physical Security Programs directs the security standards of the Overseas Security Policy Board (OSPB) and DOS policies and procedures associated with the physical security, construction security, transit security, secure procurement, defensive equipment, and armored vehicle programs at U.S. missions. The office provides oversight on the implementation of these programs abroad to ensure compliance with the OSPB security standards. The mission of the Diplomatic Courier Service is to provide secure and expeditious delivery of classified, sensitive, and other approved material between U.S. diplomatic missions and DOS.

The Office of Security Technology supports diplomacy by deploying agile technical security systems to match emerging threats. ST uses courageous professionals and insightful leadership to accomplish this mission at operating locations worldwide. As threats evolve around the world, so does the organization. There are now several missions within the ST, which include Security Technology Operations (STO), Countermeasures Program (CMP), Facility Security Engineering (FSE), and Security Systems Integration (SSI).

The STO Division enhances security for all Department facilities worldwide to reduce risk and ensure a safe working environment for U.S. government employees and visitors. To meet present and future security challenges, the Division is charged with providing reliable, appropriate, and professional technical security support. STO is comprised of four branches: Naval Support Unit (NSU), Overseas Support Branch (OSB), Security Engineering Services (SES), and Quality Assurance and Liaison Branch (QAL). NSU provides the U.S. Department of State Bureau of Diplomatic Security (DS) with cleared, trained, equipped Seabee personnel to provide technical security systems support to advance the United States' interests overseas. OSB provides management oversight, funding, staffing, coordination, and logistical support to overseas Engineering Service Centers (ESC), Engineering Service Offices (ESO), Technical Security Offices (TSO), and Regional Technical Offices (RTO). SES is dedicated to establishing, maintaining, and evaluating technically secure work environments for domestic facilities, Secretary of State related missions, and Marine Security Guard training. QAL elevates personnel and information security at DOS facilities through active quality management of technical security solutions.

The remaining divisions that round out the Office of Security Technology include Countermeasures Program, Facility Security Engineering, and Security Systems Integration. The CMP division ensures the integrity of United States' intelligence worldwide by serving as DOS's point of contact for all domestic and overseas technical countermeasure operations.

CMP manages the research and identification of technical security threats and vulnerabilities and the development and implementation of risk mitigations to advance Diplomatic Security strategies. The FSE division develops, supplies, installs, and maintains technical security systems to help ensure a safe and secure environment for DOS's conduct of diplomacy. The SSI division provides global security connectivity, integration, and monitoring solutions for U.S. Foreign Affairs' stationary and mobile platforms.

In addition to the divisions of the Office of Security Technology, SEOs also serve within the directorate for Cyber Security Technology, and some receive additional training to earn the title of Regional Cybersecurity Officers (RSCO).

The Directorate of Cyber and Technology Security (CTS) is a center of excellence. It brings together cybersecurity, technology security, and investigative expertise to present a unified capability on these critical and emerging issues for the Bureau of Diplomatic Security and DOS.

Much of the specific work done by ST is classified and most of these professionals require high-level Top Secret Sensitive Compartmented Information (TS-SCI) clearances. The ST's work is often overshadowed by the great DOS mission. Their best work is invisible; however, the mission they carry out is critical to national security and the protection of thousands of U.S. citizens abroad.

2

The United States

Navy Seabees

Prior to WWII, construction for the United States Navy was carried out by contractors under the Bureau of Yards and Docks led by Civil Engineer Corps (CEC) Officers. The CEC Officers in charge of the Seabees rotate between expeditionary positions with the Seabees and shore duty assignments under what was the Bureau of Yards and Docks and later became Naval Facilities Engineering Systems Command.

The Bureau of Yards and Docks was established in 1842 to oversee the U.S. Navy's domestic shipyards on the eastern seaboard and latterly those on the Pacific coast. In 1867, the CEC was formally established, and a surge in work began after the Spanish American War in 1898 with construction of naval stations in Puerto Rico, Guam, and the Philippines. In 1911, Congress designated responsibility to the Bureau of Yards and Docks for the design, construction, and maintenance of all U.S. Navy installations, including magazines and hospitals that were formally designed and constructed by the Bureau of Ordnance and Bureau of Medicine, respectively.

During WWI, there was another large expansion of the Department of the Navy (DON) footprint. However, as has been the case throughout history for the service branches, there is often a reduction in the size of the standing forces during extended periods of peace. Between WWI and WWII was no different. There was a slight uptick during the Great Depression in an attempt by government to offer more jobs, but by the time WWII broke out, there were only 200 CEC Officers, and the U.S. Navy was woefully unprepared for a major conflict, which was evident during the events following the attack on Pearl Harbor, "a day which shall live in infamy."[7]

In the months after the attack, plans were drawn up by the newly appointed Commander in Chief of the Pacific Fleet (CINCPAC), Admiral Chester Nimitz. An island-hopping campaign was planned to push back the Japanese from all the islands they had invaded since the beginning of the war. From the main island of Japan, south to Papua New Guinea and Indonesia, and as far to the east as Guam, the Japanese had spread their forces across the Pacific to gain necessary resources to maintain the growth of their empire. The island-hopping campaign by the United States was to be extensive, bringing its forces into combat with Japanese forces on every island, as well as in the waters surrounding them. For the United States to advance, they would need to build or repair air strips on each island to enable their bombers to refuel and rearm in order to extend their reach further westward, eventually flying over Japan's main islands. The crucial problem was deploying civilian contractors into a warzone without arming them or training them to defend what they were building.

Rear Admiral Ben Moreell, Chief of Civil Engineers and Commander of the Bureau of Yards and Docks, had an answer. On December 28, 1941, he proposed the formation of U.S. Navy construction units that would have the skills required to build or repair airstrips on virgin soil, as well as the military training needed to defend themselves should they encounter the enemy.[8] After only a week, on January 5, 1942, his request was approved in full with only one exception: the units were to be commanded by U.S. Navy line officers, not CEC officers. CEC officers are staff corps officers or restricted line officers, as opposed to unrestricted line officers, such as surface warfare officers and aviators. Moreell immediately saw many problems with the proposed dual command structure and went directly to the Secretary of the Navy to amend the decision to allow CEC officers to command the units. On March 19, 1942, the amended request was approved.[8] This accomplishment is one of the most important in a lifetime of major successes for Moreell. Because of this, to this day, CEC officers maintain command over naval construction units during times of both war and peace.

Admiral Ben Moreell, "Father of the U.S. Navy Seabees."
Photo courtesy of Naval History and Heritage Command

Just before the decision on CEC officers, March 5, 1942, the Construction Battalions were born. Taking the first letters of Construction and Battalion, which phonetically read "cee-bee," the nickname "Seabees" was coined for members of the battalion, the term they are still known by today.

The official Latin motto of the Seabees is "Construimus Batuimus," meaning "We Build, We Fight."[9] There are seven U.S. Navy ratings for Seabees: builders, steelworkers, construction electricians, utilitiesmen, equipment operators, construction mechanics, and engineering aides.

Between 1940 and 1945, over 10,000 CEC officers were recruited from civilian life to lead a force of 325,000 Seabees in the island infrastructure construction program critical to the United States' ability to win the war in the Pacific. However, during WWII, the Seabees supported the war effort in both the Atlantic and the Pacific theaters. In the Atlantic, they stormed the beaches at Normandy as part of Navy Combat Demolition Teams, clearing obstacles on the beaches. Seabees also formed the earliest Naval Combat Demolition Teams that evolved into modern day Navy Sea, Air, and Land teams (SEALs), Explosive Ordnance Disposal (EOD) teams, and Underwater Construction Teams (UCT). Today, the Seabees still support the SEAL and EOD units that they helped form.

In the Pacific, the Seabees joined the Marines in amphibious landings on every island in the Pacific campaign. A force of 325,000 enlisted men and 12,000 CEC officers at its peak, Seabees were more numerous in WWII than sailors in the U.S. Navy today. One of the last islands the U.S. Marines took back from the Japanese among the Northern Marianas islands, Tinian, became the loading point for the two atomic bombs that were dropped onto Nagasaki and Hiroshima. The island's infrastructure to support the endeavor was completely built by the Seabees. Even the loading of the bombs onto the planes received support from the Seabees, due to the bombs immense size.

Since WWII, the Seabees have been involved in every United States-led conflict around the world. During the Korean War (1950–1953), the Seabees grew their legacy and fame by executing the "Great Seabee Train Robbery." After a successful amphibious landing and invasion at Inchon, tons of materials and equipment were offloaded onto a pontoon causeway assembled by the Seabees, constructed despite thirty-foot tides. However, taking these supplies further inland presented a different obstacle that had so far eluded the U.S. Army. Enter the Seabees, who "tactically acquired" abandoned locomotives behind enemy lines. In a nighttime expedition, they evaded mortar fire and brought back a number of locomotives that they turned over to the Army Transportation Corps to facilitate the movement of all the supplies and equipment waiting at Inchon.[10]

The conflict in Vietnam was different to WWII or Korea due to the predominance of guerrilla and jungle warfare. Building advance bases and expeditionary airfields, as they had done across the Pacific, the Seabees came under attack more frequently. CM3 Marvin Shields became the first Seabee to earn the Medal of Honor for his actions carrying a critically wounded shipmate to safety and taking out an enemy machine-gun position.

Following Vietnam, in the 1970s and 1980s, the Seabees were instrumental in the construction of telecommunications stations around the world, providing substantial construction support for the advancing naval computer and telecommunication systems. Three of the main locations are Guam (western Pacific), Diego Garcia (an island in the British Indian Ocean Territory), and Nea Makri (Greece).[10] In other locations, such as Sigonella in Sicily, Roosevelt Roads in Puerto Rico, and Keflavik in Iceland, the Seabees maintained construction sites for many years, building out U.S. Navy installations.

Throughout those two decades, the Seabees continued to expand into niche areas of support within critical infrastructure programs. Some of these duties included support for the deployment of Mobile Utilities Support Equipment (MUSE), support for the Naval Telecommunication Stations, and support for the White House Military Office (WHMO). MUSE is supported by Seabees who are highly trained in diesel engine-driven generators, substations, and switchgears. MUSE technicians are often deployed to provide non-permanent support for pier-side power to submarines or other critical military assets when reliable land-based power grids are not available.[11]

In the same way that the Seabees evolved over time, so did Naval Facilities Engineering Systems Command. In May 1966, the U.S. Navy underwent a reorganization that resulted in the Bureau of Yards and Docks becoming NAVFAC, with the Chief of Engineers reporting to the Chief of Naval Material as a systems command. Under another reorganization in the mid-1980s, NAVFAC began to report directly to the CNO through the Vice CNO when Naval Material Command was disestablished. At the end of the 1980s, with the collapse of the Soviet Union, NAVFAC led the Base Realignment and Closure Program for the U.S. Navy, which disposed of seventy-two defunct bases. In 2003, Commander Navy Installations Command (CNIC) was established, and NAVFAC as the technical authority for shore facility design, construction, real estate, environmental, and public works would still report to the CNO, but also have additional duty to CNIC and Marine Corps Installations Command.

Support for the executive branch has also been delivered for decades at the Presidential Retreat at Camp David, also known as Naval Support Facility Thurmont, in addition to direct facility and construction support under the White House Military Office (WHMO). WHMO also provides facility management for the White House, the Vice President residence, and Camp David.

The reputation the Seabees built during WWII by paving the way to victory had captured the attention of decision makers, and the Seabees became every senior executive's go-to unit to address service or support gaps in any clime and place. In the late twentieth and early twenty-first centuries, the Seabees were drawn into every wartime engagement, including operations Desert Storm and Desert Shield, as well as Operation Iraqi Freedom, Operation Enduring Freedom, and the Global War on Terrorism, among others.

Today, the Seabees maintain all seven ratings and serve in a wide range of units, performing critical tasks in support of the fleet and, most often, Humanitarian Assistance and Disaster Relief (HA/DR) operations. The DOD also widely employs Seabees in Phase 0 (zero) operations (operations that set conditions for successful follow-on potential theater engagements are Phase 0.)[12] Performing Phase 0 operations does not mean that war is imminent in any of these countries. Rather, Phase 0 is intended to develop a beneficial relationship between the United States military and the citizens of these nations, showing that the military is there as a force for good. These operations are peacetime deployments that often build schoolhouses or medical clinics in low- or middle-income nations. Closely coordinated with the host country, the Seabees usually work in partnership with the country's own version of the Seabees. Going further, some of these deployments take the form of Civic Action Details. Most notably, in Palau, Seabees work closely with local citizens to teach specific trade skills and provide apprenticeship certifications that help them gain employment within the local economy.

3

The Cold War and Espionage

The Cold War began shortly after the conclusion of WWII as nuclear proliferation took hold. The world stood by as two superpowers—the United States and the Union of Soviet Socialist Republics (USSR), also known as the Soviet Union—vied for nuclear supremacy. They developed bigger warheads and rockets that could carry weaponized missiles further, mutually assuring destruction should one or the other launch a nuclear attack on the other. In the heat of this, the two countries were also in a space race. Famously, in 1961, U.S. President John F. Kennedy announced a goal of landing a man on the moon. Who could make a bigger bomb faster and who could get to the moon first changed the world forever. The phrase "keeping up with the Joneses," originally coined as a title of a comic strip in 1913, was appropriate with regard to which country would out-do the other.[13]

The best way to keep up with someone is to watch them and watch them closely. The United States and Soviet Union trained highly advanced operatives to collect information by eavesdropping or simply stealing state secrets, commonly referred to as spy programs by the general populace. The Americans' Central Intelligence Agency (CIA) and the Soviets' Committee for State Security (KGB) were established in 1947 and 1954, respectively. Both agencies operated under different names before, but these two names were what became synonymous with each spy program for many years to come. Today, the CIA remains; however, the KGB was dissolved when the USSR collapsed, evolving into the Russian Federal Security Service and Foreign Intelligence Service.

Spies have been employed by the United States as early as the Revolutionary War by General George Washington. They were used to gather information regarding the movement of British troops in order to respond more quickly, minimizing losses and maximizing effectiveness of follow-on engagements. However, by the 1950s, these covert operatives were doing much more. Now they were infiltrating foreign organizations to gain access to state secrets and finding schematics for weapons and technology to either use themselves or to prepare to defend the United States against.

Other than the CIA, the United States has established a plethora of other intelligence agencies. All in all, eighteen agencies fall under the U.S. Intelligence Community umbrella. The two independent agencies are the Office of the Director of National Intelligence (DNI) and the CIA.[14] There are nine within the DOD: The Defense Intelligence Agency, the National Security Agency (NSA), the National-Geospatial Intelligence Agency (NGA), the National Reconnaissance Office (NRO), and each respective element of the Army, Navy, Marine Corps, Air Force, and Space Force. The remaining seven agencies fall under various branches of governmental departments. These include the Department of Energy's Office of Intelligence and Counterintelligence; the Department of Homeland Security's Office of Intelligence and Analysis and U.S. Coast Guard Intelligence; the Department of Justice's Federal Bureau of Investigation (FBI) and the Drug Enforcement Administration's Office of National Security Intelligence; the Department of State's Bureau of Intelligence and Research; and the Department of the Treasury's Office of Intelligence and Analysis.

In the 1960s, DOS wished to build a new embassy in Moscow that would better support the large staff there. As is often the case in diplomacy, if one country wishes to secure a property to build an embassy or acquire a building, the host nation must approve it and will often trade for a building site of their own in the requesting country. As outlined in Articles 21–25 of the Vienna Convention on Diplomatic Relations of 1961, the embassy and consulates of a foreign country are not to be searched by the host nation.[15] This does not mean that the property is sovereign territory of the foreign country, but certain privileges and immunity are placed on the Head of Mission and other diplomats to freely conduct their mission. This is reciprocated for the host nation at the embassies and consulates in the foreign country it holds relations with. Giving up land that is administered by a foreign nation to build their embassy or consulate generals and restrict access is a significant gesture of good will and trust.

In the case of the United States, the construction of new embassies in Moscow has a storied history, including findings of listening devices, tunnels, and other evidence of espionage. It was not until the construction of the most recent building in Moscow began in 1985 that American labor was used to construct all secure spaces of the embassy. Throughout the twenty years prior, DOS had called on U.S. Navy Seabees to surveil the construction being carried out by local construction companies because that had always been the common practice. One significant example of this occurred in June 1978, when two Technical Security Officers discovered a Soviet listening post in the Moscow embassy. An unclassified summary of the events was provided in the History of the Bureau of Diplomatic Security of the United States Department of State, page 233:

They opened the chimney wall and found a dish-shaped radio antenna connected to a cable that ran down the length of the chimney. At the base of the chimney, the cable continued down a tunnel, large enough for a human to crawl through. The tunnel continued under the U.S. Embassy grounds to a Soviet apartment building next door. The antenna-tunnel find was an active listening post, and Soviet personnel were discovered using the tunnel. Bainbridge and Frank tested the antenna system and found the cables to be "energized." A Navy Seabee, working with Bainbridge and Frank, "surprised" a Soviet technician crawling through the tunnel, prompting U.S. workers (likely Seabees) to build a brick wall to seal the tunnel. Despite an active antenna, SY and U.S. Government technical engineers could not determine from what or where the antenna received signals, although they suspected the Central Wing of the chancery building, which housed the Ambassador's offices, was a possibility. The antenna/tunnel find revealed that the Soviets had severely breached the security of the U.S. Embassy.

One of the Technical Security Officers who made the discovery, John Bainbridge, recalled this inspection as being his first inspection in the Foreign Service. While traversing the tunnel, in addition to several devices determined to be in active use, another hatch was found that provided access to the tunnel from a cleaning room used by the local nationals who cleaned the embassy under Marine escort. Due to the investigation into the hatch, the cleaning crew was called off that day. Unfortunately, the disruption in service tipped off the KGB. Reportedly, "a Russian entered the tunnel and was met head on by a Seabee." Bainbridge adds, "To prevent any further incursions by our neighbors, the Seabees quickly erected a wall in the tunnel at the property line to ward off the KGB."[16]

Learning from the experiences of the past, the United States now constructs embassies with the utmost focus on security of all materials and equipment from the time it leaves the United States to the time it is installed in the foreign nation. Special care is taken to ensure that cleared Americans are the only personnel to step foot inside of controlled spaces, from the time of groundbreaking to the end of the useful life of the facility. This security is a testament to the protocols and practices put in place and followed by the professionals within the Department of State who are dedicated to carrying out its mission.

United States' diplomats and other official visitors traveling and working in countries with high threat counterintelligence activities, such as Russia, China, Vietnam, and Cuba, are cautioned about the threat and warned of the need to remain vigilant. An undated unclassified memo to all American official visitors from the St. Petersburg Consulate General RSO lays out the following guidelines to consider while traveling to and staying in a country:

- *Assume all conversations are monitored. Never discuss classified or sensitive information on the telephone or in an unapproved environment.*
- *Do not "talk around" classified information. The accumulation of such tidbits can help a professional to deduce classified information.*
- *There are not effective methods to protect conversations outside the approved conference rooms. Whispering or attempts to mask conversations with music or noise are no longer effective against the technical threat we face.*
- *If you are staying in a hotel room or apartment outside the consulate, you should assume that your room will be entered while you are away. Do not leave anything in your room you don't wish to share with others.*
- *Assume that anything you discard in a trash receptacle will be recovered and scrutinized.*
- *You are a desirable target of a foreign intelligence service regardless of your position, status, or affiliation. Simply the fact you have*

access to places, people, and information that is of interest to the foreign intelligence service officer makes you a potential target of their attention.[17]

The 1961 Vienna Convention on Diplomatic Relations laid out some boundaries and guidelines with regards to diplomatic and consular privileges and immunities for diplomats abroad. Contrary to portrayals in Hollywood movies and thriller novels, such as Tom Clancy's Jack Ryan series, foreign diplomats traveling to a country do not have complete immunity from the laws of the host country. They may not end up serving time in prison for significant crimes; however, the diplomat may be served a *persona non grata* letter to leave the country and never return (*persona non grata* means an unacceptable or unwanted person). The host country of that diplomat must abide by that letter and remove the person from service at that post or risk significant damage to their reputation and relationship with the host country. The Vienna Convention on Diplomatic Relations provides a customary international law with respect to diplomats that is still adhered to by almost all nations of the world.

In 1987, a memorandum to Diplomatic Security (DS) was issued as an authoritative statement on the nature and extent of diplomatic and consular privileges and immunities for diplomats abroad. The concern at the time was that many in the Diplomatic Security Service, including the Seabees, who had the same privileges and immunities, did not have a clearly defined understanding of what those privileges and immunities were:

Centuries ago, sovereign States discovered that it was not possible to maintain useful diplomatic relations with other nations if their respective diplomatic envoys had to live in fear of being thrown into the dungeon for carrying unfavorable opinions to the host government or for other real or imagined offense to the host State. Similarly, when these early diplomats began to reside in the host State, it was realized that they needed a certain security in their persons, homes, and official papers in order to effectively accomplish the work that both the sending and receiving States agreed that they should accomplish. [18]

To ensure these diplomatic privileges, customs, and immunities were fully understood, they were developed over time.

Holders of a diplomatic passport must not assume they have all the same privileges and immunities as the Ambassador. The diplomatic passport holder is simply afforded courtesies for easier transit in and out of a country. Their baggage is not opened or screened, and their biometric data is not recorded. Inviolability of official papers and correspondence and freedom from search and seizure for any reason are also commonly afforded to an official diplomat.

There are different types of diplomats. There are diplomatic agents, and their administrative and technical support staff, who are engaged primarily in the diplomatic intercourse between the two states. The agents and their staff are entitled to immunity from the criminal jurisdiction of the receiving state; however, diplomatic agents enjoy more extensive immunity from the civil and administrative jurisdiction of the receiving state than the members of the administrative and technical staff. Although, in some countries, such as Russia and China, the same civil and administrative privileges and immunities are extended to the administrative and technical staff in bilateral agreements with the United States. Typically, family members do receive the same privileges and immunities as the active employee of the U.S. government when serving in an official capacity and on assignment in the host nation. Finally, the waiving of diplomatic immunity can only be done by DOS, not the individual:

Persons enjoying diplomatic privileges and immunities are, at least in a literal sense, "above the law" of the receiving State. All States which enter into diplomatic relations with other States accept this encroachment on their sovereignty as a necessary cost of being a member of the world community. The immunity concept would never have endured; however, if its application left the receiving State helpless to react to the commission of serious crimes in its territory or without recourse when the civil law rights of its citizens are continuously abused by these diplomatic foreigners. [...] It is for this reason that, parallel with the diplomatic immunity concept, there developed the principle (now enshrined in the applicable treaties) that all persons enjoying privileges and immunities have also the obligation and duty to respect the laws and regulations of the host State. The receiving state may declare any person entitled to these privileges and immunities persona non grata at any time and without stating a reason. Persona non grata means the person so designated must depart the country within a reasonable time or face pending legal actions civil or criminal.[18]

Today, intelligence operations continue to be conducted on visiting diplomats, but surveillance operatives are much less prone to harass Americans openly if the Americans don't agitate those that are following them. American diplomats traveling abroad to certain countries are often followed for one of two reasons. First, to gain information about them and their purpose at the consulate or embassy. Second, to protect the diplomat from petty crime or crimes of opportunity, which could create international incidents that neither country wants. While Lieutenant Adam Gerlach was visiting Havana, Cuba, in 2017, he reported walking to dinner with the resident Seabee when they came upon a group of children. When they were within fifty feet of the group, there was a whistle from behind them and the children scattered.[19] Gerlach's tail wanted to make sure that the diplomats were not accosted to avoid any embarrassment that might worsen fragile relations between both sides at that time.

Despite the incredible lengths that countries go to facilitate diplomatic relations, improve national security by gathering information from all corners of the world, and protect their diplomats abroad, a small percentage of personnel are insider threats. Insider threats are people who pass on classified information to foreign intelligence officers for money, malice, or by accident in acts of treason. Alger Hiss, Robert Hanssen, David Boone, Aldrich Ames,[20] and Chi Mak[21] are a few examples of high-profile cases where the individual passed along information to foreign intelligence agencies, such as Russia and China. Often, these are average people, but many have extenuating circumstances or have become resentful toward the U.S. government for any reason.

Another one of those individuals who traded state secrets was ex-Marine Sergeant Clayton Lonetree.[22] In December 1985, former NSU Seabee Joe Simpkins was posted to Moscow, and was there when the news of the treason broke in January of 1986. The impact on the remainder of the military population in Moscow was great. The entire Marine Security Guard detachment that was there with Lonetree was replaced with a handpicked group of MSG Marines, and once they arrived, the MSGs were on heavy lockdown. Their potential for interaction with Russians was made near impossible, and the restrictions affected all other embassy personnel.[23] Fortunately for Simpkins and the other Seabees working in Moscow, they were able to avoid much of the crackdown and didn't experience a big change to their daily routines. However, every military member was sent to Frankfurt in Germany for polygraph tests. Thankfully, everyone passed and came back.

To minimize the potential of an insider threat, every country heavily scrutinizes and screens their personnel to try to prevent loss of information due to spies, double agents, or "compromised" individuals (people with risky lifestyles that leave them vulnerable to outside influences). This is done in the form of security clearance background investigations, and new investigations on a regular basis.

Gaining a security clearance at any level in the U.S. government brings with it an increasing level of responsibility and accountability. Clearance levels are Secret, Top Secret, Sensitive Compartmented Information (SCI), or "Yankee White" (for those working in direct contact with the President of the United States), and gaining clearance is a long process. The first step in this process is completing a Standard Form 86 (SF-86) and fingerprinting. The prints are run through the international database to confirm who you are and to confirm that you are not on any watchlists in the United States or abroad or have any warrants for your arrest. The SF-86 asks you for personal information dating back at least five years. For the highest-level clearances, they often go back more than twenty years. They will ask you for information about family, friends, current and former residences, foreign travel, and all foreign contacts. This is in addition to drinking habits, any traffic citations, civil or criminal investigations, debt, investments, and social media activity. All this information creates a profile to assess risk. The contacts of your family and friends will be called and many interviewed. Most will be asked to name two or three other people that the investigator could contact to further validate the information. This is because most people will only provide contacts who can give a positive report. It's the second and third order contacts, who aren't usually listed, that often give a less biased and filtered version of the individual in question.

The background check is also designed to reveal any vulnerabilities for blackmail or coercion. Gambling debts, heavy drinking, soliciting sex workers, and evidence of other vices can leave the individual exposed for exploitation by foreign entities to gain information or documents in exchange for compensation that enables them to continue their risky lifestyles.

4

A Partnership Begins

In the mid-1960s, the Foreign Building Operations, in close coordination with the Office of Security, was struggling to find enough trusted personnel readily available to perform construction security surveillance overseas. They had to find an entity they could trust to perform construction surveillance at minimal cost and on a short timeline. The workers would need to be not only experienced construction workers but also United States' citizens with security clearances so that they could be trusted to deal with whatever threat they uncovered during the construction. Looking across the federal government for support, they discovered the storied Seabees, and in early 1964, DOS employed the Seabees in Jakarta, Indonesia, for a small construction project. The result of this initiative far exceeded expectations. Perhaps this same entity could help again.

The Seabee Detachment deployed in Jakarta was from Naval Mobile Construction Battalion ELEVEN. Their success led to the more significant request for their involvement in the next project, in the summer of 1964. The Navy provided two Chief Petty Officers to the DOS for a survey of the proposed work areas. From September to November 1964, a Seabee detachment consisting of one officer and forty-nine enlisted men were assembled from both East and West

Coast battalions. They needed the Seabee skills to perform work that they were unable to get civilian contractors to carry out because of the sensitive nature of the security program, the discipline required to carry out such a program, the speed of implementation required, and the non-availability of civilian personnel with the skills and clearances necessary for such assignments. This first detachment did everything DOS asked, which ultimately led to a follow-on request for a larger detachment—known as Detachment NOVEMBER—from Naval Mobile Construction Battalion FOUR. As the name suggests, this follow-on detachment deployed in November of that year.

The success of the initial projects, the speed with which the U.S. Navy responded to the request for Seabees, and a decision by DOS to initiate a program of surveillance of construction overseas led to preparations for enlarging and making permanent the Seabee support program. However, at this time, the United States was heavily involved in the war in Vietnam, where the Seabees were also concentrated. If DOS was going to get their Seabee unit permanently, they were going to need to fully reimburse and pay for the billets from DOD. DOD has funding formulas for the number of servicemembers they can afford in a budget year. By reimbursing DOD for the Seabees assigned to them, DOS mitigated any impact on the total Seabee force able to be deployed to Vietnam. It was in September 1965, in consideration of the long-term aspects of the new program, that the U.S. Navy initiated a formal agreement for the Seabees to be assigned to DOS. By December 1965, an agreement had been drafted and a proposal submitted. DOS agreed with the proposal, and on April 21, 1966, the Secretary of the Navy established the Naval Support Unit, State Department (NAVSUPPU STATE DEPT) under the direction of an Officer in Charge (OIC).

In the DOD today, a request for forces, like that from DOS in 1964, would not be as simple. Today's Global Force Management

(GFM) system requires an entity to submit their needs to DOD, whose readiness reporting system determines what unit, regardless of branch, is available for deployment while maintaining all the capabilities requested. Today, units comparable with the Seabees exist in other branches of the armed forces. In the Air Force, there are units called the Rapid Engineer Deployable Heavy Operational Repair Squadron, Engineer (RED HORSE) and Prime Base Engineer Emergency Force (BEEF). And in the U.S. Army, there is the Corps of Engineers. But in the 1960s, these other units, with similar skill sets, simply did not exist or were not as flexible for small missions. The type of work done today still has its foundation in the construction trades but has increasingly become more technical to include systems networking and programming.

Detachment NOVEMBER Seabees were initially tasked with construction surveillance. These would be skilled Seabee tradesman, usually with five to fifteen years of naval construction experience. Many came in with private sector experience. Their job would be to provide site security by monitoring the construction activity every day, which not only ensured the local contractors were following the plans and specifications but also identified any work that was inconsistent with regular construction practices. This was usually in relation to more sensitive parts of the building, such as missing rebar in a wall or floor that would make it easier to chisel through from a tunnel. Sometimes the construction techniques being employed could compromise the integrity of the building. Or perhaps the construction workers were taking an inordinate amount of time in one area or on one piece of construction that would normally be done much faster. Such inconsistencies could only be spotted by an experienced tradesman, i.e., a Seabee.

The first time the Seabees arrived in Moscow was immediately following a find of wired devices by the Technical Security Officer during inspections in 1964.[24] This find fully justified the Seabee program and led to over 100 other discoveries at U.S. diplomatic facilities in Iron Curtain countries during the Cold War. The effort to repair damage caused by the removal of the wired devices at a number of facilities resulted in Project DEMO (short for demolition) that the Seabees were tasked with. This project was an all-hands-on-deck effort. The crew assigned to the job experienced "extreme restrictions" and "cramped living conditions." In a letter of appreciation written by then Senior Chief Robert Goudy, he noted the nighttime hours, which avoided disruption to regular embassy operations. Lunch was scheduled for 11:30 PM, and "the Embassy wives provided hot meals and apple pie. This greatly assisted in keeping the crew in high spirits."[25] The arrangements in follow-on locations improved along the way, but the apple pie was referred to more than once in the summary memo.

It was after these instances that DOS realized the true value of having Seabees on construction sites to observe foreign nationals in countries where sophisticated foreign intelligence gathering was widely practiced—mostly Eastern Europe and communist countries influenced by the Soviet Union at first. Today, this type of environment exists in countries such as China, Russia, Iran, and North Korea, or where violent extremist organizations and transnational criminal organizations operate. All these entities were identified in the December 2020 edition of "Advantage at Sea," published by the Secretary of the Navy, as well as the 2018 National Defense Strategy published by the Secretary of Defense.

PART II

Building a Legacy

5

The Naval Support Unit

The Naval Support Unit (NSU) was formally established on April 21, 1966, at the request of the Chief of the Bureau of Yards and Docks (now the Commander, Naval Facilities Engineering Systems Command). The NSU provides the expertise and labor requested by the Department of State; its mission is to provide DOS with cleared, trained, and equipped Seabee personnel to carry out technical security system support in the diplomatic mission to advance America's interests overseas. The Seabees, Sailors, and officers of NSU are colloquially known as the "Professionals Around the World."

The unit is funded on a "cost reimbursable basis," paid for by DOS to provide the necessary resources to operate. This arrangement alleviates the strain on the Naval Construction Force resources, funded via the Department of Defense.

At the time NSU was established, the United States was in the middle of the Vietnam War. Had this agreement not been made, the successful Detachment NOVEMBER may have been the last detachment to support DOS until at least the end of the war nearly ten years later, if ever again. This agreement is unique compared to most other Seabee Units. Most other units fall under Naval Beach Group or Naval Expeditionary Combat Command within the Naval Construction

Force, composed of two Naval Construction Groups. Under NAVFAC, the unit is most similar to the Mobile Utilities Support Equipment (MUSE) Division under Naval Facilities Engineering and Expeditionary Warfare Center (EXWC). However, no other unclassified naval unit exists to primarily support another agency's operations like NSU.

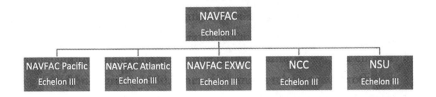

The NAVFAC Organizational Chart for Echelon II and III commands per the Standard Navy Distribution List

While NSU was operating as a detachment, they fell under the operational control of the Atlantic Division of the Bureau of Yards and Docks and managed out of Davisville, RI, the birthplace of the Seabees. When NSU was formally established, it was created as an Echelon IV command to report administratively to the Chief of the Bureau of Yards and Docks, that in turn reported to the Chief of Naval Materials. In May 1966, the Department of the Navy went under a significant reorganization, and the Bureau of Yards and Docks became what is known today as Naval Facilities Engineering Systems Command (NAVFAC) and began reporting to the Chief of Naval Operations. Meanwhile, the Chief of Naval Materials was disestablished.

NAVFAC is an Echelon II command that reports directly to the CNO, an Echelon I. NSU has always organizationally fallen under NAVFAC as an Echelon III command since the reorganization in 1966 and continues under NAVFAC today. Other Echelon III commands under NAVFAC include NAVFAC Pacific, NAVFAC Atlantic, Naval Facilities Engineering and Expeditionary Warfare Center (EXWC), and the Navy Crane Center (NCC).

Over the years, despite organizational changes all around it, the NSU organizational structure has not changed very much. In 1964, Detachment NOVEMBER began with an OIC and forty-nine Seabees. As the detachment stuck around longer, and before it was formalized in 1966, some administrative support was provided via U.S. Navy reservists who were assigned to oversee orders, pay, and logistics.

DOS originally asked for 155 Seabees, but due to lack of funding and availability of Seabees, that number was not achieved for nearly twenty years. By the mid-1980s, more than fifty NSU Seabees were posted to thirty-two countries to support the Department of State's Bureau of Diplomatic Security mission. Today, there are 139 personnel that fall within NSU, but the program is still led by a single U.S. Navy Lieutenant Civil Engineer Corps Officer.

The headquarters of NSU also evolved over time to better support the work being performed around the world with the addition of a formal AOIC and Senior Enlisted Leader (SEL) position as well as Operations and Administrative Staff.

History of NSU Personnel Allowance	
1964	50
1974	75
1983	109
1985	118
1986	165
1988	168
1989	139
1990	120
1993	112
1997	103
1999	150
2000	120
2018	129
2020	139

The OIC reports to the Commander of NAVFAC through the Chief of Staff at NAVFAC. The OIC's reporting senior on their annual Fitness Report (FITREP— an annual performance evaluation for a military officer) is the Chief of Civil Engineers and Commander, NAVFAC—a two-star admiral. The Assistant OIC and Senior Enlisted Leader (the same person in NSU) work closely with the Force Master Chief of the Seabees to provide feedback on any personnel and administrative issues. The Immediate Superior in Command (ISIC) is reported to by the junior command. For NAVFAC, other Echelon III commands are led by a Rear Admiral Lower Half, Senior U.S. Navy Captain Civil Engineer Corps Officer, or Senior Executive Service Civilian.

The reporting structure is both an opportunity and a challenge for a lieutenant who is reporting as an OIC of an Echelon III command to a two-star admiral. On the one hand, you get exposure to the inner workings of command headquarters and get face time with the most senior Civil Engineer Corps Officer, providing their perspective and advice on your career, performance, as well as visibility with the most senior officers in the community on correspondence. On the other hand, the challenging aspect is the intimidation of reporting to a highly experienced two-star admiral. Regardless of rank, the NSU OICs are held to a high standard on all administrative requirements, and any Commander's Critical Information Requests (CCIRs) that are reported go straight to the top.

Operationally, the unit reports to the Division Director for STO, a Senior Foreign Service Officer civilian. Adjacent branches include Overseas Support Branch, Security Engineering Services, and Quality Assurance and Liaison Branch. These are headed by Foreign Service Officers at the FS-1 paygrade, or a military O-6 pay equivalent. Again, the OIC is matched on equal footing with very senior personnel. It may seem intimidating for the OIC, but those they work with welcome the OIC as an equal in responsibility for program management. The relationships and mentorship from these senior personnel is an opportunity of a lifetime. The OIC, as well as all the Seabees in NSU, have an opportunity to share their military experience with an organization thirsty for outside input and perspective when it comes to strategic planning and team leadership.

A question that often comes up is if there is such a gap in experience, why is the OIC of NSU only a Lieutenant? Why would it not be a Captain (O-6) or at least a Lieutenant Commander (O-4)? Much of this simply has to do with the size of unit. A 139-person unit is similar in size to a company in a Naval Mobile Construction Battalion or that of a Marine Corps unit. A U.S. Navy Lieutenant or U.S. Marine Corps Captain often leads between 129 and 149 personnel. At face value, this is the main reason that a senior lieutenant—who is often close to promotion to Lieutenant Commander while in the OIC position—is most often selected to serve as the OIC of NSU. However, when determining what rank of officer to place in command of a unit, there are considerations such as mission type, adjacent units, and risk.

The mission that NSU has and supports within DOS's Bureau of Diplomatic Security is highly technical and global. Most Seabees are serving independently at a U.S. embassy. There is no unit like this that sends First and Second Class Petty Officers to operate independently in foreign countries, seeing direct unit leadership only two to three times per year. However, at each post, the Seabee is overseen with what the military calls "tactical control," by a SEO or a seasoned STS, who are Foreign Service Officers. This onsite leadership provides day-to-day management and direction. Because of this, the 80 or so NSU Seabees who serve overseas do not require daily management and direction from headquarters. This reduces the 139 to approximately 60 personnel in the vicinity of NSU headquarters (Washington, D.C.). Of the remaining 60, approximately 24 are in a training pipeline that is run by the Department of State Technical Security Engineering Division, leaving approximately 30 personnel for daily management and direction from headquarters. Despite the global mission and the overall administrative responsibility, the operational requirements are greatly reduced compared to a typical unit, which requires management of 4 to 5 times the amount of personnel.

There are a couple of adjacent military units that operate within the DOS, which NSU encounters on a regular basis. The two main units are the Marine Corps Embassy Security Group (MCESG) and the Defense Attaché Offices. The MCESG is led by a U.S. Marine Corps Colonel and the Defense Attaché Office, referred to as the

"DATT," is also led by a military officer of the O-5 or O-6 rank. In addition to these military units, as mentioned earlier, the STO branch colleagues of the OIC are also O-6 equivalents. This could easily justify the selection of a U.S. Navy Commander (O-5) to fill the OIC role. However, if the Senior Leader of the unit was to be O-4 or higher, the title could convert to being a Commanding Officer. There are significant differences between a Commanding Officer and Officer in Charge on paper, although in execution, the differences are more subtle. Mostly, the differences are administrative. An OIC is usually a lieutenant or lieutenant commander. They may be the only officer with the unit, but an O-4 would typically have at least one other officer with them as their Assistant Officer in Charge. An OIC also only has certain authorities granted to them under U.S. Navy doctrine and policy but is ultimately allowed to carry out nearly all the same functions as the CO, except for specific types of discipline cases or administrative actions. They also are not allowed to wear either the command ashore/project manager or command-at-sea insignia pin worn on the uniform of a CO. A CO is allowed to wear the command insignia pin when in a designated billet and has increased authority for administering discipline under the Uniform Code of Military Justice and Non-Judicial Punishment. A CO is also able to sign a certain threshold of awards, such as the Navy and Marine Corps Achievement Medal. Beyond these administrative differences, the execution of operations and general administration of the command is very much the same day to day.

The last consideration to review is that of risk. A determination must be made as to the amount of risk there is to have a lieutenant manage a program as geographically expansive as NSU, when they are often outranked in every engagement with adjacent units or colleagues. This risk is mitigated by the screening done for selection of both the OIC and every Sailor in the unit. Due to the unique nature of the command, a thorough interview and screening process is conducted to prevent many common discipline cases. This results in a group of above average Sailors entering the unit at the recommendation of their prior chains of command. It is not a perfect system; like any command, the majority of a leader's time is taken up by a minority of personnel. However, good order and discipline is much easier to maintain because everyone wanted to come to the command, which compels them to put their best foot forward. Many do not want to leave the command once they arrive. The discipline cases that are encountered are usually when a lapse in judgment occurs. These situations, however unfortunate, usually culminate in the transfer of the personnel from the unit because of the high risk, high reward environment. Independent duty carries with it a great amount of trust. A discipline event normally results in a loss of trust in the unit member's ability to carry out their duties without direct supervision.

The last consideration to determine the rank of the unit leader is how many officers it needs. For the entire existence of NSU, only one officer has ever been assigned to the unit. It was briefly suggested that multiple officers would be needed across the unit to cover the regions. However, Chief Petty Officers were found to be more than capable of being both a technician and regional leader. The idea of bringing on more officers never resurfaced in any official correspondence. Much of this, I believe, goes back to how the unit is managed in Washington, D.C. Despite the travel demands of the OIC and AOIC, a second officer to act as the AOIC, deputy OIC, or executive officer has not yet been required. Should the demands of the position become burdensome, or the size of the unit goes over 150 personnel, it may be justified for the Navy to request the DOS fund a second officer billet. However, this additional officer creates second order effects. The two most prevalent effects would include impact on developmental tours of a junior officer and a preference to clearly delineate the chain of command by rank.

In the Civil Engineer Corps community, junior officers—i.e., an Ensign, Lieutenant Junior Grade (LTJG), and Lieutenant (LT)—begin their careers with two development tours that are each two years long. The two tours generally include a construction management tour and a battalion tour. By the time they complete these tours, the LTJG will have been promoted to Lieutenant, as long as they meet the basic qualifications as determined by the U.S. Navy. Currently, with a Lieutenant as the OIC of NSU, an AOIC of the rank of LTJG would make sense, were it not for these development tours. The NSU officer billets are considered staff billets, and without completing the first two development tours, the LTJG would be at a competitive disadvantage among their peers if they did not gain the requisite experience normally achieved by completing those tours. Considering this, it would be most sensible to have the Assistant OIC be a Lieutenant and the OIC be a Lieutenant Commander (LCDR). This would provide a clear delineation in the chain of command and would prevent one Lieutenant from being the reporting senior for another, which would be extremely disadvantageous to the Assistant OIC. The same question could be asked about the AOIC position filled by a Lieutenant. There are two examples of a LCDR filling Commanding Officer billets in the Seabees, and those are with the Underwater Construction Teams (UCT) and the Construction Battalion Maintenance Units (CBMU). There, the executive officers are Lieutenants within a much larger organization, which is more demanding in nature and so requires more than one officer to maintain the daily execution of the command's mission.

Balancing these considerations and any second order effects in determining the rank and the title of the leader for NSU is constantly weighed. For over fifty-five years, the decision has been to maintain a senior lieutenant as the OIC of NSU. I believe much of this is a result of the selection of the individual for the OIC position, as well as their ability to continue to deliver results and provide professional support as a representative of the U.S. Navy to the DOS.

In addition to the contemplation of title and rank of the OIC, these factors also contribute to the rank and title of Assistant Officer in Charge (AOIC). As mentioned earlier, the size of NSU is approximately the same size as a company within a Naval Mobile Construction Battalion. The leadership structure of a company in a battalion includes a Senior Enlisted Leader (SEL) with the rank of Master Chief. Likewise, that was determined as the best fit for NSU. The U.S. Navy requires a Command Master Chief (CMC) for units greater in size than 250 personnel. With NSU being approximately half that size, a formal CMC billet was not created. Instead, AOIC and SEL were both assigned as concurrent titles. For NSU, nearly all SELs historically were filled by prior NSU Seabees. This allowed them to bring institutional knowledge with them to the position when advising the OIC. However, today, this is not a hard requirement.

Both the OIC and AOIC typically serve three years in their respective billets. Three years is common for an accompanied shore tour but less common for command leadership billets. There is a case to be made for both two- and three-year assignments to command leadership billets. These billets are typically more demanding and create a drain on the individual in those billets. A two-year command billet also provides more opportunity for others to have command of a unit; whereas a three-year billet allows the commander of the unit to see through changes they may implement and become an expert in their position.

NSU is unique in that it operates wholly within DOS, which is often a completely unknown entity to the incoming OIC and AOIC, who have their own book of acronyms and means of conducting business. Foreign Service Officers also are accustomed to three-year assignments, similar to military officers. The NSU job also requires extensive travel, and it takes approximately two years for the leaders to visit all the locations NSU Seabees are posted. Because of this learning curve, the time it takes to visit all the posts, and close association with typical Foreign Service Officer rotation plans, a three-year OIC and AOIC billet is a logical term length.

The remainder of NSU is split between Administration, Operations (OPS), and Training. The headquarters element is composed of ten personnel: OPS, Assistant OPS, Training, Command Career Counselor, Independent Duty Corpsman, Yeoman Chief as Administrative Officer, three Personnel Specialists, and an additional Yeoman. The training program oversees all Seabees in the training pipeline. OPS oversees all the deployable Seabees within the unit, including the resident Seabee program, which posts the Seabees overseas at diplomatic embassies and consulates. A handful of others support SES. The remainder are in the temporary duty pool.

Due to the amount of time intended to be spent on temporary duty traveling to various countries to perform work, the assignment for Seabees to NSU is a type-two sea duty, which means an overwhelming majority of NSU Seabees are deployed on temporary duty assignments of 150 or more days per year. This is the same type of sea duty as serving in a Naval Mobile Construction Battalion, with deployments of six to eight months.

Sea duty for the Seabees is not what most people think of for U.S. Navy Sailors. Seabees are most often found in deployable land based naval units, which are more aligned with Marine Corps operations than a regular naval vessel. Units ranging from ten to fifteen personnel, and upwards of 600 are flown into a theater to set up forward operating bases or camps to live and work from. This is recognized as Seabee sea-duty time.

A shore command for a Seabee would be a non-deployable assignment with NAVFAC or a Public Works Department (PWD) or a training or recruiting billet. A non-deployable assignment would be providing facility maintenance at a U.S. Navy or Marine Corps installation under the PWD or in a Seabee Project Shop, where a team of five to ten Seabees will execute small projects. Other shore programs may include Naval Construction Groups, Construction Battalion Maintenance Units, Naval Construction Training Centers, Camp David, White House Military Office, White House Communications Agency, MUSE, and Naval Communication Telecommunication stations. Other sea duty assignments for Seabees include Naval Mobile Construction Battalions, Amphibious Construction Battalions, Naval Construction Regiments, and Underwater Construction Teams. Seabees serving with Naval Special Warfare, Explosive Ordinance Disposal Groups, or Coastal Riverine Groups may serve on either sea or shore duty, depending on the specific unit or element they are attached to.

Naval Support Unit is always ready to deploy to manmade and natural disasters, as well as to support technical security projects, construction projects, and decommissioning of old facilities anywhere in the world for periods of deployment ranging from as little as five days to five or more months. Whether stationed abroad or operating from the TDY pool in Washington, D.C., NSU Seabees can be involved in numerous types of work. Typical TDY projects have included Construction Security Surveillance (CONSEC), Post Communications Center (PCC) installations and renovations, installations of Uninterrupted Power Supply (UPS) systems, installation of power distribution systems, classified information handling systems, installation of vault doors and emergency egress hatches, parent room preparation, secure conference room erection, and installation of secure telephone booths. To do this type of work takes a plethora of skills that are attained both from in-rate Navy training and a six-month training pipeline conducted throughout Northern Virginia.

Throughout the Seabees' history, they have been turned to when a crisis occurs and have had to quickly teach themselves how to take on the challenge. "No good deed goes unpunished," and for NSU Seabees, this meant after performing a task well, that task quickly became part of a list of regular tasks, stretching their original mission. To counteract excessive "scope creep," the unit has a Memorandum of Agreement. The original MOA (January 1967) served as a charter, broad in context, for supporting construction security. As new requirements were placed on the Security Office, the Seabees were often the first ones sought to address the new demands until permanent civilian or foreign service personnel were hired by the DOS to carry out the tasks long term.

In 1976, Lieutenant Hoff wrote to the Deputy Assistant Secretary, Mr. Viktor Dikeos.[26] What came from the letter was a regular review of the NSU Memorandum of Agreement (MOA). In 1978, the first revision to the original MOA from January 7, 1967, was signed, but the next MOA was not signed until 1984. Another long gap in MOAs ensued until 1997 before some level of regularity was standardized. MOAs have been signed approximately every six years (2003, 2008, 2015, and 2021).

The MOA is reviewed by the U.S. Navy and DOS to ensure the integrity of the program is maintained and that the Seabees continue to carry out significant and important duties in line with their skill sets, or that they receive adequate training for whatever they are doing on a long-term basis outside of the basic rate skill set. The key idea for this is to ensure Seabees continue to volunteer for NSU assignments. Some Seabees only want to build within their rate. But what NSU is well known for is doing work outside of a Seabee rate for much of the time, falling back on the skill set to adapt to the evolving mission and being ready for whatever may be next.

The program has had its ups and downs in terms of reputation. For a while, the unit had poor retention and advancement. A lot of that had to do with poor test scores for advancement, something that is a constant battle. Also, because the skill set and experience gained are extremely marketable, Seabees often separate or retire from the unit and walk back through the DOS doors shortly after separation, making twice as much pay while now performing as a civilian, or making three times as much as a contractor executing the same function they were while on active duty. Knowing what an E-5 and E-6 (enlisted paygrades) makes each year, no one can fault smart Seabees from recognizing the opportunity they have to transition and create a better life for themselves and their families; especially when advancement quotas have often been extremely small each year for the Seabee ratings.

6

A Particular Set of Skills

In addition to the skill sets NSU Seabees have acquired at traditional Navy training schools, they also receive training from the Department of State. When the unit was first established, training was only six weeks long. Topics included construction security surveillance techniques, technical security threats, counterintelligence briefings, improvised explosive devices, lock school, and coping with violence abroad.

Locksmith training was added to the program in the 1970s. The locksmith skills have been utilized by Diplomatic Security (DS) much more extensively as time has passed than the construction surveillance skills. Despite concerted efforts by NSU leadership over the years to refocus the unit's mission on construction related projects, instead of technical security, locksmith skills have been the bread and butter for well over forty years.

Seabees receive training closely associated with their rate. Builders and steelworkers who perform vertical construction using wood, concrete, and steel are known as "Charlie types" because they historically make up Charlie Company in a typical NMCB organization. Utilitiesman and construction electricians carry out work above and below ground to install or fix plumbing/piping and high/low voltage electrical work and they are known as "Bravo types" because they make up Bravo Company in a typical NMCB Organization. Construction mechanics and equipment operators in a NMCB organization make up Alfa (not Alpha) Company, and these "Alfa types" perform horizontal construction, such as paving and earthmoving. Someone somewhere knows why it's spelled "Alfa," but that person isn't me!

The last rating is Engineering Aide (EA). The EA has historically found themselves in the headquarters company of a battalion because they work with all other types, surveying, testing materials, and drafting plans. Throughout time, all these rates have found themselves in NSU. They may have been brought in for certain tasks, but all have evolved to be able to carry out any task that the Office of Security Technology asks them to perform today.

In 1964, against the backdrop of the Cold War, DOS was in dire need of a ready workforce comprised of Americans who had security clearance and were also experienced construction workers. This is where the in-rate training Seabees got a foot in the door at the DOS. Their primary task through the remainder of the 1960s and into the 1970s was to perform Construction Security Surveillance (CONSEC), i.e., observing the definable features of work (DFOW) being performed on a construction project. These DFOW may be excavating, installing rebar, and laying the foundation, building walls, laying brick, masonry, electrical, plumbing, HVAC, windows, doors, painting, etc. However, to be able to identify something amiss; the individual performing the surveillance must be trained to perform the construction properly and experienced enough to spot something wrong.

All Seabees that come to NSU are warfare qualified—second tour or later Seabees who are Second Class Petty Officers or more senior. In a construction battalion, these petty officers would be crew leaders or project supervisors with three to five years of experience in construction at minimum. In addition to the training received from DOS, they have the tools to identify anything being built in that isn't in the designs and specifications. For many years, this was the focus until the Foreign Building Operations required all contractors to only employ cleared American contractors to work on a building's controlled access areas. After this change, the demand for the Seabees transitioned from construction to technical security as advances in technology created new opportunities for a "Can Do" organization.

Less than ten years into its existence, NSU had begun to shift away from its primary support operations of CONSEC, focused on general large scale embassy construction projects. Originally involved only with CONSEC on a Temporary Duty (TDY) basis evolved into resident posting assignments overseas as an economical solution to larger construction projects. For a period, NSU Seabees were being used for construction projects in non-restricted spaces or non-sensitive areas of diplomatic posts. Today, this type of work is strictly off limits to NSU Seabees. To many, this may seem contradictory. Why would a unit of Seabees, expert construction workers, be opposed to performing construction work? The reason is that the purpose of NSU was to perform construction work in *classified* spaces, where cleared Americans were required or foreign nationals needed to be surveilled. This regular construction work was not only less prestigious, but it was not the intention behind the unit's creation.

Also, at this time, Seabees began training as locksmiths. Lock setting and defeating quickly became associated with NSU, and soon the Seabees were the go-to experts for lock-related issues. Locksmithing is a skill very much outside of the in-rate knowledge for Seabees. But, in 1976, the then NSU OIC Lieutenant Hoff highlighted the divergence away from the original mission in a letter to the Deputy Assistant Secretary for Security. Hoff argued at the time that it was a "skill not known or needed before or after two years of their tour in this unit."[26] Hoff may have been right in 1976; however, it did not change the training the Seabees received. In fact, it could be argued it accelerated the conversion to heavy focus on technical security system training that is in high demand today across DOS and a sought-after specialist skill within the Department of Defense.

Locksmithing is still a primary training program for NSU Seabees; however, unlike in the 1970s, the skill set has been used in other Seabee billets across DOD, including Naval Support Facility Thurmont, better known as the Presidential Retreat at Camp David, and the Pentagon. There are numerous stories told by former NSU Seabees of having to step up to the plate at Navy installations and other federal agencies to fix difficult locks or broken mechanisms without loss of information or materials. The Seabees have been saving the government untold amounts of money in locations all over the world because the government does not always have a contract for someone with a security clearance to come in and open the locks.

In 2020, the NSU Seabee posted in Dubai, United Arab Emirates, was called upon by a U.S. Navy ship that pulled into port with a damaged Sensitive Compartmented Information Facility (SCIF) door and broken lock. The Seabee met the ship in port and proceeded to make repairs to the door and lock to bring their SCIF back into compliance and able to store classified materials. This timely support is just one example of the incredible skills NSU Seabees attain while with DOS and their ability to respond wherever and whenever around the world.

Ultimately, NSU Seabees became identified as locksmiths as the years passed. Making keys or changing combinations, the Seabees are expert "safe crackers." The skills and certifications they gain in training carry over to all government safes and locks. This skillset earns a Navy Enlisted Classification (NEC) code that indicates they can be used across DOD and other departments and agencies in the federal government.

The go-to experts in DOS, the Seabees regularly recover safes without needing to destroy them to gain access. However, even the most expert locksmith sometimes needs to take out the drill or saw to get in. This can also be a result of a safe breaking. The default for a safe, if a mechanism breaks, is not to break open but break closed. For certain facilities, busting a hole in the wall is the last resort, but if all else fails, the Seabees find a way to recover the contents of a safe, which may include classified documents, devices, munitions, or cash.

Aside from CONSEC and locksmithing, additional skills have been added to the NSU Seabee toolbox, and they have grown evermore advanced and expansive. By the 1980s, with the advent of the personal computer, the Seabees were getting trained on technical security systems before being posted overseas to assist with upgrading the quickly evolving technology. The technical security systems the Seabees have been trained to use and fix over the years include remote buzzers, magnetic locks, physical barriers and gates, silent alarm buttons, secure video systems, high-security alarm systems, uninterrupted power supplies, tear gas systems, acoustic deterrent systems, shredders, x-ray machines, metal detectors, Forced Entry/ Ballistic Resistant (FE/BR) doors and windows, shielded enclosures, and, of course, locks and safes.

Another in-rate skill eventually put to use within DOS was that of construction mechanics. Originally, NSU Seabees were mostly builders, steelworkers, utilitiesmen, and construction electricians. However, construction mechanics quickly followed.

The mechanics were tapped into when NSU Seabees and SY were tasked to execute a vehicle armoring program after multiple kidnappings and killings of U.S. Ambassadors in 1968. The Seabees had already been performing maintenance on Ambassador vehicles in various countries, but now the stakes were raised significantly. The program took on the challenge to armor vehicles because the Seabees were already familiar with the vehicles, making them an instant resource for DOS. Fast forward forty years, as terrorist forces got more sophisticated, the need for armoring of vehicles greatly increased. Seabees in

Iraq and Afghanistan alike began armoring Humvees until the new MTVRs arrived in the countries to better protect personnel in convoy. This type of work demonstrates how adaptable the seven Seabee rates have been, and continue to be, in ways that would have not been comprehended in 1941, when they were first authorized to assemble.

According to Lieutenant Hoff's letter, the vehicle armoring program commenced as a small, insignificant program for DOS and one Seabee. Seabee Master Chief C.C. Walker was asked to provide technical advice and a prototype for DOS to utilize. The program ultimately grew tremendously into a primary objective of NSU. At the time, DOS was also agreeing to armor vehicles for other agencies, despite no DOS employees being extensively involved or knowledgeable of the armoring process. The Seabee construction mechanics involved in the vehicle armoring program were drawn from an automotive preventive maintenance program for Chief of Mission vehicles. The construction mechanics were the auto mechanics for overseas vehicle assets already when vehicle armoring was added to their duties. The two programs that developed from this were the Light Armoring Vehicle (LAV) Program and Chief of Mission Fully Armored Vehicle (FAV) Program. The LAV program consisted of aluminum plating fitted inside the doors, behind the seats, and a few other locations, providing some protection from small arms (pistol) fire. Lexan plastic inserts were also made for the windows.

One vehicle armoring team based out of Panama City, Panama, in 1981 was challenged to provide a fully armored vehicle for the U.S. Ambassador in La Paz, Bolivia. Fully armored vehicles have more robust engines with fuel injectors so that the extra weight of the armor will not limit the vehicle from making evasive maneuvers that are sometimes required. However, La Paz sits at an elevation of approximately 12,000 feet. At this elevation, regular fuel injectors are not enough. It was determined that for La Paz, a supercharger may need to be installed in the Chevrolet Caprice to maintain performance at the high elevation. Retired SEO George Herrmann recalled that after the vehicle was finished in the states, it had to be shipped to Bolivia, arriving at sea level on the Pacific coast. The two Seabee mechanics were to meet the car at the port and drive it up the mountain roads to La Paz. Herrmann said, "As arrangements were being finalized, the speed shop had a question for them: did they want the car shipped with the low altitude fuel jets, which would have required a stop about half-way up the mountains to insert the high-altitude fuel jets, or did they want the car to simply be shipped with high altitude jets in place, which would result in a race-car like ride up the slopes?" Herrmann asked the Seabees, who both said the high-altitude jets would be the way to go. "The Seabees met the car [...] and took turns driving it up the road to La Paz. They said later that it was possible to burn rubber off the tires at any speed allowed by the mountain roads [...] The Ambassador discovered quickly that he could easily lose his Bolivian motorcycle escort whenever he wanted to, and realized he had the fastest car in all Bolivia."[27]

Six to ten Seabees were assigned to these armoring programs through the late 1990s. Over time, every U.S. embassy had its allotment of fully or lightly armored vehicles, and eventually, as with all vehicles, they would come to the end of their useful service life. However, disposal of these vehicles was complicated. They could not be simply resold on the open market overseas due to the armoring. They would either need to be scrapped, used as U.S. military training targets, or dumped at sea to become marine life habitats, but none of these options were determined to be the right solution. The interim solution was to pool the vehicles that were past their prime at strategic locations where VIP visits from the SECSTATE or other cabinet members were common, i.e., NATO, EU, UN, and so on. However, by doing this, it created more maintenance issues if the cars sat too long. The Seabee team in Frankfurt, Germany, proposed to rotate the vehicles to be driven on a somewhat regular basis by members of the ESC team. But, as Oscar Wilde once wrote, "No good deed goes unpunished." According to George Herrmann, nearly all the armored vehicles were high-end, either Cadillacs or Chevrolet Caprices. As the ESC members were driving the vehicles around with "flagstaffs on the front fenders," the embassy began hearing complaints from other members of the embassy community about not being able to drive the vehicles around. In the end, "the inability to equitably regulate the loan of fully armored vehicles to other consulate personnel" meant that the vehicles "became bound to the parking lot."[28]

It wasn't until 2019 that the last Seabee left the Protective Technologies Branch as a Contracting Officer Representative overseeing contractors performing the armoring of vehicles. Today, the SEOs, STSs, and Seabee Technical Security Specialists all receive the same core training. However, each receives some additional skills that the others do not. SEOs are more geared toward project management and countermeasures, and the STSs receive additional certifications for networking and itemizer machines. The Seabees bring their in-rate construction skills for tasks that SEOs and STSs are not utilized for. Otherwise, the STSs and Seabees are true technicians performing maintenance and repairs nearly every day.

Some STSs and Seabees have been known to take their skills to the next level by their exceptional tinkering and resourcefulness. Director Ron Stuart recalled a handful of Seabees and STSs who would find the cause of a lock or other security system failure but, instead of replacing the entire component, would replace the specific part. This can save money; however, keeping inventory of old and replaced locks or systems to salvage for parts takes up precious space and time to be properly inventoried. Without meticulous organization and communication, this ends up creating more work later and can cause someone to unintentionally install a broken component instead of a new component if not aware of the surplus inventory.[29]

In the wake of the Dar es Salaam and Nairobi bombings in 1999, the STS position was created as a permanent member of the Office of Security Technology team. The STSs are true subject matter experts, often with decades of technician experience developed in the private sector or military, and they hone their skills with DOS. STSs often serve as certifiers and inspectors of the technical security work performed and are incredible sources of information and technical knowledge for NSU Seabees just starting out. DOS requested thirty-four STS personnel from Congress in the wake of the bombings. The Office wanted a group of highly trained specialists they could "keep on duty after all the training and experience invested." Retired ST Office Director John Bainbridge recalled that "integrating three very different occupations, i.e., U.S. Navy Seabees, Engineers, and Technicians into a cohesive workforce deployed around the globe at roughly 100 sites was challenging, but [...] it has been an extremely rewarding amalgamation of talent dedicated to keeping America's Foreign Service personnel safe and secure from terrorism and governments which employ clandestine services to ferret out our secrets."[30]

Just as important to learning the technical skills in the schoolhouse is being able to work alongside individuals with varying backgrounds and understanding the skills everyone brings to the mission is critical. All SEOs have degrees in science and technology fields, such as engineering, computer science, or physics. STSs typically come in as master electricians, information technology specialists, computer technicians, or even former Seabees. Seabees have experience in their respective construction rates as well as in project management and small unit leadership.

Ron Stuart, also a former U.S. Marine, recalled occasionally sending Seabees to certain posts due to their command presence and leadership in an effort to help show young SEOs what natural leadership looks like. The soft skills gained from small unit leadership, as well as having endured years of sometimes blistering feedback, the Seabees can often enter an environment and quickly discern the morale and effectiveness of leaders. The Seabees would show up ready to work, take control of the tasking and lead the team of technicians to a successful project completion all while mentoring the SEO on how to engage and focus the team's efforts. After the Seabee would leave, the SEO would sometimes ask Ron if he sent the Seabee on purpose to mentor them. "Absolutely," he would respond.[29] Building a level of trust amongst the three labor types is paramount to be effective in the field on day one. Knowing all members of the team can perform at the same high level, but with a different background, creates a beneficial learning environment for all and a confidence that the right resources and experience are available, strategically postured all around the world.

7

The Early Years

(1964-1982)

The fifty personnel tasked to form Detachment NOVEMBER in 1964 were likely told they were going on a classified mission that was critical to national security. They may have been told they were going behind the Iron Curtain into Moscow to perform construction related tasks. Seabees who had been building and fighting in Vietnam for nearly a decade were now entering the most sophisticated technical threat environment of the Cold War. One can only imagine the thoughts going through their heads on their voyage to Moscow, but perhaps some Seabees had dreams of Russian vodka. Regardless of what they thought they would experience, they knew, once again, that the Seabees were going to be the first to do something.

While deployed in Moscow from 1964 well through the 1980s, NSU was formally established to create a more permanent presence of Seabees within the Department of State. After all, as the story goes, when you give a mouse a cookie, it is going to want a glass of milk. The presence was small at first. NSU Seabees were strategically positioned around the world at various embassies in what became known as the Seabee Residence Program. This program placed a contingent of

Seabees at large U.S. diplomatic facilities located near international travel hubs. These larger hubs were known as Regional Technical Centers that were later renamed Engineering Services Centers (ESC). The first four locations that Resident Seabees were located were Frankfurt, Germany; Manila, Philippines; Panama City, Panama; and Beirut, Lebanon.

As operations expanded, Seabees were also posted in other strategic locations with the same scope of mission but tied to a smaller area of operations. These locations were known as Maintenance Centers but eventually became Engineering Services Offices (ESO). Whether at ESCs or ESOs, Seabees were under the daily control of a SEO. These ESCs and ESOs operated regionally within a hub-and-spoke strategy. From their hubs, they would travel out to perform work at various other locations. At the ESCs, Special Projects and Construction Security Surveillance (CONSEC) were a significant portion of the work. These projects or activities included minor construction projects, post communication centers, and other special work.[31] The post communication centers were in Controlled Access Areas (CAA), which are areas within a building where classified material may be processed, that foreign nationals were not allowed to work in. There are also areas known as Limited Access Areas (LAA). These areas are typically adjoining spaces to a CAA, such as the corridor leading to CAA spaces.

The Maintenance Centers, or ESOs, had fewer Seabees, and their focus was both vehicle maintenance and Technical Security System (TSS) maintenance. Overall, NSU Seabees would maintain TSS with increasing volume as each year went by. This volume of work became most of the daily work for some NSU Seabees. By 1972, this fact resulted in an official request to NSU to perform maintenance on TSS and relieve Technical Security Officers (SEOs today) to be able to perform higher priority work, such as planning and new TSS installations or upgrades.

This shift in focus away from construction did not stop at TSS. For a brief time, Seabees were also assigned to logistic support, including shipping-container construction for the DOS armory in Washington, D.C. This was similar to work already being performed to support the shipping and receiving of vehicle parts overseas under the vehicle maintenance program.

Within the armory, they would repair standard pistols and rifles in addition to teaching new RSOs and TSOs on their function and operation. This wasn't the responsibility of the Seabees; however, like that mouse with a cookie, when you give someone a Seabee, they're going to ask for other things, too. Weapon handling skills are a military necessity that Seabees have been trained for, but that's not something they typically receive enough training on to be considered experts. In 1885, the U.S. Navy created the Gunner's Mates (GM) rating to perform this type of function as their primary duties.[32] The majority of Seabees' experience using weapons would likely have been high; however, their expertise in performing the tasks of a GM to train new RSOs and TSOs would have been amateur in comparison.

Diplomatic Security Service training in the early 1970s was still mostly limited to protective services for U.S. ambassadors and foreign dignitaries. However, following the diplomatic killings in Khartoum, Sudan, in 1973, training quickly modernized in response to the new threats, and they no longer left it to the Seabees for their small-arms introduction. The Seabees' involvement quickly lessened to mostly shipping and receiving security commodities, such as munitions and weapons, before completely tapering off by the late 1970s. The vehicle armoring program also came under fire during this time for similar reasons. Work that either took the Seabees away from their in-rate skills or could have been performed by civilians or contract labor was an easy target for NSU leadership, who moved personnel away from those tasks.

During these early years, despite some mission creep away from their core tasks, NSU was involved in several events at embassies around the world that tested their core mission in Moscow. Amidst the Prague Spring in 1968, a fire erupted in the upper floors of the eighteenth-century building that was home to the U.S. embassy of what was then, Czechoslovakia. The old building was extremely vulnerable to fire, which threatened to engulf the building without a quick response. The resident Seabee, William Darrah, at great risk to himself, was highly commended for preventing a major fire: "Due to a curfew, the local fire department was unavailable. In response, the members of the embassy staff, U.S. news correspondents, and private American citizens formed a bucket brigade and managed to control and extinguish the fire. The U.S. Ambassador to Czechoslovakia said, 'By general agreement, the person who merits the highest praise is Seabee William B. Darrah, who knew his job thoroughly and showed great personal courage.'"[33]

Shortly thereafter, a team of NSU Seabees was sent to Prague. Working around the clock and, despite material delays and other shortfalls due to the invasion by the Soviet Union, the team restored the upper floors of the damaged chancery within a matter of weeks without additional disruption to embassy operations.[34]

During an emergency mission in response to a magnitude 6.2 earthquake that hit Managua, Nicaragua, on December 23, 1972, the Seabees made extensive repairs within hours of arriving. Approximately 3,000 aftershocks devastated much of the city for nearly two weeks.[35] They sifted through debris and collected classified and sensitive documents and equipment. The tremendous effort of the Seabees insured the United States' financial losses were kept to a minimum and that the integrity of its classified holdings was maintained.

While one team was assisting in Nicaragua, NSU Seabees were also some of the first DOS personnel sent into China after the establishment of a U.S. Liaison Office in May 1973.[36] There was an abrupt and immediate need for a secure facility with minimal planning, but the Seabees proved their worth by constructing a facility that was both "aesthetically pleasing and superbly functional," according to Victor Dikeos, the Acting Assistant Secretary of State for Administration. This work earned a meritorious unit commendation citation recommendation that went on to state: "The examples cited above were chosen not because they represent the high points of the overall NSU effort during this period, but because they are suitably illustrative of the kind of success against bewildering odds that the Department of State has come to expect of Seabees."[34]

Another significant event occurred in early 1973 that forever altered the culture and nature of business for Diplomatic Security and NSU Seabees. On March 1, 1973, the Saudi Arabian Embassy in Sudan was stormed by the Black September Organization, resulting in the killing of three Western diplomats.[37] These individuals included the U.S. Ambassador to Sudan Cleo Noel and the Deputy Chief of Mission George Curtis Moore.

By 1974, NSU had grown from fifty to seventy-four Seabees and was also operating from ESCs in Nairobi, Kenya, and Hong Kong, a British Colony, in addition to the four original locations. They were about to grow more. Following this atrocious act of terrorism in Sudan, an amendment for 21.8 million USD was made to the 1974 U.S. congressional budget.[38] The result of this amendment was an explosion of technical and physical security installations and upgrades at diplomatic facilities abroad that also included thirty new NSU Seabee positions. Twenty of these positions were for the Resident Seabee Program, five were to support the Vehicle Maintenance Program from Washington, D.C., and the remaining five were to be posted at Maintenance Centers to perform vehicle maintenance and light armoring in the field.

DOS immediately began to hire additional Technical Security Officers with electronic engineering backgrounds to monitor new security system devices and, in haste, assumed the Seabees could and would absorb the preexisting aspects of the ST program on a permanent basis. These aspects broadly included the maintenance of any existing systems while a number of new technologies were being planned and implemented by the TSOs. For some time, as discussed earlier, the Seabees took on this role in the dynamic environment with the influx of work and strained manpower to keep up with the high demands of Congress and the public to drastically improve protection for American diplomats abroad. Some of these activities included installing and monitoring sophisticated electronic equipment, extensive lock modifications, x-ray operations, vehicle armoring, bomb searches, protective services for the SECSTATE and other U.S. government dignitaries while on travel, as well as on occasion, performing duties as couriers. The Seabee toolbox had grown to carry out tasks across the spectrum of DSS Special Agents, Couriers, and Technical Security Officers, let alone their original construction-based assignments.

As the unit grew and the mission continued to evolve, on August 10, 1977, NSU Seabees were part of the original team to re-enter Havana, Cuba. Diplomatic relations had ceased in 1961, following a series of properties of U.S. corporations being nationalized by the Cuban government, led by Fidel Castro. This advance team was sent to prepare the existing U.S. Embassy that was originally opened in 1953 and is still in use today. (However, the facility today is extremely dilapidated, due to its position on the coast and decades of hurricanes that have pounded its façade.)[39] Just a few weeks later, on September 1, 1977, an agreement was signed with Cuba by the Carter administration to establish a U.S. Interests Section under the protection of the Embassy of Switzerland.

Around the same time, on the night of August 26, 1977, a fire broke out in the upper floors of U.S. Embassy Moscow. This fire led to widespread damage that gutted the eighth and ninth floor and caused significant water and smoke on the seventh and tenth floors, as well as the attic. It was believed that an electrical fault within the facilities haphazard wiring caused the fire. There were two other theories of how the fire began: a tea kettle left on too long and the intense microwave radiation that was suspected of being emitted directly at the embassy by the Russians from the rooftop shed across the street, causing the electrical devices to overload and cause a spark. The building was crammed with U.S. personnel, as the Cold War raged, and it was constantly being renovated to accommodate more people. A couple of Seabees from the Naval Mobile Construction Battalions were asked to supplement the NSU Seabees already there to assist with the significant repairs from the fire.[40] Negotiations for a new embassy building were underway, but not moving quickly enough. Nevertheless, in response to the fire, eight Marines and Seabees were called in as well as two structural engineers, likely from FBO.[41]

In St. Petersburg, the TSO at the time, Bob Bryan, recalled that the Seabee shop on the fourth floor of the consulate had become a "dumping ground" for construction material since its opening in 1972. Prior to the fire in Moscow, they had "excavated" the room and disposed of a lot of "sensitive junk," but they also found large amounts of good material, which they set aside for a rainy day. A lot of that material was shipped from St. Petersburg to Moscow after the fire, and the Moscow Seabee team was busy for a week making repairs while they waited for additional materials to arrive. The fire must have helped the United States negotiate for a new building.

The never-ending stream of work in Moscow continued in 1979. Seabees of NSU were assigned to provide CONSEC of the new embassy office building that was finally approved and now under construction. CONSEC duties may simply be defined as the responsibility to detect and report any suspected or actual attempt by construction workers to surreptitiously introduce listening devices, conduits, or channels which may be used to technologically penetrate sensitive working areas.[42] These CONSEC duties were confined to the office building itself and did not include any of the housing or recreation and support facilities in the new embassy complex. In this iteration of diplomatic tit-for-tat negotiating with Russia, the United States (i.e., Seabees) were not allowed to monitor fabrication of the precast floor panels, wall panels, or columns that were all constructed off site. Structural materials, such as reinforcing bar, steel beams, and interior brick, were required to be manufactured in the Soviet Union. During construction of the new embassy, as columns began to be put up, the Seabees identified inconsistencies in construction practices and techniques. Upon further investigation, it was discovered that the Russian contractors were installing listening devices in the columns of the building. This was the most significant find by the Seabees since the unit was conceived. Work on the embassy was brought to a full stop, and it took years for construction to get back on track.[43]

Outside CONSEC, Seabees were neither tasked nor expected to provide construction quality control of the new office building. This was, and remains, the sole responsibility of the DOS's Bureau of Overseas Building Operations (OBO), formally known as the Foreign Buildings Office. However, as tradesmen who find it impossible to keep "constructive criticism" to themselves, Seabees regularly reported inferior construction practices or materials to appropriate officials. This information was unsurprisingly met with mixed reviews.

On February 14, 1979, the U.S. Embassy in Tehran, Iran, was overrun for approximately two hours by armed Iranian gunmen. Leading up to this was a series of events recalled by retired SEO Paul Tubbs. The United States had supported the elevation and election of the Shah, Reza Palavi, in the 1950s. Over the years, the exiled Ayatollah Khomeini spent most of his time in Iraq waiting to make his return. In November 1978, the Shah departed Iran for medical reasons and traveled to Egypt and Morocco to receive treatment. Eventually, he ended up in Panama. Leading up to the Shah's departure in December 1978, as the political environment became more volatile, the U.S. Ambassador asked personnel if dependents would want to depart the country as part of an unofficial authorized departure. Every dependent volunteered to do so.[44] The months leading up to this, embassy personnel and their families had been witness to a rising tide of demonstrations against the United States. They would also receive regular security notices about "keeping your TV and radio turned down low," due to the English broadcasts that would identify them as Americans.

Tubbs said, "Travel to and from the embassy, in the U.S. government armored vehicles, became a daily exercise [. . .] In mid-February, some powerful group had demanded that the U.S. Embassy refrain from raising the American flag and, of course, that demand was refused. The next day [February 14, 1979] the embassy compound was attacked and taken over." Tubbs further noted that two Seabees were in the chancery at the time of attack, while he was in the nearby ESO building. After the Marine Security Guards gave up their final positions, since "the continuing defense of which was futile," the American employees "gathered and it was arranged for Pan American Airways to supply three Boeing 747 aircraft the next day to begin evacuating those who either insisted on such, or those whom the Ambassador decided should depart. Tubbs departed the following day on a 747 that "had nearly a dozen people sitting in the aisles."[44]

The embassy was eventually returned to United States control by Iran's revolutionary forces by the direction of Ayatollah Khomeini after all U.S. Marines' weapons were seized.[44] In immediate response, and once the Marines were resupplied, two NSU Seabees made emergency repairs to a bullet-riddled generator at the U. S. embassy later that same month while under Marine guard. Thomas Tracy, the Assistant

Secretary of State for Administration wrote in his recommendation to Secretary of the Navy Edward Hidalgo that this accomplishment "restored power and a semblance of order to the facilities there after the facility was first overrun."[45] Subsequent innovative security improvements made by the Seabees in the wake of the embassy takeover greatly improved the post's physical security posture. However, on November 4, 1979, the U.S. Embassy in Tehran was again overrun but this time by student militants that resulted in 66 hostages taken for 444 days. This is now known as the Iran Hostage Crisis. Therefore, despite the improvements made and due to the ensuing events, the embassy closed on April 7, 1980, when diplomatic relations were officially severed with Iran.[46]

In the wake of the capture of the Marine Security Guard detachment in November of 1979, NAVFAC, the ISIC for NSU, took significant concern for the conduct of military personnel in a hostage or terrorist situation. The point of concern was who was to assume command or take lead during a hostage situation. In an event purely of war or armed conflict, it is likely that only military members would be taken as Prisoners of War or hostage. However, with non-state sponsored terrorist actors, it is likely that military personnel could be taken hostage, in addition to higher ranking civilian foreign service diplomats, such as the ambassador or Deputy Chief of Mission (DCM). At any time, it would be somewhat counterintuitive to have an E-6 or E-7 servicemember take charge in the presence of a what equates to a 4-star military flag officer equivalent. The U.S. Navy requested that DOS provide feedback for subject conduct in these situations for policy to be developed and promulgated.

During armed conflict, if captured and held captive, military personnel are trained to follow the six articles of the code of conduct, which provides instruction on the behavior and obligations expected of them during combat or captivity.[47] In 1980, following the hostage crisis in Tehran, where the Marine Security Guard Detachment was taken hostage during the student militia takeover of the embassy, NAVFAC requested guidance from the Chief of Naval Operations for how military members not in armed conflict were to act. NAVFAC referred to DOD Directive 1300.7, dated May 23, 1980, which stated that military members during instances of detention outside of armed conflict would require "special instructions." NAVFAC was now asking what these "special instructions" were to be given to NSU's multiple overseas resident Seabees.

Code of Conduct for Members of the United States Armed Forces[47]

I: I am an American, fighting in the forces which guard my country and our way of life. I am prepared to give my life in their defense.

II: I will never surrender of my own free will. If in command, I will never surrender the members of my command while they still have the means to resist.

III: If I am captured, I will continue to resist by all means available. I will make every effort to escape and aid others to escape. I will accept neither parole nor special favors from the enemy.

IV: If I become a prisoner of war, I will keep faith with my fellow prisoners. I will give no information or take part in any action which might be harmful to my comrades. If I am senior, I will take command. If not, I will obey the lawful orders of those appointed over me and will back them up in every way.

V: When questioned, should I become a prisoner of war, I am required to give my name, rank, service number and date of birth. I will evade answering further questions to the utmost of my ability. I will make no oral or written statements disloyal to my country and its allies or harmful to their cause.

VI: I will never forget that I am an American, fighting for freedom, responsible for my actions, and dedicated to the principles which made my country free. I will trust in my God and in the United States of America.

Working in concert with multiple other agencies, the Marine Security Guard Battalion produced a training concept card to gather lessons learned as to best survive with dignity without compromising the code of conduct in response to the events in Tehran. However, one aspect that it still did not address was what might occur if the military members were held hostage with civilians, or more pertinently, career foreign service officers or political appointees, such as the U.S. Ambassador, Chargé d'Affaires, Deputy Chief of Mission, or Consulate General.[48]

Articles II and IV both reference "command." The idea is, of those captured, whoever is the most senior military member present will be the leader or spokesperson for those in captivity. What if a Lance Corporal, a Second Class Petty Officer, a Lieutenant Colonel, or a Commander were the most senior in the military, but they were in the company of the U.S. Ambassador? Certainly, this scenario was plausible, given events at the time. Having a plan in place for who takes command in this situation would be incredibly important to avoid disagreement about how to act or respond to the captors given the code of conduct. In May 1980, a proposal was drafted by the Office of the Judge Advocate General that discussed the code of conduct during peacetime hostage situations specific to when an embassy is overrun.[49] It was eventually determined that while the Ambassador of the U.S. mission in the country of interest is still able to lead, they would remain in charge of any military personnel that were operating under the authority of Chief of Mission within the hostage situation. Should the Ambassador be incapacitated, then the senior military member could assume the leadership role for all personnel present. This is because the Ambassador holds privileges in their country assignment with the host nation government as a direct representative of the head of state. For the United States, an ambassador posted abroad is a direct representative of the President of the United States within host country. If an embassy or consulate general was overrun while only a Charge d'Affaires or Consular General is on site, i.e., officials who do not hold the same privileges or representation as the Ambassador and direct representative of the head of state, then the senior military leader could assume the leadership role immediately, despite any paygrade disparities.

It may seem rash to have a military member immediately take over for the Chargé or Consular General; however, military personnel receive training on survival and being prisoners of war in their basic training and every time they deploy overseas. However, in no way would the military member take the leadership role as long as the diplomatic facility was still in control of U.S. personnel. It is also not a forgone conclusion that the senior military member takes over immediately, as every situation is different, and a certain amount of diplomacy should be attempted to avoid any further escalation. Unfortunately, as history has shown, that is not always possible. The military will work with the senior diplomats at post to respond to any forces that ultimately overrun an embassy in order to secure their safe passage out of a country or ensure they are provided with hygienic conditions as diplomats under the Vienna Convention on Diplomatic Relations. The complexities surrounding military personnel serving overseas as a diplomat in often hostile conditions while under Chief of Mission authority are innumerable. Conducting oneself under peacetime hostilities is no exception.

On the other side of the world, in response to the eruption of the civil war in El Salvador, 1979, emergency support was requested to construct access controls at the U.S. Embassy in San Salvador, the nation's capital. NSU responded with a carefully researched and planned project that was completed well ahead of schedule despite the country being stricken with severe political instability and violence. The NSU team of Seabees also made significant contribution to improve the working and living conditions for post officials and made time-critical repairs to embassy vehicles that later facilitated the tense and dangerous evacuation of personnel from the country.

In 1980, while the work continued, the U.S. Ambassador to El Salvador queried NSU regarding the handling of weapons. NSU Seabees are not meant to serve as a protective force for an embassy, even though they are military personnel with weapons training and their motto: "We Build, We Fight." Nevertheless, today, in the capacity that Seabees serve DOS, handling weapons in an official capacity is not allowed without prior OIC approval. Throughout the 1980s, however, after multiple bombings and in locations where personal safety getting to and from the embassy was extremely dangerous, some Seabees were issued sidearm weapons to protect themselves while at a post.[40]

It must be considered what overseas conditions were often like in the 1980s. Most embassies had only ten to twelve Americans working at the facility with local nationals carrying out many of the duties. The RSO program was only slowly increasing in scale with slim human resources. The local guard forces that are employed today were nowhere to be found at that time. Ultimately, it was officially determined that if the Ambassador directs the Seabees in extreme circumstances (such as a bomb attack or invasion of the facility) to use weapons, the Seabees would be able to act utilizing their military training to defend the facility, personnel, and information until properly relieved or evacuated from the property.

Emergency recovery support was provided to U.S. Embassy Islamabad, Pakistan, following its destruction by a hostile mob in November 1979. NSU participated in both the initial survey of damages and the immediate reconstruction of secure communications facilities at post. The planning team assisted DOS in setting up temporary operations, restoring order to the myriad safe/file containers filled with classified documents, and planning future manpower and material resources to reconstruct the mission's required secure areas in response to the destruction.

The early years of NSU were highlighted by a considerable amount of work in Moscow and in other countries in the Eastern Bloc, as well as the numerous high visibility events they responded to worldwide. As the skills and expertise of the Seabees became ever more potent, the application of Seabee labor began to grow well beyond the original scope of work that the Seabees were first brought in for. Despite this recognized scope creep and alarms sounded by NSU through repeated memos to U.S. Navy and DOS leadership, the work continued to be taken on. Additional training for the Seabees to become experts in the new field of work of technical security also became intentional, rather than ad hoc on-the-job training.

The Seabees in general find it hard to say no and love to be the solution to a need or problem. They cherish the role of solving the seemingly unsolvable. Within DOS, there are a number of experts and skilled technicians, but the type of work they do is not well known by the public, and finding personnel to hire is difficult. This work entails regular international travel and living abroad, far from extended family and friends, in often remote and austere locations. On top of this, the need for personnel with advanced technical degrees makes recruiting challenging, to say the least. The integration of the

Seabees into DOS helped fill a critical gap in the absence of adequate civilian hiring.

If not already, it will become evident that this dynamic labor pool has been able to adjust to the needs of DOS whenever needed. Despite straying far from its original scope, the U.S. Navy never decommissioned the unit, which probably has a lot to do with the financial arrangement between DOS and the U.S. Navy, as well as the pride of seeing manifest the Seabee ethos of "Can Do!" The Navy will always be committed to providing personnel to billets that are funded, even in time of war, as they have since the Vietnam War. By 1982, the unit had doubled in size to 109 personnel and its growth wouldn't stop there.

8

A Changing Environment

(1983-2000)

In the southwest Asian country of Lebanon, a civil war began in 1975. Syrian, Israeli, and UN interventions attempted to diffuse the situation but to no avail. A multinational force, including American troops landed in Beirut in August 1982. At first, it seemed this force would be successful, but soon after its departure, just weeks after arriving, tensions escalated following a massacre of Palestinian refugees and the multinational force returned. This multinational force included U.S. Marines and Seabees.

On April 18, 1983, the U.S. Embassy in Beirut, Lebanon, was bombed by Islamic activists. A truck packed with about two thousand pounds of explosives killed sixty-three people, including the suicide bomber and seventeen Americans. Islamic Jihad, a group linked to Hezbollah (a Lebanon-based terrorist group), claimed responsibility for the attack. Although this attack seemed to have come from nowhere to most Americans, Beirut was a ticking timebomb. Not much changed until after October 23, 1983, when the U.S. Marine and French barracks were bombed, killing 243 U.S. military members and fifty-eight French soldiers. Within four months, the Reagan administration removed all remaining U.S. Marines as part of the original force.

Former Office Director of Security Technology John Bainbridge was assigned to the Regional Technical Security Office in Athens, Greece, in 1983. His office was responsible for overseeing facilities in southern Europe and a large portion of the Middle and Near East, to include Lebanon. He recalled the numerous movements of U.S. embassy operations in the wake of the first attack, arriving in Beirut a few days later after the first bombing: "As the U.S. embassy was shattered beyond use, the British allowed [U.S. personnel] to establish operations in their embassy until [the United States] could find another building to renovate [...] The decision was made to renovate a building in West Beirut." However, while Foreign Building Operations readied the site by installing "ballistic windows, door access controls, vehicle barriers, CCTV, alarms, and even a 50-caliber rooftop gun placement," the area was becoming less stable, so the U.S. government abandoned the site and moved across the so-called Green Line to a more secure location in the eastern portion of the city.[50] The Green Line separated the Christians in the East and Muslims to the West between the 1970s and 1990.

Meanwhile, the interim U.S. Embassy had moved from the British Embassy and was operating out of the U.S. Ambassador's residence in the southeast suburb of Yarze. As the environment continued to evolve, after the U.S. Marine barracks were bombed on October 23, 1983, access to Beirut's U.S. Mission was only possible by U.S. military helicopter if the "security situation on the ground was deemed suitable for a landing." "This was the third U.S. Embassy in Beirut to be abandoned since the civil war began a decade earlier [...] Another site was chosen near the Baaklini Annex and designated as the Temporary Office Site that was also later abandoned." Before it was abandoned, several Seabees were assigned from the Athens office as part of a crew assigned to install security equipment at the new site.[50]

Amid the bombings of the U.S. embassy and the Marine barracks in Beirut, on November 11, 1983, Naval Mobile Construction Battalion ONE (NMCB 1), then deployed at Rota, Spain, was alerted of a potential tasking in support of the U.S. Marines, who were part of the Multinational Peacekeeping Force in Beirut. The tasking consisted of improving the living conditions of the Marines located at Beirut International Airport. On November 14, NMCB 1 sent a survey team to Beirut, and on November 24, Thanksgiving Day, Detail Bravo Lima departed for Beirut. The tasking was completed with Seabees and sixty-one pieces of equipment returning on March 1, 1984. This was the first involvement of Naval Construction Force Seabees under combat conditions since the Vietnam conflict.[10]

After the initial Beirut bombings in 1983, on December 12, 1983, the U.S. Embassy Kuwait City, Kuwait, was also struck with a vehicle bomb. A solo NSU Seabee was there. At the time of the blast, he was performing maintenance on the roof of the chancery. Former NSU OIC James McConnell recalled the story told to him, which was that the Seabee was nearly blown off the roof by the blast but managed to grab onto an antenna to keep himself from going over the edge. When the Seabee got off the roof and went to look at what happened, he realized the bomb had hit the consular section where his wife worked. At the time, he did not know his wife had, fortunately, left to run an errand and was not in the consular section at the time of the blast.[51] At least two people were killed and over fifty injured by the blast. Seabees and their families can often be in danger at posts in hostile environments, like Beirut, then and now.

On September 20, 1984, a Seabee team assigned to the new site in Beirut was completing installations in the Marine Security Guard booth and on the roof when another incident occurred: "a van came around the corner and stopped short of entering the basement entrance only because the visiting British Ambassador's bodyguards opened fire on the vehicle. A vehicle barrier lying next to the road would have prevented the van's access but was not yet installed." The blast killed twenty-three people, including two U.S. Military personnel from the Defense Attaché Office in Beirut. [50,52]

Stephan Haycook, a Builder First Class Petty Officer (BU1) in NSU, was at the Baaklini Annex along with four other Seabees on the team in Beirut the day the bomb hit, September 20, 1984. The following is his firsthand account of that morning:

Just prior to the blast, I was in the Consular Section of the Embassy with the FBO Project Manager and one of the contractor's foremen going over work that was to begin there that day. From the consular section, I went in the lobby and then out the main door of the embassy. Since it was almost lunchtime, I was headed outside to the front to smoke a cigarette and then go for something to eat.

I had not heard any of the shots that were fired at the bomb truck as it forced its way through the gate leading to the embassy and was simply on my way outside. I had just cleared the building and stepped onto the drive when the blast occurred. I was only 30 to 40 feet from the point where the blast went off. The blast lifted me off my feet and threw me backwards about eight feet back inside the foyer of the building. I found myself lying flat on my back, covered with debris and the ceiling of the foyer.

The blast hit me pretty hard, and it took a couple of seconds for me to come to my senses... I knocked the debris off myself, stood up, and went back into the building. Hearing screams, I made my way to the Consular Section and started carrying people out. At this time, I didn't know what exactly had happened, only that there was an explosion. When the ground floor of the building had been cleared, I headed upstairs and continued to dig people out and carry them outside

[...] After they had cleared the building of people, it was time to start gathering and removing the classified.[53]

It was not until September 23 that Haycook was able to see a doctor and then again on September 25. Both of these times were with state medical personnel from the embassy during the mass casualty recovery period. Despite still not having had a chance to see an ear, nose, and throat specialist, all the doctors determined he had a ruptured left ear drum; an injury sustained while conducting life-saving acts to recover injured personnel and secure classified information. On September 27, he was able to catch a helicopter out to the *U.S.S. Shreveport* (LPD-12), in the Mediterranean at the time. The ship had been flying in support to the embassy from their position at sea.

The primary reason BU1 Haycook was flying out to Shreveport was to accompany materials to be used at the embassy. BU1 Haycook was tagged to go. Dressed in what civilian clothes he had and carrying a backpack with some of his other belongings, including a bologna sandwich. The secondary reason he was tasked to take the flight was to get checked out by the Navy doctors onboard, given his injuries from the blast. When he landed on board, most assumed he was a civilian, since he was not in uniform, and he came known as "Mr. Haycook." When he did land on deck, he found a Chief Aviation Boatswain's Mate (ABHC) and asked where the materials were that he was supposed to accompany back to the embassy. As it turned out, the helicopter they passed on the way to the ship was carrying the materials, they had gotten cleared to go while he was getting picked up. Without a need to hurry back, he checked in with medical. There they learned he was a First Class Petty Officer and a Seabee Builder.

After their assessment of him, they determined he should get follow-on care in Rota, Spain, where they were sailing to next. He would be able to stay on board and then get back to the United States from there. What the ship didn't realize was that BU1 Haycook needed to get back to the embassy and finish the mission. Through some scuttlebutt in medical, he learned there was a detachment of Seabees supporting minesweeping operations in the area, and they were, in fact, onboard in the well-deck. BU1 Haycook immediately made a beeline for the well deck and met up with his fellow Seabees. They took him in and got him set up in the galley with some fresh food so he didn't have to eat the stale bologna sandwich in his bag.

Overnight, he stayed in the medical berth. One night on ship was enough for him, though, and in the morning, he was "ready to escape."[40] Going back up to the flight deck, he found the ABHC again and presented his diplomatic credentials as "Mr. Haycook" and asked when the next flight to the embassy was. The Chief told him to standby and that he would put him on the manifest for the next flight leaving within the next half an hour. The wait was just short enough. As he was boarding the aircraft, he faintly heard over what is commonly referred to as the 1MC, or public address circuit: "BU1 Haycook, report to sick bay. BU1 Haycook, report to sick bay." Just in the nick of time, he escaped the ship and was no longer at risk of being sent home due to his injury. After returning to the embassy, he worked there for a couple more weeks before the Reagan Administration decided to remove all non-essential personnel from Beirut and stop preparing an embassy for operations. In that time, Haycook was able to discard his trusty bologna sandwich that made it with him over the entire two-day trip.[40]

This dedication of the Seabees would be even more crucial moving forward. The 1980s had already started off with President Reagan's intent to build a 600-ship U.S. Navy. Since the end of the Vietnam War, the fleet had quickly downsized from 847 in 1970 to 538 in 1980.[54] Throughout the 1980s, up until the Berlin Wall fell on November 9, 1989, the catalyst for the decline of the Soviet Union and the end of the Cold War, the United States invested heavily in strengthening its forces in anticipation of war with Russia. However, for NSU and the DOS, the U.S. embassy bombing and the Marine barracks bombing in Beirut were the first major dominoes to fall that eventually led to the establishment of the Bureau of Diplomatic Security, the Diplomatic Security Service, and multiple requests for additional Seabees.

On November 5, 1984, Assistant Secretary for State for Administration Robert Lamb wrote to the Assistant Secretary of Defense for Manpower, Installation, and Logistics Lawrence Korb, in a request for fifty more Seabees for a two-year period to "staff out existing program and new activities." The activities were to provide "security related construction and repair and construction surveillance."[55] This was in immediate response to mandates by congress to expand State's security program.

Shortly after this request, reorganization (in conjunction with the Foreign Relations Authorization Act of the same Federal omnibus bill in 1986, discussed in Part I), formally established the Diplomatic Security Service as a United States Law Enforcement Agency with criminal investigative authority and ability to arrest suspects and execute warrants in every country around the world with an U.S. diplomatic presence.[4] The DSS is the only overseas Law Enforcement Agency for the United States, and its agents are trained to perform many of the same missions and tasks as the FBI and Secret Service; however, the expanse and reach of DSS is across more than 270 countries around the world.[56]

The FBI does have offices overseas, known as the Legal Attaché, or "Legat" for short. The Legat does not conduct foreign intelligence or counterintelligence investigations. Their primary role is to coordinate on investigations of interest to both the United States and the host country.[57] Comparatively, DSS performs investigations abroad, often related to passport and visa fraud. Human smuggling and trafficking as well as transnational crime are the two other major categories of investigations that occur.[56] The Secret Service primarily protects U.S. dignitaries and visiting world leaders, elections, and national-level events. Although this will take them all around the world, they, like the Legat, work with local law enforcement agencies abroad but do not conduct investigations in those countries.[58] The DSS provides protective details for U.S. Ambassadors overseas in addition to protective details for foreign diplomats traveling in the United States, similar to the Secret Service.[56]

Around the same time, in South America, there were many hostile actors operating throughout El Salvador, Nicaragua, and Honduras. Prior to BU1 Haycook's support in Beirut in 1984, he was sent on a three-month mission through these three countries to support the vehicle armoring of approximately forty vehicles in response to the assassination of U.S. Navy Lieutenant Commander Albert Schaufelberger in San Salvador on May 25, 1983.[40] BU1 Haycook would find himself in the middle of multiple hostile activities throughout his time in NSU.

Leaving Nicaragua on the same trip in September 1983, he was being driven to the airport by an embassy driver. As they were driving up to the airport, two Cessna aircraft flew over. One began dropping homemade bombs over the airport in an attack on the control tower. The other focused on nearby residences of senior officials. Anti-aircraft fire brought the Cessna down, but it crashed into the tower after being hit.[59] Needless to say, the driver immediately turned the vehicle and headed back for the embassy. BU1 Haycook would not be flying out of San Salvador that day.

Returning to San Salvador in June 1985, where the Seabees helped evacuate the embassy during previous civil unrest at the outbreak of El Salvador's civil war in 1979, two Seabee mechanics were on a regular TDY trip to support the vehicle armoring program. Operating out of Panama City, Panama, they frequented the posts throughout Central

America on a regular basis. Retired SEO George Herrmann recalled when the two mechanics were sent to San Salvador during the continuing civil war: "Their plane arrived on a Friday, they checked into their hotel and then into the embassy." They visited "the RSO and [outlined] their work plan. They then checked in with the Marines." Over the repeated visits to San Salvador, the Seabees had grown a close relationship with the Marines, often exercising with them and spending their liberty time together. After a couple of days on the ground, the Marines invited them out to a restaurant to eat and down some beers. However, "on checking out the Ambassador's Cadillac, the Seabees found that one of the suspension parts had been badly damaged, and it appeared as if the front axle might have been slightly bent. Fortunately, spare parts were available at post, so they set to work. The Seabees had to tell the Marines that they had to skip the festivities because they needed to work late."[60] On that same evening, June 19, 1985, several gunman opened fire with automatic weapons and killed thirteen people, including four off-duty U.S. Marines who had invited them to the Zona Rosa restaurant that evening.[61] Herrmann said, "Had it not been for the bent suspension parts, (NSU) may have lost both Seabees as well."[60]

After a few years of highly superlative work and actions, NSU received a Navy Unit Commendation (NUC) in 1984. This type of commendation, awarded by the Secretary of the Navy to any unit of the U.S. Navy or Marine Corps, recognizes outstanding heroism in action against the enemy, "or to any such unit that has distinguished itself by extremely meritorious service, not involving combat, but in support of military operations, rendering the unit outstanding compared to other units performing similar service."[62]

This was the first NUC the unit received. The award was presented during a ceremony at the Department of State's Harry S. Truman Building. In attendance was then Secretary of State George Shultz and Chief of Civil Engineers, RADM John Paul Jones Jr. The NSU OIC was Lieutenant James McConnell. McConnell recalled, when he was reading the introduction for Secretary Shultz, he stated that Mr. Shultz "was" a Marine. From behind him, he heard Secretary Shultz correct him, "I am a Marine!"[51]

Secretary Shultz served as an artillery officer with the U.S. Marines during WWII. During this same time period, the unit attracted the attention of Vernon Walters, a retired Lieutenant General, who had risen to the highest ranks after beginning as a Private in the U.S. Army during WWII. Serving as a roving U.S. Ambassador during a portion of the Reagan years, he often found his way into NSU spaces when they were headquartered at the Harry S. Truman Building. According to McConnell, Walters enjoyed colorful conversations with the Seabees as a former enlisted himself. Walters served as the Deputy Director of the CIA, U.S. Ambassador to the Republic of Germany during reunification, and the U.S. Ambassador to the United Nations.[63]

On September 9, 1985, our good friend BU1 Haycook found himself back in the middle of the action. This time he was in Bangkok, Thailand, during an attempted military coup. Thankfully, he was not in proximity to the fighting that ensued for approximately ten hours. However, his time in Bangkok was not going to be without an up-close eruption of fire. The U.S. Embassy in Bangkok is today on one piece of property a few hundred feet up the street from the old embassy that was retained and is now an annex building for additional office space. BU1 Haycook was on site with another team of Seabees, executing a Post Communication Center (PCC) renovation. The top of the facility, built following the Vietnam War, had a helicopter pad on the roof in case of the need to evacuate, as in Saigon in 1975. Under the helicopter pad was a storeroom, and this was where a bunch of the materials for the renovation were. Also on the roof, were a number of old Vietnam-era document "destruct barrels." These barrels are fifty-five-gallon drums lined with cardboard and ignitable materials that would burn so hot that even the barrel would melt in on itself. The resident Seabee posted in Bangkok, who was not assigned to the project, was supposed to be removing these barrels. However, before moving them, it was determined that the ignitors needed to be removed due to degradation of the plastic to prevent an accidental ignition. Although, in theory, this may have been a good idea, how it was executed was less than ideal. The ignitors ended up being tossed into a pile. The ignitors that were removed were safe enough when kept separate. However, during a lunch break, one of the Seabees began playing with the ignitors to see if they'd light, throwing the spent ones into a barrel. One of the ignitors thrown did not make it into the barrel and instead ended up in the pile of ignition material meant to burn extremely hot and fast. Flames erupted from the massive pile with an unbearable heat. The Seabees scattered. The resident Seabee went in one direction and ended up on the opposite side of the roof than the team of Seabees from the PCC project. BU1 Haycook recalled the resident Seabee disappearing off the roof and praying that he landed safely below.[40]

At this point, the Seabees needed to tell someone the roof was on fire and also put the fire out quickly, if they could. BU1 Haycook ran downstairs. Not trying to cause a panic when he made it to the RSO's office, he knocked on the door and calmly informed the RSO that the roof was on fire. Of course, panic ensued. As the RSO worked to get the building evacuated and called for the Thai fire department for back up, the Seabees were running to find all the fire extinguishers. One found a fire hose in the stairwell and Haycook ran with it up to the roof. Unfortunately, when they turned the water on, they realized the hose had rotted, and the water was spraying from the connection and none of it was getting through the hose to the roof. While Haycook was on the roof, he had eyed a cart with two cylinders on it. Originally, he thought they were oxygen and acetylene tanks for welding but then realized it was a "crash cart" in case a helicopter crashed on the roof and started a fire. Grabbing the nozzle from this cart, he pulled it around to direct it at the fire. When one Seabee opened the valve, the pressurized fire suppressant came out at a high velocity. However, instead of putting the fire out, it pushed the flaming material over the edge of the roof, and it began to rain down on the ground below. In a matter of seconds, the fire was out on the roof, but now it was scattered to the wind. Thankfully, the remaining materials burned themselves out and no one was injured on the ground. However, our protagonist, BU1 Haycook still didn't know what happened to the Seabee who went over the edge! BU1 Haycook remembered this and ran over to where he last saw him. To his relief, the Seabee was on a ledge one story below; he appeared to be in a lot of pain. He had landed on the ledge of the balcony, and he caught himself from falling off and in doing so had broken both of his wrists.

At this point, the Thai fire department had arrived but, as with any post, the Marines did not want to let uncleared local nationals onto the compound unless absolutely necessary. With the fire out, the need was not as urgent; however, they would need to let them recover the Seabee on the ledge of the building and take him to the Thai Hospital's emergency room. While the Seabee was being cared for, an assessment of fire damage was being made on the inside of the building. Although the fire was put out relatively quickly, the intensity of the fire had quickly burned through the roof and melted some wires to the communications box, which took the system offline. For most posts in the 1980s, this would not have been a big deal. However, due to the size of the mission in Bangkok, it was one of the few overseas locations that kept an open line with Washington, D.C., at all times. When the line went dark, D.C. immediately began calling to find out why. Soon, everyone in D.C. learned that a fire had been started on the roof causing some damage. This was not a great day for NSU, but it was another day that lifelong lessons would be learned for all involved.

Due to rising threats of terrorism and bombings at diplomatic and military facilities overseas, there was a tremendous increase in the construction of New Office Buildings (NOB) and upgrades for existing buildings. The building work was a significant portion of the Omnibus Diplomatic Security and Anti-terrorism Act of 1986.[64] This sudden construction demand also resulted in a request by DOS for sixty additional NSU Seabees through Fiscal Year 1988 to perform construction security surveillance at the numerous overseas locations. NSU was granted an additional three-year surge of sixty Seabees. These extra billets increased the temporary authorized manning ceiling from 118 to 178 personnel. To meet this surge, prior NSU Seabees were pulled from other assignments across the NCF and NAVFAC to return to the unit to meet demand. By April of 1987, 165 personnel were assigned to the unit.[65]

As the world continued to adjust to the new terrorist threat, the same Lebanese terrorist group, Hezbollah, struck again, this time taking the life of a Seabee. Following completion of a routine repair project at a base in Greece, Steelworker 2nd Class Robert D. Stethem, USN, and four other members of Underwater Construction Team 2 were returning to the United States aboard TWA Flight 847 when the terrorist group hijacked the flight and diverted it to Beirut, Lebanon. The terrorists singled out Stethem and another Seabee, Clinton Suggs, and they were brutally beaten. While the aircraft sat at the Beirut airport, the terrorists beat Stethem over a prolonged period, as he refused to submit to the terrorists demands. The terrorists finally killed him with a bullet to the head on June 15, 1985. After lengthy negotiations, the remaining passengers were finally freed. A total of thirty-nine passengers were held hostage for seventeen days. The four terrorists made good their escape into Beirut, but one was later apprehended in

Germany and convicted of air piracy and murder.[11,66] SW2 Stethem was posthumously awarded the Bronze Star and Purple Heart. Later, he would have a U.S. Navy destroyer named after him, *U.S.S. Stethem* (DDG-63). Throughout the hostage situation, the NSU OIC served as the intermediary between NAVFAC and DOS.[51]

In 1986, following the Iran hostage situations in 1979, the killing of Robert Stethem in 1985, and the three bombings in Beirut targeting U.S. government and military personnel, the NSU OIC made an important change to their operating procedures by temporarily permitting NSU Seabees to travel on their tourist passports vice diplomatic or official military passports. This attempted to mask their military affiliation while traveling internationally throughout regions of the world where America had fallen out of favor. All military are instructed to respond affirmatively if questioned by host government authorities whether they are U.S. military personnel but are not required to divulge that information up front. They may present their diplomatic credentials first.

As a result of the significant amount of work being conducted overseas at diplomatic posts during the late 1980s and into the 1990s, NSU Seabees quickly found themselves offered many opportunities for outside work while posted overseas. Due to stricter security requirements, contractors were extremely interested in employing off-duty Seabees.[67] Sailors are generally allowed to hold a second job, as long as that job does not interfere with the performance of the individual's official duties and does not reflect adversely on their military service. Typically, members must request approval from the chain of command prior to commencing work. Title 5, U.S. Code section 5536 prohibits military personnel from directly receiving pay from another government. However, it does not prohibit them from receiving pay from a contractor under contract with the U.S. government. Of course, the individual cannot be responsible for establishing the contract in the first place.

What this ultimately meant was that NSU Seabees could conduct their official duties during regular working hours and then check-in with the second job with a contractor at post to perform skilled labor usually within their Navy rate as a steelworker, builder, electrician, or utilitiesman. Seabees could then make an additional 15–20 USD per hour (around 40–55 USD in today's money). As an E-5 or E-6 in the U.S. Navy, this additional money was attractive. Today, pay has increased for U.S. Navy Sailors, but it still trails the private sector in terms of what their skillset would be worth in outside employment.

Mikhail Gorbachev took over as the leader of the USSR in 1985 and led it up until its ultimate unraveling in 1991. Prior to the end of the Cold War, and when the Berlin wall fell in 1989, President Reagan made a visit to Moscow, the first visit by POTUS in nearly fourteen years. In advance of his visits, SECSTATE George Shultz made numerous visits, as well as Colin Powell as his National Security Advisor. Each time they visited, they stayed at the Spaso House, which is the Ambassador's residence. The Seabees would scan and clear the residence each time. During Reagan's visit, a live television broadcast was being made from the embassy. For the Seabees, this was a rare opportunity to see what it took to make a telecast. Despite the significance of the broadcast, they had trouble filling the room, so using some TV magic, they repositioned people and made it look full in front of the cameras.[23]

When the USSR all came crashing down in the last few months of the year, it left in its wake fifteen independent republics. This incredibly swift fall of the communist state, which had existed since 1922, led to the United States and other nations to seek diplomatic relations with these new states outside of the control of the Russian Federation. Many of the consulates and embassies previously in Eastern Bloc countries would now upgrade these existing facilities, or either build or acquire new ones to give legitimacy to the new independent states, hopefully preventing them from being pulled back in by the Russian Federation under the leadership of Boris Yeltsin. Predictably, NSU Seabees played a significant role in the preparation of all these new or enhanced diplomatic facilities.

During the same period, there were a number of severe natural disasters around the world. In Manila, Philippines, Mt. Pinatubo caused the second largest eruption in the twentieth century. The effects of the volcano spewed ash, and the follow-on Typhoon Yunya then hit the area, causing a number of roof collapses and an onset of disease among the 20,000 newly homeless citizens.[68] Around 350 Filipinos were killed during the initial eruption, and the aftermath of the eruption ultimately claimed the lives of 722 more from disease, roof collapses, and/or mud flows that overtook many communities living on the mountainside. NSU Seabees were called in to help with the cleanup at the U.S. Embassy in Manila and make repairs to a facility that has survived since before WWII and is still occupied today.

NSU was also involved in recovery efforts following the earthquake in Cairo, Egypt, on October 10, 1992, that killed 545 people, injured 6,512, and collapsed or damaged approximately 9,350 buildings in the city, leaving 50,000 homeless.[69]

Lastly, when Hurricane Andrew struck Florida in August 1992, a category-5 hurricane that made a direct hit on Miami-Dade County, the Department of State domestic facilities in Miami were part of the 25 billion USD worth of damage.[70] Due to the extensive damage, the Florida Regional Center in Fort Lauderdale was commandeered. This is where the Western Hemisphere Affairs leadership for STO moved in the wake of Hurricane Andrew. For diplomatic Couriers, Miami was, and still is, a major hub to access facilities in the Caribbean and both Central and South America.

During the beginning of the Gulf War in January 1991, the Seabees assigned to U.S. Embassy Abu Dhabi, UAE, volunteered to remain in the area of conflict and provided vital security engineering support to diplomatic missions located in the Gulf. Three Seabees were sent into Kuwait immediately after the liberation of Kuwait City alongside U.S. Special Forces in March 1991 to help secure the embassy and reopen the facility. Under the risk of personal injury from mines and sporadic gunfire, the Seabees lent their construction skills and special expertise in locks and the installation of alarm systems, allowing the embassy to reopen in record time. Additionally, throughout the crisis, a traveling team of NSU Seabees conducted the light armoring of vehicles in the Gulf at various DOS missions.[71]

During a second Moscow embassy fire that occurred in March 1991, NSU Seabees found themselves in the middle of another major event. Eight Seabees working on security projects in Moscow at the time of the conflagration provided outstanding contributions to extinguishing the fire, evacuating embassy personnel, administering first-aid, escorting Russian firefighters, and securing the building. In the aftermath, they provided critical support for security, construction, repair, and materials handling. The source of the fire has never been officially determined, but welding work being conducted in the elevator shaft of the building was one possible cause.[23,40] This same elevator was notorious for getting stuck. The Seabees were charged with maintaining it to the best of their abilities, but it was an uphill battle. Whenever the elevator broke down, one of the Seabees would have to go up to the mechanical room to lower the elevator car to the next floor to release the occupants. It was rumored that SECSTATE Henry Kissinger got stuck in the elevator during one of his visits and it was up to the Seabees to get him out.[23]

In 1991, when the fire broke out, there were operations around the clock within the embassy's Communications Program Unit and even more people in the facility than were already there in 1977.[72] In order to make repairs for these fires and perform any other construction work throughout the Cold War, materials had to be shipped in from the other side of the Iron Curtain, often from Frankfurt, Germany. This was not due to concern over the materials being compromised, but because the availability of materials on the open Russian market was so limited. Conditions were so dire in the USSR that Simpkins recalled watching the Russians start small fires underneath their vehicles in the winter to warm the fluids up enough to get the vehicles started. Antifreeze was hard to come by, as it was being diverted to the military. Simpkins "could not believe that this was the other superpower."[23]

The fire was the catalyst that resulted in congressional approval on October 6, 1994, of the 240 million USD to execute the project nicknamed "TOPHAT." Leading up to this event, retired ST Office Director John Bainbridge was again involved with planning and coordination efforts associated with the new embassy construction. John recalled that when he was assigned to this project in 1986, after his work in Beirut attempting to outfit a suitable embassy building there, details were light. When he asked where he would be working, the answer was the CIA. He was to join a group of engineers, scientists, and other specialists from NSA, CIA, DOS, and the military services. After three polygraph tests, he was finally cleared to work for the CIA. Still unsure what exactly he was going to be doing, details finally began to reveal themselves. Since many of the building components were being made offsite, "the Intelligence Community was concerned that having U.S. Navy Seabees watch the workers construct the building may not be enough security to prevent listening devices from being implanted." Bainbridge said, "Convincing senior DOS management to cease all Russian construction after the building was topped off was no small undertaking and took considerable effort to accomplish." For the next few months, with the help from talented scientists from America's premier academic institutions, the "inspections began to unravel the puzzle." The group provided highly classified briefings every week to the intelligence community and congressional offices and included a "tour of the penetrations" that had been found during intrusive inspections with the U.S. Ambassador to the USSR and the Secretary of State.

"At the end of the tour, [Bainbridge] was asked what [DOS] should do with the building to remedy the intrusions, and [he] replied by suggesting [they] remove half of the building and reconstruct it securely without the aid of the host government." This was the idea that ultimately prevailed. The U.S. Embassy Moscow compound that originally began construction in 1979, was going to be partially rebuilt only using cleared Americans. In January 1997, a contract was finally awarded, and work commenced in September of the same year. This effort took until May 5, 2000. Personnel were able to move into the new facility twenty-one years after construction began.[73] A project that began at the cost of 25 million USD, had grown by nearly ten times. Despite the cost, it was home to "the most advanced countermeasures ever applied to a DOS New Office Building." One of the main lessons learned from this project was "to not have your adversary construct a building for you if you need to conduct classified operations when it is occupied."[74]

When construction began again, NSU was heavily involved in the Moscow Secure Chancery Facility project under the oversight of the Moscow Embassy Building Control Office (MEBCO).[75] Three NSU Seabees were provided to conduct a number of activities to include inspection of construction materials, certification and decertification of secure containers, installation, maintenance, and repair of technical security equipment, project technical security oversight, assistance with Technical Surveillance Countermeasure Inspections, and assistance in testing and repair of parent room and enclosure shielding to ensure contract compliance.[75] A Master Chief Store Keeper, a U.S. Navy fleet rate, was also assigned to NSU to support the MEBCO project. Their job was to oversee the container yard and warehouse facility where all the supplies and materials were kept for the project.[40]

Shortly following the fire in Moscow, in August 1991, an attempted military coup took place in Moscow, led by Soviet Loyalists, in an attempt to keep the Soviet Union from fracturing. The coup failed, but enough damage was done that Gorbachev resigned on December 25, and Boris Yeltsin took over to lead Russia into the post-Soviet era. Amidst the coup, and on extremely short notice, NSU Seabees spearheaded the planning, coordination, and execution of the offload of two Air Force C-5 aircraft carrying equipment and supplies required to maintain embassy operations.[76] Three Seabees caught up in the coup attempt in August provided continuous observation and reporting of Russian troop movements. Working in continuous shifts throughout the coup attempt, they also provided perimeter security watches and assisted communications staff with the proper disposition of classified documents and information.[77] Yet again, NSU Seabees proved invaluable, providing benefits beyond their core mission.

In 1992, NSU established a formal agreement with the Foreign Building Operations to provide eight Seabees to perform installation, maintenance, and repair of Forced Entry/Ballistic Resistant (FE/BR) doors.[78] At the peak of this program, twenty-two Seabees were assigned. The teams were sort of nomads. They would take three trips per year of approximately three and a half months long. This meant they were on the road for over 300 days a year! Prior to this agreement, Seabees on loan to FBO were mostly only performing as Construction Security Technicians. These Seabees were also becoming less competitive for promotion than their peers who were working within the DOS mission. Due to this growing concern, it was determined by the leadership in 1998 to discontinue the agreement. Full time support would be contracted out by the FBO.[78,79] Today, Regional Security Technicians have supplemented the Seabee and STS ranks to support perimeter physical security that is not located in controlled access areas. NSU Seabees are still trained on FE/BR doors due to the magnetic locks and other mechanisms, but only in a secondary support role. Overseas Building Operations, formally FBO, remains the purview of the primary owner responsible for the maintenance and repair of FE/BR doors.

Throughout the 1990s, NSU was actively involved in maintaining security at U.S. diplomatic facilities throughout the former Yugoslavia as war broke out on numerous fronts across the region.[80] After the outbreak of hostilities, the NSU Seabee posted in Belgrade, Serbia, conducted security-support trips to constituent posts that included securing the U.S. Embassy in Sarajevo, Bosnia, to provide a safe working environment throughout the Bosnian War. Additional NSU Seabees provided support on the ground shortly after U.S. Forces arrived as part of the NATO peace keeping mission to bring an end to ethnic fighting in Bosnia and Herzegovina in 1996. In Pristina, Kosovo, a team was sent in to establish a secure environment at the U.S. Information Service Office. As NATO and U.S. forces intervened in the Kosovo War in support of the Kosovo Liberation Army in late 1998, the Office began operating as the diplomatic mission of the U.S. in Kosovo shortly thereafter.

During this period, there were evacuations of U.S. embassies during times of unrest in multiple locations. In Kinshasa, Democratic Republic of Congo (now named Republic of Zaire), during the relentless fighting over the resources, U.S. diplomats were evacuated in September 1991 as rebel forces threatened Western citizens in the capital city. The Kinshasa Seabees maintained document-destroying equipment and security monitoring systems until the last of the embassy staff departed the compound. They also installed makeshift armoring on the evacuation vehicles and performed as convoy drivers to the airport.

In Lima, Peru, the Seabee was directly involved in, or in the vicinity of, several terrorist attacks directed toward the U.S. embassy or American companies operating in Peru. The attacks were believed to mostly be led by the Túpac Amaru Revolutionary Movement and Sendero Luminoso terrorists throughout 1993.

On September 17, 1994, President Clinton ordered U.S. forces to be prepared for military intervention in Haiti under Operation UPHOLD DEMOCRACY.[81] The vehicle armoring program under DOS quickly tasked a Seabee team with constructing a ballistic resistant protective enclosure to protect Jean Claude Aristide of Haiti in Port au Prince in anticipation of his return to power.[82]

After a relatively calm period since the end of the Gulf War, the world of DOS changed significantly on August 7, 1998. Two simultaneous bombings occurred in Dar es Salaam, Tanzania, and Nairobi, Kenya, at the respective U.S. embassies, killing 224 people, including twelve Americans.[5] Previous assassinations, facility takeovers, fires, and planted microphone systems were all game changers for embassy operations. However, the 1998 bombings were the straw that broke the camel's back, shifting the Bureau into what it resembles today.

Not surprisingly, NSU Seabees responded to this atrocious attack in their typical fashion. At the helm of NSU was Lieutenant Carmelo Melendez and Master Chief Stephan Haycook—the same Seabee who found himself within fifty feet of the Beirut bombing fourteen years earlier. There was perhaps no better person to be the AOIC and Senior Enlisted Leader of NSU through this phase of DS history. Carrying out these two bombings were Osama Bin Laden and Al-Qaeda. The terrorist organization continued to grow in strength and sophistication over the next three years, culminating in the plane hijackings on September 11, 2001, that left 2,977 people dead. These three years would be extremely active for NSU. Melendez recounted the series of decisions and events that took place once he found out about the bombing:

I was in India at the time and got a call from Washington, late at night from the ST Office Director in Washington, D.C. I was informed of the bombings in Nairobi and Dar es Salaam and that one looked worse than the others. DOS was trying to send agents there and was hoping I would get there, too, to see what the Seabees could do. I departed the following day as soon as I could get tickets. I immediately began thinking about what we were going to need on site, such as tools, materials, and security equipment. I began putting together a list of my NSU superstars that I knew I could call upon to meet me there to pick up the pieces. I called a few of the regional centers and SEOs to get ahold of the Seabees and requested to have them prepare to send the Seabees with equipment. They were tasked to imagine what tools and equipment you would need if your post got blown up.

I first traveled to Nairobi and immediately went to the site and saw its massive devastation. The post was days away from thinking about physical security, as they had to recover a significant number of bodies first. I went back to the airport and continued onward to Dar es Salaam. After arriving at the second site, I felt NSU Seabees could help make a difference there immediately. I told the RSO on site we could get a group of Seabees there quick if they wanted it. Of course, they said yes.

The order of importance for recovery from any bombing is the same. Identifying any remaining casualties or body parts, recovering and/ or destroying classified, and then setting up physical security wherever operations could be resumed. The mission in Tanzania was going to take about three to four weeks. When the team arrived, we split them up to both help the FBI and agency wherever they needed support first. Then when they figured out where they were going to reconstitute the embassy presence, we would start creating the infrastructure necessary to do so.

We were able to acquire some shipping containers and had them delivered to the Deputy Chief of Mission house. We also took some

FE/BR windows that were still useable, air-conditioning units, and other materials from the embassy site that weren't necessary for the investigation to assemble a Post 1/Operations center to get some level of function back. The FBI was very appreciative, as well as Secretary of State Madeleine Albright. The Secretary arrived a few days after us and she was ecstatic over the hard work by the Seabees and the rest of the team. The RSO had me come along with him to tour her around the site. In the short time on site, the Seabees had brought a sense of stability to the site and after four weeks of non-stop work, the Seabees mission had come to an end having done all they could.[83]

During Carmelo's stop in Nairobi, the Special Agent he met with asked if he thought the Seabees could help. Knowing NSU didn't have the capacity for what was needed in Nairobi, Carmelo mentioned reaching out through DOD to request Humanitarian Assistance/ Disaster Relief Seabee support. The agent ran with the idea to the Defense Attaché Office for them to communicate with U.S. European Command, the geographic combatant command that covered Africa at the time, to request a detachment of Seabees to deploy to Nairobi to assist with the recovery operation and clear the scene.

Melendez gathered an elite group of nine NSU Seabees, who were all on the ground in Tanzania within forty-eight hours of the bombing.[84] One of those Seabees at the time was BU1 Steve Fox. Fox was in Cairo, Egypt, on a TDY trip and received the call to pack up everything he had available that he would need if a post had blown up, get tickets, and wait for the go ahead.[85]

Due to the early on-site presence of the NSU Seabees, the leading RSO in Dar es Salaam informed all FBI, CIA, and DOS experts who arrived a couple days later that the only way they would get into the building was if the Seabees authorized it. The first part of the job was to make the crime scene secure by shoring up the facility, as well as combing the debris for remains. Melendez told the NSU team that if anyone didn't feel comfortable helping with this part of the job, they could work on a different part of the tasking. BU1 Fox recalled that it was a "shitty job but it had a motivated crew." They all stepped up. Drafting their plans on napkins, the Seabees diligently worked with the FBI evidence collection teams, gathering body parts and any evidence that would lead them to the perpetrators. Fox found a piece of metal with the Vehicle Identification Number (VIN) that ended up on the third floor of the building.[85] SECSTATE Madeleine Albright cited the team for making the site safe and ensuring the success of the FBI investigation. They had all the hard evidence to secure and apprehend the culprits working with the local authorities.

Hot-wiring two government trucks that no one could find the keys for, the Seabees got around town and got to work on the new Post 1, after clearing all of the classified information and materials from the scene.[85] Within fifteen days on the ground in Dar es Salaam, a new embassy was established with makeshift security posts constructed from shipping containers. The cases that each of the team members packed all miraculously combined to provide all the tools and materials they needed to execute the work to build a Post 1 at the temporary embassy that was established at the DCM residence.[85]

NSU Seabees unpacking materials brought
to recover from the Dar es Salaam embassy bombing.
Photo courtesy of Steve Fox.

Because of the simultaneous attacks in Nairobi and Dar es Salaam and Carmelo's recommendation to the Nairobi RSO, Carmelo called NAVFAC to see if a request had been received. The Naval Construction Force had indeed received a request for Seabees in Nairobi, and NAVFAC worked with the Naval Construction Brigades to find a ready unit. A detachment of thirty-one Seabees from NMCB THREE, already deployed to Guam, were redeployed and were on the ground in Nairobi within forty-eight hours.[84] In total, forty-one Seabees responded to the attacks.[5] SECSTATE Albright noted that the Seabees were the number-one presence at both sites and were critical to enabling DOS to get their operations back up and running. More details of the story of NSU in Dar es Salaam following the bombing is recounted by retired UT1 James Renken in his book, *Mission Tanzania*.[84]

SECSTATE Madeleine Albright meets NSU team in Dar es Salaam, Tanzania. Photo courtesy of Carmelo Melendez.

When the mission was complete, BU1 Fox returned to Cairo but was immediately recalled to Nairobi where the other bombing had occurred. When he got there, the detachment of Seabees from NMCB THREE had already departed, and he supported the establishment of a temporary visa location in an old residence. Today, that building is still being used. Fortunately, the NSU Seabee stationed in Nairobi was in town getting supplies and came back after the blast. He would've been in the basement, where the shop was, and likely not survived.

Fox eventually retired as a Chief and went to work for Diplomatic Security as a Civil Servant. Today, he works in the Physical Security Programs Branch and reviews OBO plans for quality assurance to ensure they meet the DOS's physical security standards, such as stand-off distance, etc. Coincidentally, more than 20 years after the bombing, he has come full circle and is working on reviewing the plans for the

NOB in Nairobi, a building that will finally replace the "temporary" visa location he helped establish in 1998.[85]

The bombings and other events that NSU responded to over the years are the underlying reason NSU has a Temporary Duty (TDY) pool available in Washington, D.C. Aside from the special projects conducted, one of the Required Operational Capabilities for NSU is to respond to natural and manmade disasters around the world. This adjustment was minor in NSU operations; however, instead of a TDY pool meant solely for special projects as the primary purpose, this was now a secondary purpose of the mission with manmade and natural disaster response taking precedence. Just over a month after the bombings in Africa, Seabees made damage repairs to the U.S. Interests Section facility in Havana, Cuba, caused by the destructive forces of Hurricane Georges that struck the island on September 23, 1998. The storm dropped over twenty-four inches of rain on parts of Cuba and left 100,000 people homeless in its wake.

Throughout the late 1990s, NSU Seabees were also involved with construction support at the Mount Weather Emergency Operations Center. Mount Weather is a fallback location for the continuity of the U.S. government. It is used as the center of operations for the Federal Emergency Management Agency (FEMA). For years, Naval Mobile Construction Battalions provided 14-person detachments to perform work at the site but would often run into issues with security clearances to fill out the roster. If NSU had the capacity, they would often lend out a few Seabees to support whatever work was being done.[40]

Leading up to the opening of the new embassy in Moscow in 1999, NSU personnel assigned to the Moscow Embassy Building Control Office (MEBCO) were tasked with the installation and maintenance of a two million USD state-of-the-art security system at the new embassy building. This system ensured the integrity of material shipments against clandestine penetrations by foreign intelligence agencies. Once construction was complete, NSU planned, coordinated, and executed the critical move and decommissioning of the existing office building to the new U.S. Embassy Moscow, which they had been waiting nearly twenty years to occupy. Working with the Department of Defense Interagency Coordination Group and NAVFAC, NSU secured the approval from the Under Secretary of Defense to augment the NSU TDY Seabee Team to be led by Command Master Chief Stephan Haycook and eighteen Seabees previously assigned to NSU, to include BUC Fox. Haycook first supported the new embassy building in 1983, performing construction surveillance. Sixteen years later, he would finally see it finished. Demonstrating meticulous attention to detail, NSU successfully completed both the move and decommissioning ahead of schedule.[86] With little fanfare and continuing to support the never-ending mission in Moscow, NSU deployed a total of twenty-four personnel to Moscow, Russia. In April 1999, it was time to support the final move from the old and defunct embassy building to the new embassy compound. Haycook recalled that the move was scheduled to be done in a week. The detachment of Seabees decided that a week was four days too many. Working around the clock, they completed the move in just three days.[40] Completing this move was a major milestone in the history of the new embassy building in Moscow that began in 1979.

At the same time the embassy was nearing its opening, in January 1999, President Clinton proposed the Expanded Threat Reduction Initiative (ETRI) that would "significantly increase funding for cooperation with Russia, Ukraine, and other New Independent States to prevent proliferation of weapons of mass destruction and the materials to make them." It was believed that "the August 1998 economic crisis in Russia and related regional economic turmoil jeopardized efforts to reduce weapons to desired levels."[87] Congress followed up with the proposal in the Foreign Operations, Export Financing, and Related

Programs Appropriation Act of 2000. It recorded that the Senate found that the proposed ETRI was "critical to preserving U.S. national security" and that "State Department programs under the ETRI be funded at or near the full request of 250 million USD."[88] The same congress ultimately appropriated 839 million USD "for necessary expenses to carry out the provisions" of the Foreign Assistance Act of 1961 and the Freedom Support Act of 1992, "for assistance for the Independent States of the former Soviet Union and for related programs." The services of NSU Seabees were called for to modify rooms at diplomatic facilities in Moscow to install safe vaults and alarm systems for the deployment and distribution of 500 million USD in new 100-dollar bills to the Russian economy in Moscow. Without the tireless work of the Seabees, this operation would not have worked to move and store that many bills.[82,87]

The twentieth century closed out at an incredible pace for NSU. The unit had grown quickly to 150 after the bombings but returned to approximately 120 by the end of the millennium. A major shift in operations was about to occur as NSU's significant effort in Moscow for nearly thirty-five years was ending with the opening of the new embassy. However, the major threat of terrorist organizations would begin to take center stage. Following another Al Qaeda attack on October 12, 2000, NSU personnel deployed to the Port of Aden in Yemen and U.S. Embassy Abu Dhabi, UAE, in the wake of the attack on the *U.S.S Cole*. The attack killed seventeen U.S. Navy Sailors and led to a significant rise in port security. It was a clear signal that enemies of the United States were becoming increasingly sophisticated and would go to any length to target American assets in any clime or place.

9

A New Age

(2001-Present)

Donald Rumsfeld took over as Secretary of Defense in 2001. He quickly began working on changing the posture of the U.S. military overseas and ensuring the services were ready to fight the guerrilla style warfare adopted by foreign terrorists. Following the September 11 attacks in 2001, the force restructuring accelerated. The DOD began looking for military billets supporting non-DOD elements that were not core to the military required operational capabilities. NSU fell into this category. Unaware of the target on its back, NSU continued to support the DOS, unaware of this potential threat looming in the distance.

NSU OIC Scott Kosnick and AOIC Stephan Haycook both recalled their experience from that fateful day of the attacks on New York City's World Trade Center and the Pentagon. At the time, NSU had all the Chief Petty Officers in Charge (CPOIC) in Washington, D.C., for the annual CPOIC week. The Chief-pinning ceremony scheduled for that week was supposed to happen at the Pentagon but had been shifted to a state annex building following the attacks. From where NSU had been evacuated to—a hotel near the annex—they could see the fires burning at the Pentagon. Kosnick remembered departing later that day from Rosslyn and heading toward the metro: "There was not a soul on the streets in this normally busy area. It was really eerie, and then, to get on the subway, there were multiple construction workers who were at the Pentagon and described watching the plane slam into the side of the building."[89] NSU Seabees would shortly be called into action.

As the fate of NSU had begun to be contemplated in Washington, D.C., bombings of Taliban strongholds in Afghanistan began on October 7, 2001. Ground forces arrived after just twelve days. And on November 14, only weeks later, the city of Kabul, Afghanistan, fell and the Taliban retreated. Following the Taliban's departure from Kabul and the signing of the Bonn Agreement on December 5, Seabees from the NSU TDY Special Projects pool, in addition to those assigned to U.S. Embassy New Delhi, India, were deployed to Kabul. They were tasked with reopening the U.S. Embassy Kabul, which had been closed since January 30, 1989.[90]

After a thorough survey by both NSU Seabees and Army Special Forces team, the former embassy facilities were declared safe to occupy and to commence security improvements. Seabees from NSU immediately went to work repairing and installing new electrical and mechanical security systems. Working under arduous and hostile conditions, the Seabees from NSU completed this incredible task in less than forty-eight hours. Re-opening the embassy enabled the Department of State to reestablish a diplomatic presence in Afghanistan as an American Liaison Office on December 17, 2001.[90]

NSU Seabees were scheduled to return to Washington, D.C., once the facility was open and conducting daily operations. Instead, Ambassador James Dobbins, serving as Director of the Liaison Office, determined that the office could not, and would not, function without a permanent Seabee on site, highlighting their importance in the eyes of the diplomats. From that point forward, at least one NSU Seabee was stationed on the ground, performing overlapping ninety-day TDYs in support of the diplomatic facilities. The reopening effort proved worthwhile, and just five days later, on December 22, the U.S. government recognized the authority of the Interim Authority in Afghanistan. Another month later, on January 17, 2002, U.S. Embassy Kabul was officially reopened.

Following the reopening of the embassy in Kabul, plans for a protective detail were prepared to secure the Presidential Palace in Kabul, and the effort initially included six NSU Seabees. The Diplomatic Security (DS) Afghanistan Presidential Protection Detail was established for newly selected Chairman of the Interim Authority of Afghanistan Hamid Karzai. Karzai would later be chosen to serve as Interim President and eventually elected to serve as President for two terms, totaling twelve years in power overall. The ST personnel of the detail assisted in turning over the facility security operations of the palace from DOD to DOS. Based on facility assessments of security personnel already on the ground, including the NSU Seabee retained by Ambassador Dobbins, several physical and technical security weaknesses were identified on the thirty-five-acre Presidential Palace Compound, known as the Arg.[91] These weaknesses could easily be exploited by local Taliban rebels. The team quickly formulated a plan to improve both technical and physical security. The execution of this tasking was a planning and logistical challenge. Working seven days a week, the team developed a rough scope of work and added over 200 items to an existing bill of materials previously created. To get all the materials on site as quickly as possible, a Russian Antonov AH-124-100, the world's second largest cargo plane ever built, was contracted to fly the materials and equipment to Kabul in one load. The team went on to offload over ninety tons of cargo in two days.[92]

DS team overseeing Antonov AH-124-100
loading for delivery to Kabul.
Photo courtesy of Diplomatic Security.

Following the offload and familiarization with their location, they immediately commenced work. The work entailed installing an entire electrical infrastructure, consisting of generators, a manual transfer switch, uninterrupted power supply, four load distribution centers, and over 3.5 miles of power and signal cable. All this work would have to be performed atop an unstable 400-year-old wall. They mounted several power supplies, a security interface cabinet, and the control center for the security cameras. Anticipating the long distances between the cameras and control center, the team set up DOS's first ever wireless Closed-Circuit Television (CCTV) system. The CCTV system worked via line-of-sight transmission, which was difficult to maintain. Two times after wind and snowstorms blew through, SEO Luis Torres-Torres was sent back to Kabul to adjust the system. Eventually, the cameras were replaced with wired cameras to eliminate the repeated adjustments, but the proof of concept was there for installations elsewhere.[93] The team also labored intensively to install security lighting around the perimeter of the Presidential Palace and putting an emergency notification system into operation.

Putting up the final cameras on the rear of the compound, Torres-Torres had an encounter with the razor wire atop the rear wall of the compound near the presidential house. It may have been due to distraction from the impalas, a type of antelope, running around behind the house, or maybe exhaustion after nearly forty days of non-stop work, but the scar left behind would forever be a reminder of his work at the compound.[93]

CE2 Chris Beck attempting to keep an impala away
on the Presidential Compound.
Photo courtesy of Diplomatic Security.

This successful mission wrapped up in forty-one days and provided ample security for President Karzai during his time in the Afghanistan

Transitional Administration. The completion of this sensitive priority project was key in the seamless transfer of protective detail operations from DOD to DOS. Throughout this time, since the DS team improved the security posture, there was not a single assassination attempt on President Karzai within the palace compound. For nearly twenty years, prior to the U.S. withdrawal from Afghanistan in August 2021, two Seabees remained posted in Kabul on twelve-month orders, helping maintain the technical and physical security systems on the U.S. Embassy Kabul compound and outlying camps.

DS team photographed with President Karzai.
Photo courtesy of Diplomatic Security.

As if the 9/11 attacks weren't enough, 2001 also brought with it anthrax attacks via mail. At least one letter laced with anthrax had passed through Dulles, Virginia, where diplomatic mail is processed before being sent overseas. Following the discovery of the letter, investigators quickly conducted contact tracing to identify what other mail bags may have been in contact with the source letter. It was determined that a few of those mail bags had been sent to the U.S. consulate in Yekaterinburg, Russia, where a team of Seabees, including Lyle Dynda, were working on a Technical Security Upgrade (TSU). The team had set up their workspace in the basement of the consulate, which also happened to be part of the mailroom. The consulate received notice that their mailbags may have been contaminated and to isolate them. However, the mail had already been removed from the bags, and only the bags remained in the mailroom. Nevertheless, when Dynda got the message, he picked up the remaining bags and sealed them in plastic bags. He didn't give it a second thought, as he was at the end of the trip and about to depart. The bags were then sent to be tested. They were examined with a twenty-four-hour test and ten-day test. Before they departed, the twenty-four-hour test came back negative, so they returned to D.C. Unfortunately for Dynda, he started feeling unwell on the way back and went to medical upon his return. Prior to leaving the consulate, the TSU team members were all given letters from the management officer that they could have been potentially exposed to Anthrax and should take the necessary precautions if they showed any signs of illness. Dynda showed this letter to the Ft. Myer medical team, and after initial shock and disbelief, they immediately transferred him to Ft. Belvoir, where he was isolated for three days. All tests came back negative for him, as well as the ten-day test for Anthrax from the mail bags in Yekaterinburg. Regardless, he was on Ciprofloxacin for ninety days just to be on the safe side.[94]

The following year, Dynda was on his last TDY trip to Lima, Peru, in March 2002. The team of Seabees was completing a TSU in advance of President George W. Bush's visit just a few days after they were set to depart. On Dynda's last night in Lima, they stayed out a little late celebrating. He flew out in the morning on March 20, 2002, and the rest of the team decided to go into the embassy a little later that day so they could work late to finish the upgrade, after most embassy workers had departed. The team was just about wrapped up when they felt the building shake. A car bomb went off right outside the embassy perimeter where they often found taxis to return to their hotels at night. It was believed that the same Shining Path rebel group that had conducted a series of bombings in the early 1990s was responsible for killing at least nine people and injuring twelve that day.

Throughout 2002 and 2003, NSU was called upon to provide personnel to serve as Site Security Managers to support the congressionally mandated six-phase Sensitive Compartmented Information Facility (SCIF) project. The tasking consisted of upgrading fifty-eight SCIF areas across the country and the new DOS Headquarters facility to meet Director of Central Intelligence Directive 1/21 standards at a project cost of 15.3 million USD. NSU personnel assigned to the project were responsible for developing and drafting the Construction Security Plans, Technical Security Specifications, coordinating accreditation teams for inspection, and managing and supervising fifty construction surveillance technicians. NSU's efforts ensured time-critical deadlines with national security implications were met allowing the continued processing of classified information and materials at DOS, which subsequently made an overwhelming positive impact on the DOS organization from the Secretary of State down.[95]

While maintaining an impressive record of successes and continuously conducting work in Moscow and numerous other sites around the world, other agencies took interest in the skills of NSU Seabees and their professional execution of operations. Between 2001 and 2003, NSU provided support for twenty-six classified projects in coordination with the CIA. Following this success, the CIA was interested in having their own detachment of Seabees and were given a window of opportunity to test them out. As Operation Iraqi Freedom was launched and federal funds were pulled to support the war effort, funding in DOS for FY2002 was reduced, and DOS was struggling to find enough money to pay for all 115 Seabee billets at the time. Coming to a mutually beneficial agreement, DOS agreed to receive reimbursement from the CIA for twelve Seabees for a one-year period. This way, DOS didn't lose the billets, and the CIA got the support they were looking for. If this sounds a little too good to be true, it is! But it worked for a while, until the Pentagon got clued in on the arrangement. The future Operations Chief of NSU, Senior Chief Shawn Milligan, was one of the dozen Seabees selected to support the CIA directly.[79]

The operations with the CIA ran the spectrum of renovating Chief of Station offices and communication centers to building out listening posts in Europe. One of the last projects they did was a result of a search for three U.S. Soldiers captured during the Yugoslav Wars. A team of five Seabees, including retired BUC Lyle Dynda, were sent out to an old, remote Albanian airfield to build a listening post to collect signals intelligence that could help find the captured soldiers. Eventually the three U.S. Soldiers were found and released to Jesse Jackson after he negotiated their release. Prior to the successful recovery, Dynda was selected for the team. At the time, he was serving in Casablanca, Morocco, when he got the call. He was asked to return as soon as possible and was quickly sent to Frankfurt, Germany, with little information to go on. He was told he would be met by someone in Frankfurt to get his follow-on travel arrangements and tasking. Dynda recalled being picked up from the airport and taken to another airfield where they flew on a Cessna to their location in Albania. Once on site, they were tasked with various projects to make their makeshift camp more hospitable. However, as the Seabees were attempting to complete the project, they realized they would run out of materials first. Due to the lack of materials and no expectation of more arriving, a flight was scheduled to leave on the upcoming Friday. Since they had nothing more they could do, the team called Chief Milligan to let him know they were getting on the flight and coming back.[94]

At this time, support for an additional project at the embassy in Tirana was requested. Two of the five Seabees were to get to Tirana, and the rest would be able to return to the United States. However, a similar issue arose. The materials for the project hadn't arrived at the embassy yet. Seabees have learned over the years, if the materials aren't on site when you arrive, be prepared to wait for days, weeks, or even months. Because of that experience, Dynda was able to convince Milligan and others that it was best for the entire team to return to Washington, D.C., and to send the two Seabees back out when the materials arrived. But Dynda received a call from an Army Major directing them to keep two people at the embassy, despite there being no materials. The next day, Chief Milligan also received a phone call from a Marine Colonel telling him to keep the team on site. Not knowing who this Colonel was, and the fact they didn't report to him, he blew him off, and the team continued their way home. However, that journey, according to Dynda, was no small feat.

As the team was attempting to fly out, the Cessna experienced mechanical problems. Taking the only alternative, they drove up to where the military forces were quartered. But, when they arrived, they had to find where the U.S. forces were. Asking around, they eventually found the camp. However, they had left three members of the team with all their gear back at their drop site while searching. Before they were able to regroup, they asked around to see about getting on a flight out. They lucked out and were able to get on a flight to Ramstein Air Force Base in Germany thirty minutes later. Thinking quickly, they found an idling truck with a driver on standby. Giving him forty USD, all the money they had on hand, they got him to help them out. They took off back down the road and picked up the rest of the party and gear, making it to the plane just in time. When they arrived in Ramstein, they stopped at the United Service Organizations (USO). They had made it out of Albania but still needed to get to Frankfurt, where they knew they could get help from the consulate to get a flight back to D.C. Fortunately, the lady working at the USO was headed to Frankfurt after her shift and offered to take them. The team finally got a break. Upon their return to the states, Dynda asked Milligan if the materials ever showed up in Tirana. They had not. In fact, they never showed up anywhere.[94]

Despite the materials never showing up, Chief Milligan received another phone call but this time from a U.S. Navy Commander reporting to the Assistant Director of Naval Intelligence for Interagency Coordination (Office Code: N2K). The Commander informed him that the agreement between DOS and the CIA was not approved by the Navy. This office's purpose was to support detachments at other agencies for work that was often classified. For example, this office would put together non-redacted awards and personal evaluations for the service members conducting the missions. Chief Milligan, Master Chief Haycook, and the OIC, Lieutenant Tarey Isbell, were then summoned to the Pentagon to determine how the agreement between DOS and the CIA could be carried out in a more "legal" way. In the end, the CIA was required to go through the N2K office for further NSU support instead of through DOS. The relationship between the CIA and NSU persisted on and off, but eventually the N2K office approached NAVFAC, and future non-technical security requests would be offered to the Naval Mobile Construction Battalions for small detachments during deployments instead of going directly to NSU.

The silver lining to this run-in with the N2K office was that they were now aware of NSU. They knew what NSU did and why it existed. The coincidental relationship that developed with the Commander was soon to pay off. The Office of the Secretary of Defense (OSD) had discovered NSU on its list and still did not know why there was a detachment of Seabees with the DOS. Similar to the assessment during the Vietnam War, when every billet was scrutinized for the war effort, DOS would be required to justify maintaining the Seabees with NSU. The question OSD had to first resolve was: What did NSU do for the DOS?

Coincidentally, 6,400 miles away in Vladivostok, Russia, four Seabees on a TDY mission to decommission the Post Communications Center at U.S. Consulate Vladivostok would happen to be staying at the same hotel as Secretary of the Navy (SECNAV) Gordon England and Commander in Chief, U.S. Pacific Command (CINCPAC), Admiral Walter Doran, during a visit to the Russian Pacific Fleet Headquarters in Vladivostok.[96] While in the hotel, the entourage recognized the four Americans not with their group and inquired who they were, thinking they must be contractors. As it turned out, it was the four NSU Seabees, including our widely traveled Lyle Dynda. After the shock wore off by SECNAV and CINCPAC that there were Navy personnel operating in Vladivostok with the DOS, they were elated to learn more.

The Seabees invited them to the U.S. Consulate Vladivostok to show them what kind of work they performed, and the invite was reciprocated for the four Seabees to accompany the SECNAV and CINCPAC to the Russian Military Base for the "dog and pony" show of Russian equipment. A "dog and pony" show is an elaborate presentation, usually part of a promotional campaign. Dynda recalls his favorite part of the demonstration was the opportunity to fire many of the Russian infantry weapons equivalent to the United States' M-2, 0.50 caliber machine gun and the MK-19 automatic grenade launcher. Dynda had previously served as a weapons instructor with the Naval Construction Regiment and was very familiar with the

U.S. versions.[94]

Ultimately, this random encounter was reported to SECDEF Rumsfeld upon SECNAV England's return to Washington, D.C. Unknowingly, the SECNAV's delight to find this little-known unit with DOS more than likely worked to the advantage of NSU to continue to operate in support of DOS without further interruption. Aside from the new Global War on Terrorism, the recent bombings in Africa, and the even greater threat of attacks on embassies where violent extremist organizations operated, NSU's support to DOS was even more critical. NSU Seabees were heavily involved in physical and technical security upgrade projects all around the world, especially Africa and the Middle East where most of these known threats operated.

Despite best efforts up to this point, it was still perceived that NSU was nothing more than a handshake agreement between DOS and the Naval Construction Force. At this point, OSD began to inquire within DOS and went to the Senior Military Advisor (SMA) for Political-Military Affairs, an Air Force Brigadier General, to see if he knew anything about the Seabees. Master Chief Haycook and Lieutenant Isbell had previously met the SMA during a meet and greet. Haycook recalled that he had seen what he determined to be a pilot's helmet on his bookcase when they met. Attempting to make small talk, he asked if he was a pilot. The response was forceful, "No. I'm an astronaut. I flew U2s." The rest of the meet and greet was a little icy, and NSU left as soon as they could.[40]

Up to this point, the General was fighting to retain his own people within DOS. When he learned that NSU was unaccounted for, he assumed he was somehow responsible for them after his brief exchange with Haycook and Isbell. OSD called the SMA to the Pentagon to meet with the head of their department responsible for bringing loaned military personnel back to DOD proper. However, due to the relationship NSU had developed with the N2K office, when the Commander heard about the meeting, he called up Master Chief Haycook and told him to get over to the Pentagon immediately. The meeting was about to occur, and they needed to prove NSU was a real unit.

Fortunately, NSU had been preparing for a meeting like this ever since their first encounter with N2K. They grabbed their materials and made it over to the Pentagon. When they met the Commander, he walked them over to where the meeting was just getting underway. He opened the door and Master Chief Haycook immediately recognized who was sitting in uniform across from the civilian responsible for determining whether billets would remain or be returned to the DOD—it was the SMA and U2 astronaut.[40] Taking a minute to gather themselves, they began to explain to the civilian how NSU came into existence, showing them documentation proving NSU to be a commissioned unit and not military attaches that reported in any way to the SMA. OSD was a little surprised that this small unit was legitimate. NSU did not even appear on a NAVFAC organizational chart; however, they were on the Standard Navy Distribution List. OSD would later present their findings to SECDEF who would have a discussion with SECSTATE about the purpose of NSU, but it ended there. By the end of the meeting, NSU was free to go and was no longer a target by DOD. Although NSU was successful in their defense, Diplomatic Security and the Office of Security Technology had taken some preemptive moves in good faith, in case they had to fight to keep NSU around. Approximately ten overseas billets were pulled back in anticipation of them being first to be cut, as they were in relatively stable regions at the time. Eventually, these ten billets would be filled again, but not for nearly twenty years.

The United States invaded Iraq on March 19, 2003, to overthrow the government of Saddam Hussein. As the coalition forces moved in, they took over the Republican Palace. This palace was the seat of power for Hussein and became the Multi-National Force-Iraq (MNF-I) headquarters. Eventually, the MNF-I secured an area called the Green Zone—a walled off and highly secure area of downtown Baghdad. Western diplomats under the Office for Reconstruction and Humanitarian Assistance, which quickly emerged as the Coalition Provisional Authority (CPA), began returning to Iraq shortly thereafter to create a new government in Iraq. The CPA neared completion of their work in June 2004. In anticipation of the transfer of power to the Iraqi Interim Government on June 28, 2004, NSU launched two Seabees to stand-up Engineering Services Office Baghdad. This same month, DOD would be turning over command and control of the Republican Palace to DOS, as it would serve as the embassy until construction of the new U.S. Embassy Iraq was completed.[97] The old U.S. Embassy Baghdad resided outside the Green Zone and was deemed unsafe to inhabit. In July 2004, the NSU OIC and ten additional Seabees were deployed in direct support of the new temporary U.S. Embassy Baghdad, tasked with contingency contracting, scoping of work requirements, and coordination to provide field expedient physical and technical security upgrades to the palace compound, as well as four additional regional sites in Mosul, Al Hilah, Basra, and Kirkuk.[98,99] Three of these sites were where CPA regional headquarters were established. The fourth, in Kirkuk, was a U.S. military airbase.

In addition to the significant work in Iraq throughout 2004, NSU responded to hurricane recovery efforts in Grenada, increased support requirements in Beijing, and technical assessments in Tripoli, Libya. Hurricane Ivan struck Grenada September 7, 2004. ESC Fort Lauderdale with support from the NSU TDY Pool and ESO Lisbon deployed an emergency team to Grenada immediately following the devastation caused by the storm. Over 80 percent of all structures on the island were damaged or destroyed. A complete technical security assessment and provisional repairs were accomplished to get the post security systems back online and operational.[99] In Beijing, China,

NSU originally deployed three Seabees to support the new 475 million USD embassy project. The construction of the U.S. Embassy Beijing was the second largest overseas construction undertaking by the DOS behind only Baghdad. The 10-acre, secure, state-of-the-art facility was completed in 2008.[100] The progress was closely monitored from Washington, D.C., across all levels of government. Tasking for NSU on this project included secure container decertification. When all materials are shipped secure, there are thousands of containers requiring surveillance from the time they leave the United States until arriving on site. When the contractor fell behind schedule, they wanted to increase to near full-time operations. To support this, container decertification also became a continuous effort. NSU launched an additional six Seabees to support the operation to help get the project back on schedule.

In 2007, with construction ongoing in Baghdad, ST Office Director Steve Romero remembered watching comments on the news from then Secretary of State Condoleezza Rice regarding video cameras to be installed in all fully armored vehicles. This was in response to an incident with contractor security details. The cameras were meant to record operations conducted by heavily armored security details.[101] He thought this was important information to know. He was responsible for the outfitting of armored vehicles overseas that transport diplomats and this was the first time he'd heard of the new requirement! ST, and the protective technology branch, scrambled to find a solution that could be installed "yesterday."[102] The NSU Seabees already on the ground in Baghdad were the ones who installed the first cameras in the armored vehicles, which are now standard in all DOS armored vehicles.

The other major activity in 2004 for NSU took place in Tripoli, Libya. Following the opening of an interest section in February 2004, ESC Cairo spearheaded the initial assessment of the former U.S. embassy facility in Tripoli over the following months. The facility had been left vacant for twenty-five years after relations failed in 1979.

However, in June 2004, the United States reestablished a liaison officer in Tripoli at the Belgian Embassy. This created a window of opportunity for the engineering service center to reenter the country and completely decommission the old facility. Multiple site visits were coordinated to ensure that all sensitive materials and equipment had been disposed of or returned after re-entry into the facility. The reopening of the Liaison Office led to full diplomatic relations in 2006, when the office was turned into an embassy. However, within five years, during the Arab Spring uprising against the Muammar al-Qaddafi (also spelled Gaddafi) regime in 2011, the environment quickly deteriorated, and embassy operations were suspended until September 2011, when the United States recognized the Transitional National Council (TNC) as the legitimate government. The United States maintained a diplomatic presence in Benghazi throughout this period, until it was attacked on September 11, 2012, and U.S. Ambassador Stevens and three other American colleagues were killed.

In the year proceeding the attack in Benghazi, a number of security upgrades were made to the Annex, as well as the Temporary Mission Facility (TMF) that was established after the TNC was recognized by the United States as the legitimate government of Libya in July 2011. The TMF opened in September 2011. The location, referred to as the Annex, housed an agency station approximately one mile from the Temporary Mission Facility. The TMF was where Ambassador Stevens, appointed to the Transitional National Council, operated from.[103] Prior to the 2012 attack, in 2011, Steve Romero was the Regional Director in Frankfurt when he received a call from the Division Chief. They needed to secure a facility in Libya for the new embassy operations. Initially, there was no plan and minimal details, but things came together quickly regardless. SEOs, STSs, and Seabees in Frankfurt took what information they had about the new facility and put together a bill of materials for physical and technical security system equipment that would be needed. Procurement was fast tracked, and two Seabees and two STSs were then sent via chartered flight from Frankfurt into Libya, where they would sleep on cots and eat Meals Ready to Eat (MREs) for the duration of their stay due to the still dicey security environment. However, while they were there, they did make a visit over to the Annex, where the agency was already set up.

There they swam in the pool and ate food prepared by the French chef before returning to the remote office. Fast forward to the attack a year later; the facility was overrun, and multiple investigations provided a number of lessons related to when to close down diplomatic facilities overseas when the host nation is no longer able to satisfy Vienna convention or other treaty requirements to adequately protect diplomatic facilities in their country.[103] One of the RSOs sent to investigate noticed that the digital video recorders' hard drives were missing. Amazingly, in light of the attack and fire, the equipment hadn't been completely destroyed. Excessive smoke from the fires that were set prevented the attackers from spending too much time in the facilities to destroy equipment. However, the recorders were stolen to be later sold on the black market. Whether sheer luck or very skilled detective work, the enterprising RSO did manage to find the recorders for sale in a local market. Against all odds, the devices not only still worked but also retained all the recorded footage from the attack. In July 2014, all U.S. embassy operations that were still ongoing in Tripoli were suspended in Libya and moved to Valletta, Malta.

Approximately a year after the attack in Benghazi, a significant attack took place on September 13, 2013, at the U.S. Consulate Herat, Afghanistan. Director Ron Stuart recalled sending two additional Seabees and a STS immediately from Kabul the same afternoon to resecure the consulate with 360-degree perimeter camera coverage and all operational systems before nightfall.[29] In both of these instances, we continue to see NSU Seabees step up to the call to go into harsh locations under high threat to perform the DOS mission time and time again. The Benghazi attack and other violence caused by the Arab Spring across North Africa and Middle East, often associated with the anniversary of the September 11 attacks, further led DOS and DOD to accept the costs associated with improving and standardizing the security of embassies to become like fortresses to protect Americans living with increasing threats all around the world.

From 2016 to 2018, NSU was on a growth trajectory. With improved recruiting and retention, it allowed NSU to grow to its maximum authorized level of 129 personnel. This ability to grow was timely. With the newly elected Trump administration in 2016, Rex Tillerson was confirmed as the new Secretary of State prior to the inauguration in January 2017. Upon arrival, a hiring freeze was imposed while there was a review of the DOS organization. For the SEO and STS skillset, this was a major problem, and the timing couldn't have been worse. As with any government program, things are cyclical. ST was experiencing a high number of retirements of eligible SEOs and STSs. Since the STS program began in 1999, many STSs were close to hitting twenty years within the organization. The Department of State Foreign Service, unlike the civil service across all branches of the government, forces out personnel upon turning sixty-five. Some rare exceptions are allowed; however, unless you are Senior Foreign Service and get a waiver to continue to serve, you are more than likely required to retire.

As most STSs hired were in their second career, many were hitting the minimum retirement age and years of service to be eligible for immediate retirement benefits. Due to this natural attrition coinciding with the hiring freeze, a gap of approximately eighty SEOs and STSs developed. The short-term solution to this problem was to have Seabees perform extended gap support TDYs to locations where STSs could not be backfilled. This increase quickly depleted the existing TDY pool from Washington, D.C., and a request to post ten more Seabees overseas, as well as add ten more Seabees to the unit, was made by DOS. The manning increase isn't always a permanent increase, as seen throughout NSU's history, but it is an available option when trying to balance mission requirements and security needs. By the end of 2020, the unit had met the request of growth. In 2019, ST also began to see a recovery in hiring SEOs and STSs after new SECSTATE Mike Pompeo lifted the hiring freeze shortly after taking over in April 2018. It will take many years for ST to completely fill every available billet it has, but one less obstacle and the support of the Seabees will allow them to still meet their mission.

As the Seabees found themselves fully employed, they were also being asked to fill roles they had never done in the past. This included tasking with the Project Management Execution (PME) Branch under the FSE and Security Engineering Services under STO. In PME, one Seabee began work as a Contracting Officer Representative in support of the high visibility initiative to install High-Definition Secure Video Systems (HDSVS) at every overseas diplomatic facility. This fifty million USD per-year push over five years was a huge lift for the Office. The HDSVS system would also enable capabilities that the department could only have dreamed of previously, as most systems went from analog to digital, enabling better storage and data collection and opening the possibility for use of artificial intelligence.

In March 2018, the United States and a number of NATO and EU nations found themselves at odds with Russia after an ex-Russian double agent was attacked with a nerve agent outside his home in Britain.[104] The United States decided to expel sixty Russian diplomats from the Russian Consulate in Seattle in response to the attack. In a quid pro quo action, Moscow forced the closure of the U.S. Consulate St. Petersburg, Russia.[105] One NSU Seabee was caught in the middle of the spat as he supported the closure of the consulate. Via a *persona non grata* letter, he was ordered to leave the country within seventy-two hours. The NSU Operations team went into high gear and was able to get the Seabee flash orders out of Russia without losing his household goods and personal items from his residence in Moscow where he was posted. For the first time since Detachment NOVEMBER entered Russia in 1964, the Seabees found themselves no longer with a permanent presence in Russia.

In October 2018, Seabees began supporting SES, the Security Engineering Services Branch. This detail supports the SECSTATE while traveling abroad to maintain classified communications with Washington, D.C., and the U.S. president. The detail maintains and operates the security equipment to keep the area secure and prevent communication observation. Supporting the Secretary on their travels often takes the Seabees to locations they would not see, even within NSU. Petty Officer Shevlin, one of the first Seabees to support SES, recalled his travels to Rovaniemi, Finland, which is situated on the Artic Circle and known as the "official" hometown of Santa Clause. Experiencing snow and reindeer farms in May were the highlights of his trip. The travel to Rovaniemi, where the U.S. doesn't have a diplomatic facility, was in support of a meeting of the Arctic Council in May 2019.[106]

A new frontier and challenge for not only the DOS but also the DOD, is Unmanned Aerial Systems (UAS)—more commonly referred to as drones. Drones can easily clear walls and with the small size of cameras today, can easily observe with incredible quality the layout of areas in addition to carrying devices that can be dropped. A couple of instances since 2019 included numerous attempts by drones to carry grenades or mortars over the wall into an embassy compound. Thankfully, none of these attempts have been successful, but they have come close. ST created a branch to counter UASs under Systems Integration Monitoring (SIM), due to the rapid growth of drone risk to the mission. The United States, along with NATO and other organizations, is trying to determine the best way to counteract these commercial drones from entering airspace over diplomatic facilities or military installations.

On July 21, 2020, the United States ordered the closure of the Chinese Consulate in Houston, Texas, in response to repeated violations of American sovereignty.[107] As with other closures, forty-eight to seventy-two hours is the common timeframe allotted for diplomatic facilities under scrutiny to be closed. Typically, countries have a good sense when a facility is facing closure because diplomatic relationships are trending down. When it hits a certain point, the amount of classified information and materials will be reduced in the event of an ordered closure. This is done to ensure a reduction in the time it takes to carry out the Emergency Action Plan/Emergency Destruction Plan to sanitize a facility.

After the facility closed and the Chinese diplomats departed, the U.S. government took control of the facility. Two NSU Seabees were called in and reported on the ground right after the closure. They were tasked with making the facility safe to operate in and assisting the search of the facility. Typically, when a diplomatic facility is abandoned due to a departure, a lot of things are destroyed, such as electronic equipment. This is done to prevent any items being salvaged or recovered for analysis. This often results in a trashed facility, such as wires cut to security systems or life safety systems, to incur the most amount of damage and make the facility undesirable and too costly to maintain or return to use by anyone else. This was the case in both the Chinese facility in Houston and the Russian Consulate in San Francisco, which was closed by the United States in retaliation for the closure of the U.S. Consulate St. Petersburg in 2018.

In June 2021, a team of three Seabees were deployed to U.S. Embassy Kabul to support the Resolute Support Headquarters transition from DOD to DOS with the drawdown of the U.S. military and

NATO forces by September 11, 2021. As has been the case throughout the history of NSU, when DOD leaves a location (such as Baghdad and Kabul), diplomatic activities typically move in behind, which includes NSU Seabees and the Diplomatic Security Service, to ensure the technical and physical security of the facilities are up to DOS standards for protecting the many U.S. government personnel and local national support staff still in action.

PART III

Diplomacy at Work

10

Officer In Charge and

Assistant Officer In Charge

The Charge of Command has been laid out by Naval leadership for decades. The most recent iteration to be released identifies four essential principles for a unit's top officer: authority, responsibility, accountability, and expertise.[108] At the apex of the NSU organizational chart is the Officer in Charge (OIC) and the Assistant Officer in Charge (AOIC). These roles are common across DOD and the Department of the Navy (DON) for small units that operate without a commanding officer or as part of a larger unit known as a detachment or detail. An attribute that makes NSU unique is that it's an Echelon III command. This categorization carries specific duties and responsibilities uncommon to most O-3, U.S. Navy Lieutenant billets. However, despite the junior rank, the intent and weight of the charge of command is no less.

An echelon in the DOD is a level of leadership. For the U.S. Navy, the Chief of Naval Operations is an Echelon I command. Typical Echelon II commands are the systems commands, such as Naval Sea Systems Command (NAVSEA), NAVFAC, Naval Air Systems Command (NAVAIR), Naval Information Warfare Systems Command

(NAVWAR), etc. Below each of these headquarters level commands, are Echelon III commands. For NAVFAC, this means NAVFAC Pacific, NAVFAC Atlantic, EXWC, and the Navy Crane Center. Each of these commands are led by a Rear Admiral (Lower Half), U.S. Navy Captain or Senior Executive Service civilian. And then there is NSU that currently falls under NAVFAC as an Echelon III command. NAVFAC was originally the Bureau of Yards and Docks before changing to Naval Facilities Engineering Command in 1966, and then Naval Facilities Engineering Systems Command in 2020. But no matter the name and how many times it has reorganized, NSU has always been within the NAVFAC organization.

Another similar, primarily Seabee command in the National Capital Region is Camp David. However, Camp David falls under the White House Military Office, due to its primary mission to maintain the privacy of the Presidential Retreat. *Inside Camp David*, written by Retired Rear Admiral (Lower Half) Michael Giorgione, CEC, USN, gives you a peek inside this incredible hideaway in Thurmont, MD.

The Vice President's Residence falls under Navy District Washington and NAVFAC Washington. Both of those entities are also shore duty commands, meaning the Seabees attached do not deploy. The other options for Seabees are to fall under the Naval Construction Force and Navy Expeditionary Combat Command (NECC) or the Naval Beach Group (NBG). The only Seabees under NBG are within the Amphibious Construction Battalion, and NECC is expeditionary in nature and purpose. These other organizations didn't make much sense for NSU to fall under due to their unique mission. NSU doesn't work for the White House, and it is a sea duty command. However, it's not truly expeditionary and doesn't fit neatly under any other organization. Ultimately, serving in support of DOS, fitting NSU under NAVFAC, despite being a relatively "junior" command, was the only viable option.

The OIC has traditionally been a senior Lieutenant who will be in line for Lieutenant Commander (LCDR) while in the unit, or sometimes already selected for LCDR. This ensures that DOS is provided with a career-focused, motivated officer who will toe the line and not need much support from DOS or NAVFAC on a day-to-day basis to lead and manage the unit. The OIC reports to the Chief of Civil Engineers administratively, like the other Echelon III commands. Operationally, the OIC reports to the Division Director for STO under the Office of Security Technology, an Officer Counselor (Senior Foreign Service) civilian.

The OIC is fully authorized, accountable, and responsible for the personnel under their leadership. As the OIC, they are granted signature authority as the reporting senior for all evaluations and charged with maintaining good order and discipline with "non-judicial punishment authority" when necessary. Not typical for such a junior level, the OIC has a lot of autonomy day to day but is held to such a high standard that any misstep could leave them in hot water on either side of their chain of command. The OIC is also responsible for setting the vision for the unit in line with its mission. The vision is critical to any unit in order for personnel to understand where the commander intends to direct the unit as they move forward. The AOIC is responsible for aligning and enforcing the guidance across the unit.

Throughout NSU's history, a larger number of OICs had been prior enlisted U.S. Navy Sailors, until Lieutenant Scott Kosnick in 2003. This unique characteristic of many past OICs was believed to be the catalyst that kept the unit operating independently without too much outside intervention. However, since Kosnick, it has been demonstrated that even officers who were not prior enlisted could still provide valuable leadership to the unit despite their relative youth and various levels of experience. Since 2003, a majority of OICs have not been prior enlisted.[40,79]

Being selected as the OIC immediately brings a sense of excitement, as well as, perhaps, a sense of being unprepared. When asked whether he felt ready for the job or knew what the unit did, Carmelo Melendez definitively answered, "No." He only learned about the job from a former detailer who mentioned Melendez may be a good fit for the job. He applied for the role, not knowing much else, and got it.[83] Many others, me included, recall similar experiences of walking into the great unknown but willing and ready to do what it takes on day one to ensure everyone in the unit is taken care of and that the mission continues.

Within DOS, the OIC position is equal to a Branch Chief, commonly filled by a FS-01/GS-15. These paygrades are in line with an O-6, or U.S. Navy Captain. This may seem odd for a Lieutenant to fill such a high-grade position, but the size of the unit (100–139) only merits a LT/LCDR for similar sized naval units. An Air Detachment in a Naval Mobile Construction Battalion is 129 personnel. This is often led by a senior Lieutenant in the battalion as a company commander making a LT/LCDR a good fit for the NSU OIC billet, too. Albeit a global responsibility that brings with it its own set of challenges, the task is challenging but exceedingly rewarding for the right OIC.

The Assistant Officer in Charge has a similarly unique billet. The other hat worn by the AOIC is as Senior Enlisted Leader for the unit. A typical navy command has a leadership triad of a Commanding Officer, Executive Officer (XO), and Command Master Chief (CMC). This triad is responsible for everything that occurs in the command, be that administrative or operational. However, NSU is built slightly differently, although in line with most units that only have an OIC. Within NSU, the AOIC is similar to the XO. Due to the type of work, having a second officer in the unit for this role would arguably be too much manpower. Therefore, as with most small details in the NCF, an Officer and Chief lead a team. For NSU, this means a Master Chief as the SEL and AOIC. The only other Seabee unit with a SEL is Camp David and the Underwater Construction Teams. For a unit to have a Command Master Chief, the command must be over 250 personnel. However, unlike Camp David, there is no XO. Therefore, the AOIC/SEL takes up many of the responsibilities for people programs that the XO would normally manage, such as sponsorship, MWR, and leading the headquarters staff, including legal, medical, and administration personnel.

As an Echelon III command, there are also extra responsibilities not normally seen by an operational unit like NSU or even a Naval Mobile Construction Battalion. However, due to being at this level echelon, there are administrative requirements and specific program structures to be maintained that NSU may not need because they don't have any units that report to them, like nearly every other Echelon III command. There is always risk of not meeting a reporting requirement, no matter how unique your unit may be, it may be worth the risk if the capacity of the staff is low and any repercussions of not reporting are likely to be minor.

The U.S. Navy has a multitude of uniforms. Working uniforms, utilities, service dress, mess dress, khakis, whites, blues ... the list goes on. However, for a unit that operates overseas in countries where personnel in U.S. military uniform can be a much greater target for hostility, NSU Seabees are dressed to blend in at their respective overseas posts. NSU Seabees have three different categories of dress: military dress, worn for official functions; a working uniform; and business dress. When someone gets promoted or presented with an award, NSU Sailors will put on their military uniform for the event but won't wear it to and from their home. Most Force Protection Condition criterion or Anti-Terrorism Force Protection measures for serving overseas is to not wear your uniform off installation or post. This is no different for those in DOS.

Most of the time, NSU Seabees are in their working uniform, comprising a collared shirt, work boots, and work pants, such as cargo utilities or tactical pants. The other category of uniform, business dress, is worn on days that the Seabees are performing their regular technical duties or are in the D.C. office. This business dress is usually a suit and tie, the typical regular diplomatic dress code. Overseas, depending on your post, this may be more relaxed, but even in Baghdad, Iraq members of the Foreign Service can be found in suit and tie.

During the times NSU Seabees wear their uniform, they earn the opportunity to wear the NSU badge. This badge was created by former Command Master Chief Rick DeBolt, while he was the AOIC of the unit from 1995 to 1999. Having previously served at the Bureau of Naval Personnel (BUPERS), formerly located in Washington, D.C., he was familiar with the process of getting uniform components approved. Having an existing personal relationship with Master Chief Petty Officer of the Navy John Hagan, he leveraged his relationship to receive Chief of Naval Operations approval for the Department of State badge in 1998.[109]

The U.S. NAVY DOS badge. Photo courtesy of the author.

The one uniform that NSU Seabees do not wear is their Navy Working Uniform (NWU), or their camouflage (NWU Type III). This uniform is not allowed to be worn by personnel in the National Capitol Region within certain facilities, including DOS facilities. The NSU headquarters is in a DOS facility and must maintain a professional appearance.

When the OIC and AOIC travel, they wear a suit jacket, collared shirt, and slacks at the facilities or casual clothes, depending on what the cultural day activities may include. On the road is where the OIC and AOIC really earn their pay while leading NSU. As part of the Memorandum of Agreement between DOS and the U.S. Navy, the OIC and AOIC are required to visit every location where their Seabees are posted every fiscal year to perform a residence inspection. To achieve this monumental task of visiting forty-eight locations (as of 2021), the schedule is split in two, and the OIC and AOIC each will visit twenty-four locations each fiscal year—a far more manageable schedule, although it still works out at an average of two visits per month.

Importantly, these inspections provide an opportunity for the Seabees to get to know their leadership. As difficult as it may be to physically get to all the locations each year, it is just as difficult to lead a globally dispersed unit when your personnel only see their leadership once or twice a year. Technology has made it easier to keep in touch, which was illustrated during the COVID-19 pandemic in 2020–2022, but there is a certain amount of leadership and relationship building that can only be performed face to face. The two-day period during which the leadership is on the ground is critical to get a good understanding of the work being performed and the operational environment, as well as carrying out an assessment of the individual for evaluation and award purposes. Without this face time, the Seabee is at a disadvantage, unless they actively communicate what they are doing through their immediate chain of command.

Each stop typically includes a workday and a cultural day. The workday is spent inside the embassy or consulate where the Seabee works. Throughout the day, the visiting NSU leadership will receive a tour of the facility and all ongoing projects. They will meet their local chain of command, which can sometimes include everyone, all the way up to the Ambassador. Leadership will also get a security briefing to better understand the threat environment from the RSO. Then leadership will also visit the residence where the Seabee and their family lives to ensure that the DOS, as part of the MOA, is providing adequate housing.

Other tasks include one-on-one mentoring or career counseling with each Seabee, in addition to updating them on the latest activities or changes from NSU headquarters and operations around the globe. This time also gives the Seabee the opportunity to bring up any administrative tasks that they haven't been able to get finished due to issues beyond their control. This enables the leadership to return to D.C., find out more about the issue, and find resolution within a few days of returning, if not before they even touchdown in the United States.

The OIC and AOIC are also inspecting the Seabee to see that they are maintaining grooming and physical standards required as a member of the U.S. Navy. This may include enjoying an early morning workout with the Seabee or general observation of their fitness level, depending on how much time is available during the inspection.

The cultural day is usually less businesslike and the more dynamic of the two days. On the cultural day, the resident Seabee gets the opportunity to take the leadership out to explore their location. These cultural days are often spent touring capital cities, and the experiences the leadership enjoy are often once in a lifetime. The Seabee also gets a day out of the office while putting them in a more relaxed environment to build a rapport with their leadership, getting to know one another better and understand each other's character and personality.

Traveling to twenty-four locations each year and spending two full days on the ground at each location quickly adds up in the amount of time spent traveling. Most trips conducted by the OIC and AOIC take two to three weeks total as they "swing" through each region, stopping at several regions' locations at once. Overall, taking into account other training courses or conferences that each must attend, the OIC and AOIC are on the road 90–120 days each year. In a three-year period, they will have spent nearly a year traveling. This pales in comparison to how much traveling some of the NSU Seabees undertake, but it is a lot to do on top of leading the entire organization. This travel is no different than being a CO for a NMCB on deployment when the Commanding Officer, Command Master Chief, Operations Officer, and Operations Chief make visits to the detachment or detail sites to build a rapport and provide the battalion leadership an opportunity to better understand the environment that their personnel encounter every day.

In addition to the resident inspections, visits to check on projects or traveling support teams are also conducted. In NSU's past, as teams went from one post to the next to service FE/BR doors, perform vehicle armoring or maintenance, and build post communication centers, the OIC and AOIC would also travel around to check on that work. Carmelo Melendez (OIC, 1996–1999) noted that he traveled 236 days in 1998 due to the bombings and commissioning work in Moscow's new embassy as well as the regular site visits.[83] Master Chief (CUCM) Joseph Maioriello noted that the travel is incomparable to any other job he's held in the U.S. Navy, including being the Operations Chief in a Naval Mobile Construction Battalion, where travel is also quite extensive, as previously discussed; however, the destinations are far less numerous.[110]

CUCM Maioriello also recalled a few leadership opportunities that were unique to serving in the military that he only experienced fully in NSU. To have a seat at the table with the Deputy Assistant

Secretary and other senior leadership within the DOS as a Master Chief, created a sense of value that was unprecedented for him. Legitimately being asked his opinion of what to do or how to handle a situation was extremely empowering and built a great deal of trust. On the DOD side, it is often normal to be asked your opinion on a problem even when the action has often already been determined. In these instances, senior leadership is only seeking buy-in from the senior enlisted leader before directing the mid-level leaders down to the most junior enlisted at the deckplate to shift to the new direction.

For CUCM Maioriello, the unit also provided an incredible leadership opportunity for junior personnel to be in a position of responsibility that they wouldn't be in anywhere else. The "Seabees knock it out of the park 99 percent of the time,"[110] so by simply providing them the opportunity to grow with the responsibility, they mature quickly and learn to operate independently without a squad leader or platoon chief checking in on them with daily tasking. Maioriello also appreciated the short organizational hierarchy within NSU. From the Senior enlisted to the E-6 or E-5, was only one level of hierarchy in between. During visits, you were able to—and needed to be— "super-candid and up front with the troops to really get to build a relationship and get honest feedback from the deckplate."[110]

Some of the lessons that Maioriello never imagined he would learn while in NSU, or at any other point in his career, was becoming the "master of ten minutes of small talk about nothing."[110] Whether meeting with the Deputy Chief of Mission, Management Officer, or other senior official, all too often, they barely knew anything about NSU. To navigate the sometimes-challenging conversations and to break the ice, Maioriello got into the habit of requesting the individual's biography ahead of time and would get the senior official to talk about themselves for the remainder of the time. By doing so, the senior official was often left satisfied having met with him, even if they didn't realize they only talked about the Seabee for the first two minutes. In one instance, CUCM Maioriello was in Abu Dhabi, UAE, and the senior official repeatedly lauded Master Chief for how sharp his Marines were at post. Unfortunately, NSU doesn't have Marines. The official had confused Master Chief with someone from the Marine Corps Embassy Security Group. At this point in his career, Maioriello also knew that sometimes it is better not to correct a senior executive when it won't cause any harm! The other life lesson Maioriello learned was how and when to wear civilian attire. After being in a military uniform for nearly twenty years, wearing civilian clothes every day was a new experience. However, after three years in DOS and depending on who he was meeting, he knew when to wear what combination of a tie or jacket.[110]

Every OIC and AOIC, in addition to any NSU Seabee who traveled extensively, picked up a few tricks of the trade or had experiences that stuck with them. Prior OIC, Adam Gerlach, relived his four attempts to land in Vienna, Austria, with a severe crosswind. However, that wasn't nearly as bad as the time he flew into Cairo, Egypt, and the plane got caught by a gust as the wheels touched down and had to abort the landing and make a second attempt. That episode was so severe that many passengers started to lose their already-digesting inflight meal.[19]

CUCM Maioriello learned to live with the uncertainty of catching flights. Flying in and out of Canberra, Australia, during the wildfires of 2019-2020, he was unsure until just minutes before take-off whether the flights would depart. He also learned to never fly through John F. Kennedy Airport in New York City when returning stateside: the JFK to Washington, D.C., leg was too easily missed or often oversold or canceled. And flying into Kabul, Afghanistan, and boarding a CH-46 Chinook helicopter for the final leg of travel to the embassy was an odd experience with smartly dressed men and women also wearing flak jackets and Kevlar helmets. To be unarmed in that environment, where he had served previously with the Seabees, left him in disbelief.

Packing for one's travels is as strategic as the flight itinerary. "Always bring a carry-on and a checked bag" was the rule of thumb to be lived by. Traveling overseas and switching airlines on any leg of the trip always increased the probability that luggage would be lost, and the traveler would be left with only what they had on their back for the next day or two. The trick was to have a set of clothes with you in your carry-on bag so you wouldn't be too out of sorts if your luggage was lost. As sensible as this sounds, successfully getting your regular size carry-on bag within the weight limits of certain overseas airlines is truly what separates the novice from the professional. It starts by first selecting high-quality, lightweight luggage, and then only packing the absolute essentials. The other personal item, rarely ever weighed, should be filled to the brim; unbeknownst to the airline, it'll likely outweigh the carry-on bag.

11

Global Leadership

The NSU OIC job is personally and professionally one of the most rewarding and challenging jobs I've ever had. The depth and breadth of leadership lessons were unique, challenging, and to say the least, thought provoking. There are many first-time experiences to work through while growing into the role. The culmination of this learning was presenting a brief at the Society of American Military Engineers Joint Engineer Training Conference in 2019 in Tampa Bay, FL, titled *Global Leadership 101*.

Master Chief Joe Maioriello and I catered our brief to junior and mid-grade military officers and civilian leaders who may be experiencing dispersed leadership for the first time or may soon in the future. We touched on four main points: "Global Command," "First Time in Global Leadership," "Alone at the Top," and "Doing the 'Right' Thing." Some of the topics were general for leadership, but the key objective was comparing how you take what you know as a leader and apply it to a workforce that isn't in the same office as you. Maybe the workforce is not globally dispersed, but even being across town or in a different state can have a significant impact on the effectiveness of a leader when he or she is not on site every day. What we did not realize, when we put this brief together in 2019, was that a global pandemic was less than a year away and knowing how to operate and lead in an environment where you don't see your personnel every day was going to be something nearly every leader in the world would have to come to terms with.

One of the biggest challenges for NSU, and any global command, is communication and reporting. Effective communication flows in both directions, and both ends need to maintain their responsibilities. Keeping everyone informed of what is going on, as well as receiving information from personnel spread across the globe, is often easier said than done. A Commander's Critical Information Request (CCIR) defines what the commander, OIC, or supervisor wants their reports to tell them. CCIRs are often things that a leader wants to know—whether the information is good or bad—to be abreast of the information in case it comes up somewhere else. A senior leader never wants to be caught off guard. There are also numerous other operational reports within each command. The CCIRs provide critical information to the leadership as speedily as possible to be able to respond or direct the appropriate resources, as needed. Laying out reporting frequency for CCIRs and other command reports is paramount to a consistent flow of information. To have reports automatically and regularly generated is a proactive approach to leadership, as opposed to reactively requesting information when needed.

Keeping a finger on the pulse of your command can be difficult without communication. By reading the reports, leaders can start putting together a picture of the situation on the ground in addition to regular phone or video calls with personnel at each location. One of the silver linings of the global pandemic in 2019 was that everyone learned how to communicate with virtual platforms better than ever before. In a time when traveling was impossible, it left a large void in the workload, and it was more difficult to monitor morale across the command, just as it became paramount to do so. With isolation and uncertainty prevalent, whether in Washington, D.C., or Astana,

Kazakhstan, morale hit an all-time low while stress was high. Vacations were canceled, separation from family was prolonged, and the novelty of the virus wore off within the first month. As a command, we were extremely sensitive to the situation the pandemic was causing for our personnel, and we pressed our regional chiefs to stay engaged at a higher frequency than normal while we all weathered the impacts of long lockdowns and quarantines. Within the first few months of taking command of NSU, we experienced the trauma and heartache of a suicide in our command and were adamant about doing our best to prevent another one at any time, let alone during the pandemic.

Sadly, suicides in the military are too common. Each one is painful, and the one in NSU made for an extremely difficult time for many who knew the member, as well as CUCM Joe Maioriello and me. We had talked with the individual just days prior and had no indication that the member was in need of any additional support or monitoring. Maioriello noted this was one of the hardest events he ever dealt with while in the U.S. Navy and something that he regularly recalls. For me, this was the first time as a leader I had dealt with a suicide. Who do I call? What resources are available? The U.S. Navy has programs and processes in place, but how do I get the ball rolling? My first action was to call my Immediate Superior in Command (ISIC), the Chief of Staff at NAVFAC headquarters. I began by simply asking for help and direction. In minutes, a phone call to the regional Casualty Assistant Control Officer was made and they walked us through the process and obtained chaplain support from the National Capitol Region. Informing the command before the news broke or rumors were able to spread was also extremely important. We then made full contact with every member in the command to ensure they knew the situation and had the resources they needed.

Master Chief Maioriello accompanied the deceased member home to the family, which is standard procedure but valuable to the families affected by a death of a serving member of the U.S. military. This last flight has a series of protocols to be followed, including flying in dress uniform. As it was the summer of 2018, Master Chief Maioriello flew back in his dress white uniform. The dress white uniform is impossible to miss. Even the shoes are white. Walking anywhere in this uniform draws attention, and it especially draws attention in an airport. Scores of veterans with some idea of what was happening approached Maioriello to offer their condolences, and plenty of other curious travelers, who knew nothing of the situation, would ask for a picture or thank him for his service. The emotional impact is unfathomable and extremely stressful for anyone.

Before boarding, Maioriello was on the tarmac to witness the coffin being loaded onto the plane, and then he was seated in the front row. The flight crew knew very well what was going on and were extremely supportive as, unfortunately, this is a regular occurrence for the military, whether it's a death by suicide or combat. When they finally landed, the captain made an announcement for everyone to remain seated until after Maioriello disembarked. The plane was silent while this happened, and Maioriello admitted to having fought to maintain his composure.

A tragic experience I had was when one of my Seabees received a battlefield injury. This will be talked about in more detail in the chapter on "Havana Syndrome," but simply stated: when someone under your leadership gets ill or injured in the line of duty, it is always worth taking the time to visit them in the hospital, if possible. When it is not possible, perhaps due to the location, phone calls with them can serve the purpose of showing empathy and support and ensuring they are getting the care they need. A fifteen-minute visit is enough to show the individual that you and the command support them and will use whatever resources are available to make sure they are taken care of. It's also a time to insist that they fully recover before returning to work and reassure them that their duties will be taken care of until their return.

Video calls did allow our CPOICs and LPOs (Leading Petty Officers) to read their personnel better than a phone call, but the virtual contact reinforced the importance of in-person contact. When a geographically dispersed team operates, they are unable to see their teammates regularly, but even a few meetings in person are enough to form a relationship with someone that makes more remote forms of contact more effective at a later time and can help one determine if someone else is truly feeling okay or if they are just saying they are okay. Having that level of connection is one of the few ways to take care of people on a personal level. Their pay, living conditions, and other material things are easiest to care for, but the emotional connection that is maintained with direct reports is what can help lead members through difficult times, such as the pandemic, as well as provide an insight into how effective the command leadership is.

Trusting a chain of command—both up and down it—and allowing people to lead in their own style is also important, as long as they are meeting the commander's intent. A Second Class Petty Officer will report to a First Class Petty Officer, who is the Leading Petty Officer (LPO). That LPO will report to the CPOIC, and the CPOIC will report to the OIC/AOIC on the state of their region. This chain of command feeds information upward. Due to the long periods of time between face-to-face meetings, trusting the direct supervisors to maintain emotional connections with their personnel is critical.

Recurring calls with your direct reports is a common practice. However, in NSU, the execution of this common practice is much more difficult across the board. Most NSU Seabees travel much of the time, in addition to the CPOICs, who are also technicians, and the OIC and AOIC. The more travel being performed, the more difficult it is to organize reoccurring meetings. If travel is minimal or mostly local and/or domestic, meetings occur weekly or monthly. Setting up reoccurring one-on-one monthly calls when everyone is traveling is difficult, despite the benefits of doing so. Being in different time zones is the first layer of difficulty. Then having access to a phone *with* a good connection *within* a controlled space can prove challenging. Finally, stopping in the middle of any task while on TDY for a call can be a distraction that disrupts productivity. Perhaps these are simple excuses for endlessly rescheduling contact that could be overcome; however, in the end, the random request for a phone call when needing to talk about something important tends to be easiest and most effective option.

During the 1980s, most communication done within NSU was via official telegrams or phone calls. Contact from Washington, D.C., to the field was minimal other than arranging a visit or when the Seabees needed something from headquarters. Receiving pay or per diem for travel was also much more complicated than today's electronic funds transfers and direct deposits. Every NSU Seabee and DOS employee was required to open a bank account through the State Department Credit Union in order to get some pay in advance of travel to cover expenses. Account information was also given to the command Disbursing Clerk (DK), in case a trip was extended. The DK could get additional monies deposited into your account that you could then access from the cashier at post. Stephan Haycook recalled the situation while preparing for a six-month TDY trip to Brazil. He took his TDY orders to the credit union, where they issued him traveler checks in the amount of the per diem he would need to pay for his hotel, meals, and incidentals. Due to the TDY being six months long, he received about 30,000 USD in advance pay. While on this trip, he realized his End of Active Obligatory Service was coming up, and his diplomatic passport was expiring, too. He needed to reenlist to stay in the U.S. Navy and subsequently receive orders to renew his passport. The thought may have crossed his mind that he could disappear into the shadows of Brazil, as 30,000 USD would go a long way there at the time; but he stayed the course and didn't become an Unauthorized Absence (UA), or Absent Without Leave (AWOL).[40] To be clear, there's no record of anyone in NSU going UA/AWOL when presented with this situation.

Before the full integration of the internet in the early 2000s and the use of personal computer stations became widespread within DOS, approximately 80 percent of all communication was done via phone. The OIC, AOIC, and Operations Chief were the only personnel in the headquarters element with a Wang computer terminal. The Wang computers could do simple word processing and send a basic form of email. Due to the limited availability, most of the Seabees in the field didn't have regular access to the terminals, which further caused the reliance on phone calls. The leadership could also send cable messages. Cables are encrypted telegrams that are still used today, although much less often. About four times a year, NSU leadership would send a cable out to all NSU Seabees posted worldwide with a general update on the unit and its operations for the quarter and any significant information to be passed to everyone.[79]

Overall, today's technology that enables instant communication with those all around the world by voice, text, or video has shrunk the globe and the distances in between. Only twenty years ago, email was still in its infancy, and the business world still relied heavily on faxes and mail. NSU was no different. Sending and receiving messages was difficult, and missing phone calls meant delays. Administrative work was slow and cumbersome, and any expectation of easy communication overseas had to be tempered.[83] Coming out of COVID-19, technology has leaped forward and produced even more tools to facilitate communication, which have left no one wanting to go back to the old days. Today, productivity has improved; however, true human connection will likely always be critical.

When I first learned that I was selected to be the OIC for NSU and in a global leadership role, I was initially overwhelmed at the sheer volume of duties and responsibilities that lay before me. As not just the OIC for a detachment or detail, but the OIC for an entire unit with the responsibility of the entire command. This would include leading headquarters staff and providing the direction for the unit in association with DOS.

Laying out my vision for the unit and commander's intent would be very important to set the tone for my time with the unit. A vision needs to be concise so that everyone can understand it, and its brevity is even more important if you expect personnel to take the time to read it through. Coming to the unit, I knew it operated well, so leading it meant maintaining a lot of things that worked effectively in addition to attempting to build upon its many years of success. The four areas of focus for NAVFAC and NCF type commands are typically people, safety, cost, timeliness, and/or quality. For NSU I wanted to again focus on safety, but communication, professionalism, and common-sense values rounded out my top objectives. These are unique to the command and critical to its function with a global presence.

I also co-opted a couple of phrases to focus the unit: "What got you here won't get you there," and "Taking us into the next decade." The first phrase refers to the type of personnel in the unit and the title of a book by Marshall Goldsmith. Many personnel are high achievers with impeccable careers, but when they enter the unit, they are now in a pool of talent that is even more impressive. It's difficult to stand out from the pack. The quote intends to impress on the individuals that only sustaining the effort that they have exerted before may not be enough to take them to the next level. The second phrase addressed the command. If there were going to be changes made, they would be focused on the longevity of the command and ensuring it is ready for the next decade as the unit rolled into the 2020s.

The four concentration areas had a slightly different focus than a typical NAVFAC unit.

1. *Safety* focused less on the day-to-day tasking, but safety in an overseas environment for the member's family and self, as well as being prepared to act expeditiously within the various threat environments NSU operates in.
2. *Communication* is obvious: being clear, concise, and responsive is key to keeping the organization running smoothly.
3. As "Professionals Around the World," *professionalism* and personal development were necessary in an interagency environment. It was important to know who was in a room with you while operating competently and independently.
4. Finally, *common sense* was needed to make decisions when no one else was around. Being honest, maintaining integrity, and remaining loyal to the mission usually would ensure the best outcome.

After the initial rollout of the vision and my intent for the command, I didn't realize how often I would refer back to it. I found that when discussing what the command was doing during my residence inspections and mentoring sessions with my Seabees, I often circled back to key points of it as I offered what I hoped was sage wisdom.

After setting clear expectations for your dispersed workforce, it is also important to reimagine how to use the tactics you are accustomed to, such as rethinking what an "open-door policy" means. How you are going to get out and see your people and set a vision for your command that crosses cultures, work environments, and time zones? An open-door policy is often employed or communicated poorly to subordinates. It is usually understood that if the door is open, you can knock and come in. If it is closed, you are occupied and shouldn't be disturbed for any number of reasons. For personnel co-located with you, you can set some parameters that may keep you from being interrupted constantly and train your personnel to be more organized and efficient in their approach. The parameters may be different depending on whether they are part of the leadership team or a superior official. For most of your workforce, the open-door policy really means, if you have an urgent problem, I'll stop what I'm doing to help you out. It's not an "all-welcome for a leisurely conversation about the game last night." Any "drive-by," as these interruptions are sometimes called, should be quick and to the point. If they need something from you, they should be able to request it quickly and be on their way. If they need to explain in great detail what they need from you, at your discretion, they should set up a meeting for when you have more time to discuss or wait for you to walk around the office and approach you in passing.

When some individuals show up to your office unannounced and inappropriately, you can respond in a few different ways. First, whenever someone enters your office, stand up. By standing up, you can address them quickly and see what they need. It's also generally perceived as a polite courtesy. You can also start walking them toward the door if you are really short on time. Sometimes going to the "head" (bathroom) is faster than letting them bury you in small talk. But by walking them to the door, they will subconsciously realize that you are busy. Rarely will the person be offended that you walked them out. You gave them attention, and if they couldn't tell you whatever they needed in the fifteen seconds you engaged with them, then it probably wasn't that important in the first place.

Everything mentioned here has to do with personnel who inhabit the same office as you. What about anyone overseas or located outside of your office day to day? How does an open-door policy work for them? There is no perfect way to resolve this conundrum, but personal preference plays a big part. I determined the best way to address the open-door policy was that if my phone rang, no matter who I was talking to (unless it was my boss), I would stop what I was doing and answer it. This is because as the OIC, you don't normally get phone calls unless there's something worth calling you about. Most people will be in a different time zone and will have made a conscientious effort to call you when you'd be in the office. For some, that will be outside their normal working hours. This is why it is important to answer any call that comes in. Others will message you first and ask if you have a minute before calling, which is even better because it gives you time to compose yourself before the call. Although I answered a ton of telemarketing calls, I did get plenty of calls from unknown numbers that ended up being my Seabees overseas, with whom I was happy to speak and help in any way I could.

Getting out and about throughout the office and to everyone you are responsible for is extremely important and advantageous. In order to learn about each of your personnel, as well as the environment they are working and living in, you must travel. If they are in different countries, the climates, cultures, and languages may all be different and add an extra level of complexity to your organization. But when traveling, I found I was getting to put a face with a name and build a relationship by spending one or two days with the individuals, and that was the most impactful aspect of my position. As their reporting senior, I was responsible for their periodic evaluations and approval of any awards. By building a bond and relationship with each of them, I was able to better evaluate their performance, even if I only ever saw them once. It also gave them an opportunity to show off what they've been working on and connect you with their colleagues and counterparts who may provide benefits or support to your operation. Just as they get to show off things to you, it is also important that you communicate to them the logic behind decisions or things that are in the works behind the scenes at headquarters so they can ask questions and even provide you feedback before something becomes official.

When I was in battalion, we were told to go to class and see what the troops were learning. I sat in on the class, but I didn't know why I was doing it at that point in my career. Was I supposed to learn something or simply be present? It wasn't until getting to NSU that I learned it was for a number of reasons. You were checking on the curriculum to see if what they are learning is pertinent, up to date, and worthwhile; you're monitoring the instructors to see how they teach and interact, or if they're just going through the motions; and you're watching your troops to see who is participating. You may not get a lot of other work done that day, but you can take away a lot of value by going. If you have personnel in training for a long time, you can use the time you spend visiting as a means of getting feedback or have them ask you questions about what is going on. NSU Seabees are in training for over six months. Therefore, frequenting the training center is an opportunity to foster relationships and gain visibility before everyone posts overseas.

Learning about the physical and security environment was another aspect of visiting the NSU Seabees around the world. Due to the nature of their jobs, there were constant threats to their safety from the environment or from nefarious actors. For a military unit that has personnel rotate every three to five years, we are constantly thinking about replacements. By understanding the physical and security environments, you can more easily find a right fit to backfill the member who's transferring. The family makeup is also an important variable in the equation, and we encourage each member to discuss their options with their family. This doesn't mean we only send families to certain posts and single individuals to the more austere locations; it is determined by the situation on the ground and the personalities that we assess during recruitment or training with the command.

NSU attracts a lot of Seabees that immigrated to the United States in their youth. Some are interested in getting posted near where they may have family overseas, while others do not want to go anywhere near where they are from. Likewise, families can be adventurous and want to go somewhere they never thought they'd live before, while others go somewhere they thought would be great only to realize they don't like it. It's an imperfect system, but when it gets down to it, the mission needs to be completed, and we do the best we can for each of our personnel to make the most of any situation. We usually do a good job at posting. There were only a couple times during my tenure that Seabees or their families were not overjoyed with where they ended up. Out of eighty-one overseas posting assignments, that's a pretty good rate of success. It is said that a leader can't make everyone happy; if you try, you will never succeed. Some people will never be happy, no matter what.

Being the senior person of a command has its privileges, but it also comes with a burden that can weigh on you the longer you are alone at the top. It is important to utilize mentors, stay in touch with your network, and work closely with your team of senior advisors to ensure you continue to stay on track with the decisions you make to lead the organization forward. As the reporting senior for the command, everyone ultimately works for you. This means that everyone is a subordinate. I say this rather bluntly to remind you that your relationships with everyone are scrutinized so that you don't show favoritism or any level of fraternization, which is extra important in a military organization. Giving everyone a fair evaluation is paramount to maintain the integrity of the systems in place for personnel management. The practices you put in place need to be repeated every time you do them in every location with every person. If you are going to take your personnel to lunch, everyone should be invited from that location. If you buy lunch in one location, you'd better do that at every location.

There's a fine line to tread every time you interact with your personnel between leadership and friendship. As the leader, you must do the right thing every time.

To have mentors is also important. While I was the OIC of NSU, I encountered many challenges for the first time. The most difficult issues were personnel matters. Experienced mentors who have been in leadership positions before and likely handled similar types of events are critical to have on "speed dial." Being able to call upon them for advice in time of uncertainty or guidance on what to do next can go a long way. It's important to know when you've encountered a situation you need support to handle. Picking up the phone and calling your ISIC for that support is okay. They are there to support your command and will be much happier to help you make a decision than to find out you took missteps that could have easily been prevented had you contacted them earlier. In the military, everyone continues to be put in positions that senior leaders believe they can handle until the individual proves otherwise. As long as you handle each opportunity well, they will continue putting you into positions of greater authority. When you hit a point where you no longer have the capacity or capability to handle situations, that is when they know you've peaked and will stop moving you up the career ladder. You may get another chance later on, but it's not guaranteed. Knowing when to call a mentor is like knowing when to turn off a bad road or keep going, believing you can make it when, instead, the mentor would know there is a cliff just around the bend.

Staying in touch with your network, in addition to mentors, is important when not interacting with them day to day. By keeping your name on people's minds, you stay in the loop on the latest developments and trends. Maintaining situational awareness of the operational picture within your organization is critical for when you are next moved to another part of the organization and want to avoid starting from scratch each time.

Finally, using your senior advisors is very beneficial. Those advisors serve as continuity for the location and often have a ton of experience and corporate knowledge. These advisors have eyes and ears across the organization and at every level. They are trusted confidants for many and will save you from yourself.

Why make a decision in a vacuum, when you could easily get advice from advisors, colleagues, or mentors who can help discern the impacts from all sides of a decision before it's ever made? In my first three months, I encountered a battlefield injury, a suicide, and a Driving Under the Influence (DUI) in a command that doesn't see these events often. How do you communicate a suicide to every person in the command? How do you get resources? You pick up the phone and call everyone you know: the ISIC, Chiefs mess, mentors, colleagues. Call in your favors and ask for help.

As the leader of an organization, everything you say or do is scrutinized and may be interpreted differently than you intended. You must always do the right thing. Avoid being too flippant in conversations and think through every one of your words when speaking to anyone. Taking the easy route and not reporting something to avoid conflict, or not taking all the required steps in a process, can create discontent in your office and paint a picture that you're above the law. By taking the time to do the right thing every time, you can avoid the pitfalls of many leaders you read about on the front page of news sources. For NSU specifically, this was one of my four main points to follow in my vision. Nearly all our personnel serve as the only NSU representative at a post. They don't have anyone in their chain of command checking in on them every day. Being by themselves overseas, they have a lot of freedom and could find themselves doing things that may be okay for civilians but not military members. Writer and cleric Charles Caleb Colton said, "Character is what you do when nobody's watching." Doing the right thing when no one is watching is what is required as a leader of an organization (and a standard everyone should live by).

Doing the right thing is also a feeling you get in your gut when making a decision. Several situations came up during my tenure that I thought long and hard about, trying to figure out every way possible to approve something within my authority without needing to go to my superiors. What I would realize in these situations was that if I had to spend two days contemplating how to avoid doing something, that meant I wasn't making the right decision. Doing the right thing is a way to cover your ass. When you're the senior person, accountability falls on you whenever something goes wrong with one of your personnel or operations. You can delegate the responsibility and authority to someone else to get a job done well, but accountability stays with you. So, "inspect what you expect." Using your resources, network, and lessons learned from your predecessors, doing the right thing can be easy, but it's not always easy to carry out the decision.

As the OIC for NSU, there are two bosses to report to. One is a Senior Foreign Service Officer Counselor (military One-Star equivalent), and the other is the Chief of the Civil Engineer Corps and Commander, NAVFAC, a two-star command. The Chief of Staff at NAVFAC is also one of the most senior Captains in the CEC and the primary conduit for relaying communications. It is important to maintain good reporting and communication to keep both chains of command up to date. Provide succinct reports on a regular basis, even if they weren't asked for.

While having two senior chains of command can be good at times, it can also be daunting. At the intersection of two agencies, I was responsible for drafting documentation on behalf of each organization when it concerned NSU. In one situation, I wrote a memo for DOS to NAVFAC to make a request for more personnel. I was then tasked with writing the response from NAVFAC to DOS. While a seemingly common occurrence in Washington, D.C., it made sense for me to write both; regardless, I thought it was funny to see my name as the drafter for each of them.

No matter how much leadership responsibility, authority, and accountability you are granted, in whatever position you are put in, you will be tested. You will be tested to make decisions in situations where nothing is clear; you will be asked to pass along bad news; you will be asked to do things you never thought you would do or were ready to do. However, every test you come across will help you grow as a leader and show your true character when the dust settles. It was a true privilege and honor to serve as the OIC of NSU, although it was challenging. Leadership isn't easy, but it's extremely rewarding when done right.

12

Western Hemisphere Affairs

The Western Hemisphere Affairs (WHA) region is comprised of North and South America. NSU Seabees are spread across six locations across both continents, not including Washington, D.C. Most NSU Seabees are posted at U.S. embassies as part of an Engineering Services Center (ESC) or Engineering Services Office (ESO). An ESC oversees other ESOs and falls under a Regional Director for Security Engineering (RDSE). In WHA, the RDSE is posted in Fort Lauderdale, FL, at the Florida Regional Center (FRC). Along with the RDSE, the NSU Chief Petty Officer in Charge (CPOIC) for WHA is also located in Fort Lauderdale.

The ST team at the FRC covers the entire Caribbean and parts of Latin America and the north coast of South America. It has a larger office to cover approximately thirteen different posts in the region that are too small for personnel to be permanently posted there. In addition to regular work, FRC is also hit by hurricanes and other natural disasters regularly. Seabees have been pivotal to the emergency response to get the various embassies and consulates reopened and operational.

The Seabees are no strangers to the Humanitarian Assistance and Disaster Relief (HA/DR) mission, as they are commonly deployed for this purpose while with the NMCBs and ACBs. The most significant recent responses have been Hurricane Maria in Havana (2017) and Hurricane Isaias in the Bahamas (2020). Seabees from FRC and additional support from the Washington, D.C., TDY pool are always on call and ready to respond. Following Hurricane Maria, a team of Seabees responded to destruction and flooding of U.S. Embassy Havana, Cuba, within forty-eight hours. Arriving so soon after the storm lifted, it was ninety-six hours before the next emergency support team was able to arrive. In that time, they secured all classified materials and equipment, in addition to getting the facilities back on generator power, pumping the flooded basement after the storm surge that breached the building, and restoring a temporary fence after a twenty-foot container floated by the storm surge repeatedly slammed the façade of the building. Hurricane Isaias caused considerable damage to the Bahamas but mostly spared the embassy. A number of cameras were knocked out, and multiple systems went offline; however, there was no structural damage, and the technical security systems were recovered relatively quickly.

Another location on the FRC constituent post list is Bermuda, a British territory. Although there are no stories of Seabees going missing in the Bermuda Triangle, one Seabee wished he had. Former ST Director Steve Romero recalled one of his first TDYs to Bermuda in the early 1990s with another STS and Seabee Chief. They were sent there to install the technical security systems for a new Consulate General facility. The facility was a two-story house being repurposed for use. Due to their longer stay, they were in a rented apartment for the three weeks. As they would be able to cook and prepare meals, the Seabee Chief told Steve Romero and the STS how things were going to work. They were going to give him food money, and he would do all the shopping and cooking if they did the dishes. Steve Romero and the STS, with only brief hesitation, shrugged their shoulders and said, "Sure, sounds good." Steve Romero said they had great meals and never went hungry while there. However, what they hadn't planned for was a dock strike that took place as soon as they got on the ground in Bermuda. This meant all their materials were held up at port. Two weeks went by before the container of materials was released, and then they had only a week to do everything. Working nearly around the clock, they managed to get everything done. But one piece of equipment they installed put them before the Consular General (CG) before they left. The office of the CG had a bathroom on an exterior wall, which had windows that a person could potentially fit through. Because of this, they installed a passive infrared sensor to set off the alarm if triggered. However, when the CG's office management specialist came by while they were installing it, the Seabee Chief jokingly told her they were putting a camera in the bathroom to watch the window. This misinformation quickly got to the CG, and the Seabee Chief and Steve found themselves having to explain what exactly they were installing in the bathroom.[102]

In 2019, the relations between the United States and Venezuela unraveled, and the embassy was closed. However, believing there was going to be a regime change, NSU placed a Seabee on standby, ready to go in with the first team to reopen the facility in Caracas when or if the time came. We selected one of our most experienced Seabees, Senior Chief Dan Baldwin, who was on standby for two weeks in D.C. waiting for a flight that never happened. False alarm.

Unlike the economic and political environment of Venezuela of today, life in Caracas in 1984 was a relaxing and friendly environment. Retired SEO George Herrmann recalled a TDY trip to Caracas while performing security enhancements at the new embassy building. George had established a relationship with the RSO, and the RSO took George and the Seabee Chief out to dinner at a food trailer beside a mountain road on the edge of Caracas. According to George, "It was a dark and seedy area." He noticed that the trailer was powered by "two long battery jumpers that were clipped onto the city power lines next to the curb." The trailer also had a drive-up window, since there was not a lot of room to park. The RSO knew the owner and introduced him to everyone, and then ordered some rounds of tacos. While eating, they watched the traffic that oddly included a lot of high-end cars. The Seabee Chief was notorious for falling asleep about 8:30 PM every night ("It did not matter whether he was lying down, sitting down, or even standing up, he would fall asleep."), and as it was starting to get late, Chief asked the RSO for the car keys. When the others went to check on the Chief fifteen minutes later, they found him asleep in the trunk of the car. He had crawled in, but left the lid up. "One of his feet was propped on the edge of the trunk, giving him the appearance of a body that had been tossed carelessly into the back of the car!" Apparently, the Chief's presence in the car did not go unnoticed among the takeout patrons in the expensive cars. Most of them "took one look at what appeared to be a dead body and sped away without ordering a thing." After about four cars passed without ordering, the owner suggested they take the tired Chief home.[111]

A nation with similarly fragile relations with the United States is Cuba, and being posted in Havana is an unusual experience. The U.S. military installation in Guantanamo Bay, Cuba (GTMO), is only accessible by military flight, and U.S. citizens serving at GTMO are not allowed to enter mainland Cuba. The single Seabee and the Marines in Havana are the only U.S. military presence outside of GTMO due to the sour relationship between the two nations since Fidel Castro took over in 1959. In Havana, the airport is tiny, but security for arriving Americans is exhaustive. At the Hotel International, they put diplomats on the eighth floor for certain undisclosed reasons.

Overall, Havana has nice living conditions, but the food situation is volatile due to continued sanctions on the nation and state-run enterprises. The grocery stores are hit and miss. One aisle may be completely full of just one item, like peanut butter. The next aisle would be barren, and so on. The open-air markets are where most people get things, often from the unregulated "black market." However, one thing was in plentiful supply: cigars.[112] Given the lack of nutritional value of cigars, personnel posted in Cuba, in addition to a handful of other countries, are allowed shipments of consumables, due to the inability to acquire many common foodstuffs and supplies on the local market. However, even such shipments cannot entirely resolve the food situation.

BUC Dustin Wallace was posted in Havana with his family from 2015 to 2017. In June 2015, Cuba and the United States reopened their respective embassies after thirty-eight years. Wallace recalled the cigar plantations and the great old-town architecture of Havana in addition to the difficult food situation. When the Wallace family first arrived, they went to seventeen different grocery stores to find all the items they were looking for, but eventually learned to be more efficient and less selective in their shopping.[112] Despite the food situation, Wallace did appreciate that the power grid was influenced by the U.S. Army Corps of Engineers when it was first being developed, and Cuba's 110V/60Hz is the same as the voltage used in the United States. Chief Wallace arrived in Cuba when relations were improving, and the Cubans made significant further improvements in preparation for the visit by President and First Lady of the United States, Barack and Michelle Obama, in 2016. He reported that Cuba paved every road and painted all the structures along the routes that the convoys would use to travel through Havana.[112]

In 1898, the battleship *U.S.S. Maine* exploded in Havana Harbor while the Cubans were rising up against the Spanish. This explosion eventually led to the Spanish-American War that left the United States with the territories of the Philippines, Puerto Rico, and Guam, while Cuba gained its independence. The Cubans built a monument in 1925 to memorialize the 266 U.S. Sailors that were lost. However, in 1951, some of the original language was changed to imply the "Sailors were pawns of an imperial power."[113] Wallace noted that after a hurricane, the golden eagle atop the monument was damaged and replaced. The original eagle is on display in the back yard of the Chief of Mission Residence (CMR). The residence itself was designed to resemble the White House and built to be a summer house for FDR; however, it was never utilized because the United States entered WWII. Today it remains as the CMR.[112,114]

The Bahamas and other islands in the Caribbean also provide a unique opportunity for travel. Because the Department of State is the oldest department within the U.S. federal government, it's travel policy still includes transit by ship. Currently, there are locations that are more cost effective to travel to by ship than fly to, including some in the Caribbean. Other locations, taking a cruise ship or a ferry to service a constituent post is also common practice—one of those locations is Montevideo, Uruguay. ESC personnel also take a ferry to Buenos Aires, Argentina, to service the embassy there.

Countries to the north and south of the continental United States each have a high number of consulates due to the significant number of people crossing the borders. Seabees support these facilities from the respective embassies in Ottawa, Canada, and Mexico City, Mexico. The U.S. Embassy Ottawa is a unique facility because it is the only U.S. embassy where a passer-by can walk up to the front door or even knock on a window. This is largely due to the close relationship the United States has with Canada and the low threat level. It's also unique because it is the only embassy post that you are allowed to drive to from the continental United States.

Ottawa, Canada, originally called Bytown, after LtCol John By, was renamed by Queen Victoria in 1855 to Ottawa, which comes from the Algonquin word "adawe," which means trade. Due to the large amount of beaver pelts traded in Ottawa, beaver tail was the name given to a local pastry—fried dough in shape of a beaver tail, coated in cinnamon and sugar and topped with chocolate. Being the northernmost post in the Western Hemisphere where NSU is located, it is one of the coldest. In case you eat too many pastries, you can work off some calories by skating five miles along the Rideau Canal in the winter, when it turns to ice.

Located on the high Mexican Plateau, Mexico City is one of the few inland world capitals. At such elevation, the temperatures are moderate throughout the year. Mexico City was founded on the ruins of the former island-capital Tenochtitlan, the center of the Aztec Empire. One of the longest continuously inhabited cities in the Western Hemisphere, it is rich in culture and tradition. There are two Aztec pyramids on the outskirts of Mexico City, and the famed Aztec Sun Stone is housed in the National Anthropology Museum in the heart of Mexico City. Our Seabees posted in Mexico City stay incredibly busy with nineteen constituent posts. Approximately half of these posts are consular agencies that do not require a significant amount of attention; however, they are still responsible for nine consulate generals there, in addition to the embassy. The El Angel de la Independencia monument is a short walk from the embassy, erected to celebrate the Mexican War of Independence from Spain that ended in 1821.

In South America, Seabees are posted in Lima, Peru, and in Montevideo, Uruguay. Peru is a beautiful country on the western seaboard of South America and presents the unique challenge of servicing posts at extremely high altitudes. This requires finding personnel who are fit enough to tolerate altitude. Unfortunately, there have been several instances of DOS personnel who weren't able to physically handle the low oxygen levels and died within the first twenty-four hours of arriving. This has also been a pressing issue at other high-altitude posts, including La Paz, Bolivia, and Quito, Ecuador, both of which are serviced by ESO Lima. Despite the risk, personnel posted to Lima often take advantage of their proximity to one of the seven modern wonders of the world, Machu Picchu, located in Cusco—a short flight or train ride.

Montevideo, Uruguay, is one of the only seven posts south of the equator that Seabees are posted and the southernmost in the Western Hemisphere. The embassy is also one of the many oceanfront diplomatic facilities that the United States has overseas. Despite the beautiful views from these facilities, it makes maintenance and operations very difficult, due to the corrosive effects of the weather to which the facility is exposed.

Montevideo is heavily influenced by both Argentina and Brazil due to occupations in the 1800s. However, a large number of immigrants from Italy also came to Uruguay, and they heavily influenced its commerce and lifestyle. It is most notable for its beef exports, making it cheaper to eat steak than many other food items in Montevideo. Leaving the city, the *gaucho*, or cowboy, cattle ranchers make up much of rural Uruguay. U.S. citizens who aren't used to the local market prices, often find ordering non-perishable items online from the states less expensive than purchasing items in local grocery stores.

When I first landed in Montevideo, I was caught off guard by the applause among the passengers. I learned that, due to the conditions, successful landings still warrant a round of applause. Furthermore, while visiting Montevideo, I'd learn that mechanical systems often need a little extra attention; it would be the second time in my life that I got stuck in an elevator. The first day at the hotel, I noticed the elevators were a little shaky. At my first duty station, Marine Corps Base Camp Lejeune in Jacksonville, North Carolina, I had a number of projects that included certifying elevators. Then, as the Production Officer for Naval Base Guam, I oversaw all vertical transportation equipment certification as well. Between nearly five years of managing elevator certifications, I had learned enough to know how an elevator should operate. Due to ingrained habit, I always keep an eagle eye out for the elevator certification that's supposed to be posted in each car every time I walk into one. On the second morning, I got in the elevator with another traveler who spoke Spanish. I took three years of Spanish in middle school and high school, so I could pick up a few words and was glad he was in the rickety elevator with me.

On that day, the elevator decided to take us for more of a ride than we bargained for. It would go to the floors it was being called, but the doors just wouldn't open. After the fourth time, we thought we may never get off the elevator if the doors never open, even though it kept moving. This is when I opened the emergency phone box and dialed out to whatever call center it was tied to. The moment the dispatcher answered in a hurried phrase of Spanish, I looked over at the other man riding the elevator, desperately hoping he could take over the call. Thankfully, he obliged and told them we needed someone to help get us off the elevator. At least that's what I'm assuming he said. After he hung up, we continued to ride the elevator up and down for nearly twenty minutes until the maintenance workers were able to stop the elevator and open the doors manually. There was only one problem: we were back on the twenty-fourth floor. We had to choose to take the other elevator or the stairs. We looked at each other and without saying it, decided "what the hell," and got on the other elevator instead of taking the twenty-four flights of stairs to the ground floor. Thankfully, we got to the bottom without further issues and were able to get on with our day. When I returned to the hotel that night, I went back up to my room to discover the key card wouldn't work. Back down the elevator I went. At the front desk I got my card reset and upon return to my room there was an apology note and chocolate-covered strawberries waiting for me, due to the inconvenience that morning. The hotel made up for it, but that day was to be just one of many adventures and experiences I would encounter during my travels.

13

Europe

The continent of Europe is split into two regions referred to by NSU as Europe and Southern Europe. The posts in Europe are full of history to include some of the oldest and most historic embassies in the Department of State's portfolio. The missions in France, the Netherlands, and the United Kingdom are the oldest. Four of the first six U.S. presidents served as Ambassadors or representatives of the United States to at least one of these three nations, including John Adams, Thomas Jefferson, James Monroe, and John Quincy Adams. Also notable was Benjamin Franklin. Their service required a long period overseas when the United States was still in its infancy. Abroad, they developed as statesmen before having significant impact on the course of the nation.

The CPOIC for Europe, the RDSE responsible for both Europe and Southern Europe, and one of the two ESC OIC's on the European continent are all co-located in Frankfurt, Germany. The consulate in Frankfurt was built in 1939, originally as a hospital for the German Air Force in WWII known as Army Hospital Plant 4377.[115] By the conclusion of the war, the U.S. Army 97th General Hospital occupied the facility beginning in 1945 until the mid-1990s.[116] There are still some remnants of the hospital's Nazi past faintly evidenced in the façade relief. It includes swastikas (painted over within the plaster) on the ceiling in some corners of the sprawling compound that are generally unnoticeable to a passerby.

In 2006, the U.S. Consulate General Frankfurt completed its consolidation of multiple facilities into a single location in the former hospital that was refurbished into one of the largest overseas diplomatic facility compounds for the United States.[117] Due to its size and location in a major transit and financial hub for all of Europe, the facility is also used as a major training and conference center by the Department of State.

It is easy to assume that most training and conferences for a U.S. government organization would be hosted in Washington, D.C., or, at the very least, stateside. However, with a dispersed global workforce that serves mostly overseas, Frankfurt is a more cost-effective location, with a vast number of non-stop flights from locations as far away as Johannesburg, South Africa, and Bangkok, Thailand. Also, being only two hours ahead of Greenwich Mean Time, it also means that most attendees don't need to cross the international dateline. And being within three time zones of around ninety U.S. diplomatic locations overseas (more than half) helps minimize jet lag for most attendees. In comparison, there are only about thirty locations in the Americas, and fifty-three in East Asia and the Pacific.

In Frankfurt, the team of Seabees primarily provide maintenance and project support to fifty-four embassies and consulates within the European region. Due to the large amount of transatlantic tourism and American corporations with foreign offices throughout Europe, consular services are in high demand. Stories of musicians and celebrities who have lost their passport while on tour abound, and the Department of State Consular Affairs section stands ready to get them back on the road, in addition to nearly 9.5 million foreign citizens seeking tourist or work visas to enter the United States each year. Approximately 36,000 visas per year are processed in Frankfurt alone.[118] Due to Frankfurt's amenities, NSU also utilizes it for its annual training. There, it conducts U.S. Navy general mandatory training, as well as peer-led training topics and discussion groups. NSU also capitalizes on the venue to bring together approximately fifty of its personnel each year to celebrate the Seabee Birthday on March 5, 1942. Producing a Seabee Ball is no small feat and each year the Frankfurt Seabee Team goes the extra mile to put together an incredible event.

As many embassies in Europe are old, updated physical security standards have prompted a number of historic locations to be vacated in pursuit of modern workspaces that allow the integration of up-to-date security systems. U.S. Embassy London, United Kingdom, is one of the most recent high-profile embassy moves. At the end of 2017, the U.S. finally relocated to the new location in Nine Elms, where an economic revitalization is ongoing. The sale of other U.S. properties in London paid for the entire property in Nine Elms, totaling approximately a billion dollars.[119] A world-class example of American ingenuity and design, the facility is on the south side of the River Thames, a short walk from Vauxhall underground station and the famous MI6 headquarters, repeatedly showcased in James Bond films since the early 1990s. The old embassy was sold to the real estate investment and development firm, Qatari Diar, to be turned into a luxury hotel. One stipulation of the sale was to never remove the historic eagles that are famously affixed to the top of the roof.[120] The new embassy offers a sophisticated work environment and impressive views of central London. The Ambassador's office overlooks the Thames to provide an enticing view for visitors. It was designed with the purpose to draw onlookers to imagine the grandeur of doing business with the United States.

For many high-profile posts, the Ambassador is a prominent political appointee. These posts are often of longtime allied nations and significant trade partners. The connectedness and celebrity status of some Ambassadors can sometimes make working at the embassies difficult. The expectations of instant results or reprioritizing of goals to a changing political landscape can often derail progress made by previous Ambassadors and their staff.

But personalities aside, the most difficult posts to work at have multiple missions that require multiple Ambassadors. For example, in Brussels, Belgium, there are three missions. The Mission to Belgium, the mission to the EU, and the mission to NATO. Three high-visibility missions and three politically appointed U.S. Ambassadors. With each trying to promote their mission as most important, each one must be treated as equally as possible and share the spotlight with the others. Or, in some cases, you just have to get more spotlights to make things work! When safes are unable to be opened, alarms malfunction, or regular maintenance work is needed, the Seabees are often tasked to work in the offices of these high-ranking officials. While visiting Brussels, a lock failed on the executive suite main door for the U.S. Ambassador to Belgium. The way to get the door open was to cut a hole through the wall to turn the doorknob. After this was completed, the lock still needed changing and a new combination set, and the hole in the wall needed to be patched. The Seabee was under pressure to get it done quickly by the Ambassador because the OIC also happened to be visiting the same day, but the task was executed flawlessly and in quick order.

The NATO building in Brussels is like walking into a scene from *Star Trek*. With its high-ceilinged atrium and eight major wings, the building is an incredible design, easily viewed from miles away due to its size and scale. There are thirty NATO countries, as well as forty non-member partner nations, which maintain offices in the grand building.[121] All together, they work on maintaining peace amongst nations around the Eurasian continent and beyond. Each office space's interior is an example of each country's technology and design. Like buying a floor to a building and outfitting it with whatever you like, the floors of each wing are all different, despite a common layout. The Seabee in Brussels also services the United States' space in the NATO building. The oldest ally of the Unites States is France. Benjamin Franklin was sent to France shortly after the signing of the Declaration of Independence in 1776. He was presented as the Minister Plenipotentiary from the United States of America at the Court of Versailles in 1778, when France recognized the United States' independence from Britain. As is often customary with diplomatic relations, the longer the relationship, the more premier embassy location the ally or partner nation may receive. The U.S. Embassy Paris building has been anything but permanent, having varying locations throughout the more than 225-year relationship as the mission in France grew. The last time it moved was when construction of the current chancery was completed in 1933.[122] Since then, it has been located across from the gardens of the Champs Elysees and adjacent to the Place de la Concorde. It's a historic building with a museum-quality interior, including original Gilbert Stuart oil portraits and original busts of some of the nation's founding fathers.

As with any old building, problems develop over time as technologies change and spaces are transformed for different purposes. For technical security systems, this usually means cramming new equipment into spaces half the size or less than they need to be. In addition to the tight spaces, many of the older facilities are also historic. Historic facilities will require coordination with historical preservation offices of not just the United States but often the local government, too. Performing renovations or simply drilling a hole to run wire can take an inordinate amount of time to get approved, if at all. Paris and Rome are two of the most historic embassy facilities in the DOS portfolio.

Like U.S. Embassy Paris's premier location on the Champs Elysees, U.S. Embassy Berlin, Germany, is also located in a high-profile location next to the Brandenburg Gate and near another significant landmark, the Holocaust memorial, which can be observed from the rear of the building. After the fall of the Nazis at the end of WWII, Berlin was split into east and west sections overseen by the United States, United Kingdom, and France on the west and the USSR, the east. As Germany was split between East and West, including the division of Berlin itself, access to the U.S. embassy built just prior to the start of WWII on Pariser Platz was lost. The former embassy was also heavily damaged during the war and was torn down by the East German government before it could ever be reoccupied. When the allied nations eventually moved back into Berlin following the fall of the Berlin Wall in 1989, the United States and others sought to rebuild their embassies in their previous locations. In 2008, the new embassy in Berlin was completed.[123] The Russian embassy remained in place, where it continues to be today, across the street from the Berlin Wall Memorial, not far from Checkpoint Charlie. Checkpoint Charlie was the famous border crossing where American and Russian forces would stare each other down daily as citizens crossed back and forth.

Sometimes, the location of embassies is extremely political, and the proximity to the city center or head of government may indicate the level of esteem between the countries or how long of a relationship a state has had with the host nation. Locations of embassies may also be determined by what the nation seeking a new diplomatic home abroad may want. Each state has its own priorities or preferences. The state could want proximity, or simply more space. The host nation will often act as liaison with property owners to facilitate the purchase or exchange of properties. For comparison, in downtown Washington, D.C., there are more than 175 embassies. The French embassy is on a premier property north of Georgetown University, the British embassy is directly next to the U.S. Naval Observatory and Vice President's Residence, and the Canadian embassy has a unique position just off the National Mall with a direct line of sight to the U.S. Capitol.

While some posts are in high profile capitals around the world, many more are in more relaxed environments and less populated areas. Helsinki, Finland, is one of four regularly cold locations that NSU has Seabees posted. The other three are Moscow, Russia; Astana, Kazakhstan; and Ottawa, Canada. Helsinki is on the southern coast of Finland, bordering the frigid Baltic Sea. The U.S. embassy has a gorgeous view overlooking the bay, just a mile from the heart of the city along a winding coastal road. Helsinki has daylight for twenty-one hours of the day in the summer and twenty-one hours of darkness in the winter. Finland is home to the greatest number of saunas per capita in the world. This practice is part of life, and the Finnish use the sauna almost daily. Using a public sauna is perfectly normal and very much a social outing, like going to the community pool. The practice of pouring cold water over yourself after getting out of the sauna is part of the typical experience. At saunas situated on the edge of the Baltic, for those adventurous enough, you can jump into the sea between each session inside the sauna. The first time jumping in the Baltic will shock your system. However, the third or fourth time becomes more tolerable after your internal temperature has risen from repeated visits to the sweltering saunas.

Saunas are either wood-burning, electric, or smoke heated. Smoke heated saunas are rare, but they all use water poured over the heated elements, such as stone, to maintain a moist environment. When I visited in June 2019, it also happened to be the warmest day of the year, at 80 degrees Fahrenheit. Coincidentally, the annual Helsinki Samba Carnival was going on, which made it feel like the hot streets of Brazil, not the Arctic Circle! Experiencing the full spectrum of activities in Helsinki, we tried the local delicacy of reindeer for our main course at dinner that night.

If reindeer isn't your thing, perhaps raclette will be more palatable. A Swiss dish, raclette is made by heating a cheese wheel and scrapping off the melted portions onto potatoes, other vegetables, bread, or meat. If you like cheese, you'll enjoy raclette when served in Geneva, Switzerland.

In preparation for posting a new resident Seabees overseas, we conduct site surveys to ensure the post is ready to receive the Seabee. My visit to Geneva was memorable. First, it was a challenge to take off from Dulles International Airport. Traveling mid-summer, it is common to encounter early evening thunderstorms rolling through the Dulles, Virginia area. After traveling internationally so many times at this point, I got accustomed to boarding the plane and turning on a movie if the entertainment system was up and running. Thankfully, this time it was. We boarded at about 5:00 PM on a direct red-eye flight into Geneva. Just as the door was about to be closed, we were notified that lightning had hit nearby and that they had to hold us for thirty minutes. I didn't think much of it as I had a movie on and didn't have a connection to make in Geneva. Once cleared, they would be able to finish loading the luggage and close the doors; however, lightning struck again before they could pull back the gangway. So, we sat there another half an hour.

By the time the storm had cleared, the aircraft had to reapply for a takeoff window, since we had been delayed more than an hour and many other aircraft were prepared to take off in their previously approved windows. We had to wait another twenty minutes before we were able to back away from the gate and taxi over to the runway. In the time it took to get to the runway, lightning hit again, and there we sat on the tarmac for another half an hour. At the end of this window, most of the storms had passed, so we just needed a new approved window for takeoff. It was at this time also that I finished my movie. Two hours into the "flight," we hadn't taken off yet, but I was one movie down. I was into my second movie before take-off. At about 8:30 PM, we finally took off, and I realized I was quite hungry at this point. I hadn't eaten much in the lounge before boarding because I had been expecting an in-flight meal shortly after takeoff.

Geneva, Switzerland, has a rare "quad mission." This means there can be four U.S. Ambassadors with competing interests in Geneva all at the same time. However, only three of the four Ambassadors sit in Geneva. The three in Geneva include the Ambassadors for the U.S. Mission to the United Nations and other international organizations, the World Trade Organization, and the UN Conference on Disarmament. Number four, the U.S. Ambassador to Switzerland, sits in Bern, the capital of Switzerland. (The United Nations operates in multiple locations around the world, and there are several other U.S. Ambassadors assigned to its various functions. The other locations that the United States has appointed ambassadors to U.N. missions include Vienna, Austria; New York City, USA; Rome, Italy; Montreal, Canada; and Nairobi, Kenya.)

The Consular Agency in Geneva is much more robust than most consular agencies due to it being home to three other missions. The facility includes one of the largest conference centers in the DOS portfolio, accommodating nearly 25,000 annual visitors. This conference center has its own entrance, separate from the main entrance to the consular facilities, to alleviate many security challenges.

Despite Geneva being at the foot of the Alps, the temperatures in Geneva are relatively moderate. Snow is rare, and extreme heatwaves even rarer. A stroll down to the water, you will observe views of the famous Matterhorn among the Swiss Alps. This historic downtown is pulsing with tourists and locals, cheese, chocolate, and more. The Swiss have such a high cost of living because they manufacture nearly all items sold in Switzerland. This creates high wages for their citizens and minimal reliance on other nations for supplies. Switzerland is a wealthy nation and host to the World Economic Forum, which gathers in the mountain town of Davos each year.

In Switzerland, depending on what region you are in, you will hear several languages spoken. English is spoken across all regions, but French is spoken in the West; German in the North; Austrian in the East; and Italian in the South.

Another location with multiple U.N. missions is Vienna, Austria. The United States participates as members in six missions under the U.S. Mission to International Organizations, which include the International Atomic Energy Agency, the U.N. Office on Drugs and Crime, the Preparatory Commission of the Comprehensive Nuclear-Test-Ban Treaty Organization, the UN Office of Outer Space Affairs, the UN Commission on International Trade Law, and the International Narcotics Control Board.

Austria was annexed by Germany in 1938 as the Nazis began taking control of parts of Europe. Austria was finally taken back by the Soviets in 1945 before the Americans, British, and French also arrived to establish an international zone and management of Austria. Unlike Germany, Austria was jointly administered instead of being split between East and West. This lasted for a little more than ten years, before an Austrian government was reestablished following the Austrian State Treaty.

I often visit museums in other countries to help determine if what I learned about each country in the United States holds true. In Vienna, the Museum of Military History houses the vehicle that Archduke Franz Ferdinand was assassinated in and gives an excellent replay of how the events unfolded leading to WWI. Austria was also one of the first countries to be annexed by Nazi Germany via The Anschluss, on March 12, 1938. This was largely due to Austria also being German-speaking and home to a large number of Nazi sympathizers. Many Austrians fought for the Nazis, as they were forced into service before later turning against the Nazis by the end of WWII. The most interesting aspect of the Austrian museum was it was the first time I had seen a large collection of old Nazi uniforms, supplies, and equipment on display.

Austria was also home to Mozart and other famous classical musicians. The theaters and Vienna State Opera continue to be venues for the classical arts. Vienna is also home to the world-renowned Spanish Riding School and Lipizzaner stallions, as well as the Schönbrunn Palace. The ornate palace is reminiscent of Versailles in France and the Biltmore Mansion in Ashville, North Carolina. It's been used as a backdrop for numerous movies, including the James Bond movie, *The Living Daylights* (1987). As if there wasn't enough to see in Vienna year-round, during late November and December the lively Christmas markets open and are not to be missed.

The CPOIC for the European region that I was traveling with, Senior Chief Mark Dickey, recounted one of his visits to Kyiv, Ukraine, just the week after the impeachment of President Trump took place. Military aid was potentially being held back until an investigation was to be opened on Presidential Nominee Joe Biden and his son, Hunter, as per a favor for President Trump.[124] Because of the investigation and interviews being conducted onsite in Kyiv, Senior Chief Dickey noted that everyone was on alert while he was there. The situation was not eased by bombs going off nearby, a reminder of the civil unrest caused by Moscow's annexing of Crimea in 2014. Seven years later, pro-Moscow separatists were still fighting with the remaining Ukrainian authorities as they attempted to take the rest of Ukraine for Moscow, which was then followed by the all-out invasion of Ukraine by Russia in 2022.

During my time in NSU, due to fragile relations with Russia, I was not able to visit Moscow, where we regularly have Seabees posted. I've heard many firsthand accounts of how beautiful the Kremlin and Red Square are, but also how rough a city Moscow is due to the cold weather and hostility toward America. As discussed earlier, the KGB's successor organizations, the Federal Security Service and Foreign Intelligence Service, are both very active. Unlike the Chinese, who do not make things obvious, the Russians aren't afraid to make it apparent they are following you. It is also important to not let on that you know you are being followed or to try to evade them. Take what precautions are possible, but they will go through your stuff at the hotel, not put things back where you left them, and perhaps cause more issues if you sabotage their attempts.

While still in the middle of the Cold War, NSU Seabee, Joe Simpkins experienced what it was like arriving with his family and traveling around the USSR while posted in Moscow from 1985 to1988. Coming into Moscow for the first time, every family had a similar experience when going through immigration, so information was given to families before arriving about what they could expect to experience going through immigration. Arriving with his wife and three kids in tow, ranging in age from six months to four years old, they were as ready as they could be. The immigration officers would look at their passports and look back at them. Then they would pick up the phone and call another officer over to do the same. This might carry on for two hours. Then, suddenly, as if nothing was amiss, they would let them through. Likely this provided them enough time to search through all their checked bags.[23] While posted in Moscow, he had to travel to St. Petersburg (formerly known as Leningrad) to perform maintenance at the consulate. However, the only way the Americans were allowed to travel to St. Petersburg was by train at night. The reason they were required to travel at night was so they couldn't see whatever was or wasn't there through the windows of the train car. In addition to traveling at night, DOS would also buy out an entire train car so there would be little to no interaction with the other Russian passengers. The only other opportunity Simpkins had to travel outside of the "inner loop"—a highway that circles Moscow—was to visit one of the two dachas (summer homes) that the embassy maintained. Transiting in and around the inside of the inner loop was fully authorized; however, if any Americans wanted to go outside the inner loop, which included getting to the other dacha, it had to be approved by the Russians, and the Americans would be followed if they went.

Former NSU OIC Carmelo Melendez did get to visit Moscow multiple times as DOS and NSU neared completion of the new embassy in the late 1990s. However, even as frequently as he visited to check on the team of Seabees there, he still ran into the occasional hiccup while traveling in and out of Russia. On one trip, he noticed the visa he received looked a little off, with some handwritten portions. Nevertheless, he thought that if he got it issued by the Russians "it must be good; what else was there to do?"[83] When he hit customs after the two-leg flight from Dulles to JFK and onward direct to Moscow, they asked him to step to the side and wait, which is never a good sign. He tried to explain to the immigration officer that the group of people behind him were waiting for him. But even with a diplomatic passport, the Russians weren't budging. They continued to delay and hold him, asking him more and more questions. Finally, three FSB agents came up to him and "asked" him to come with them. He tried to prevent them from taking him away from the immigration check point, advising them that if they called the embassy, they could clear everything up and he could be on his way; it was all just a misunderstanding. It was at that point one of the Russian agents stopped cold and said, "No, *you* don't understand."

They started to walk him back into the terminal, away from the gates where the Seabees who had come to pick him up were waiting. The agents walked him back to the gate he had just come through and put him back on the Aeroflot return flight to JFK. Fortunately, they seated him in the front row. To the bemusement of the flight attendant, she recognized him from just deplaning. She asked him if she could bring him any drinks and, accepting defeat, he piped up, "Two rum and Cokes please!" When she brought the drinks, she pointed out that the feature film on the flight was *Titanic*. Melendez responded, "Great, I watched it sink on the way here, too."[83] When he finally returned home, at about 6:00 AM, about twenty-four hours after he had left, his stunned wife inquired, "Aren't you supposed to be in Moscow?"

Three days later, Aeroflot delivered his ransacked luggage to his home. Not to be left on the sidelines long, Melendez got his visa fixed and was back in the air on his way to Moscow. This time he planned ahead in case there were to be any issues. He had booked a flight to Vienna following his arrival in Moscow in case they didn't let him in, so at least he could get some value from the trip by checking on the Seabee there and giving him time to recover. However, this time, it wasn't going to be an issue. Representatives from the RSO office met him at his gate and walked him through immigration and directly into a waiting SUV. They weren't going to mess with Melendez again. The accreditation of the embassy, which took twenty years to build, was too high of a priority for DOS to have the OIC get kicked back again.

Chief Shawn Milligan reported to NSU as the operations chief in 2000 and was immediately tagged to accompany Melendez on a different trip to Moscow just a month later. In order to go, he knew he would need to get a visa. Not wanting to annoy the administrative staff, he was determined to figure out what needed to be done to get the visa himself. Knowing he would need his diplomatic passport, he took it and grabbed a cab over to the Russian Embassy. When he got out of the cab, he wasn't completely sure where to go, but he saw a guard and went up to him. He asked him where he should go to get a visa. At first, the guard was willing to help, but as soon as he spotted a black diplomatic passport, he immediately stepped back and said, "NO! Not here! You go away!"[79] Perplexed, Chief Milligan thought maybe there was more to getting a visa than just showing up. Returning to the office a bit downhearted, the staff asked him what happened. Explaining his story, they began to explain to him that to get a Russian visa for a diplomatic passport, it had to be processed through the Russia desk at the Harry S. Truman building, and they liaise with the Russian Embassy to obtain the visa. Later that evening, when Milligan made it home, his neighbor came outside to greet him. After some pleasantries, his neighbor asked, "So what were you doing at the Russian Embassy today?" By coincidence, his neighbor worked for the FBI and sat with the Russia desk.[79]

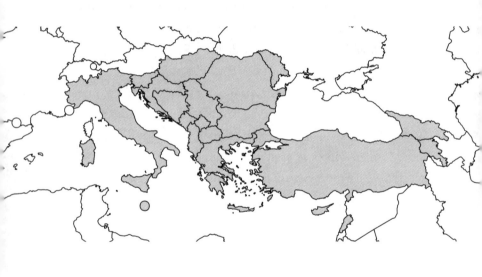

14

Southern Europe

The Southern European region is home to more ancient ancient cities than the rest of the European region, rich in culture and history. In 2020, NSU posted its first Seabee in Budapest, Hungary. The city is friendly to both the East and the West and actually began as three cities before merging into what today is known as Budapest. The three original cities were Buda, Pest, and Obuda, all sitting on the Danube River. In 1873 they united after the completion of the Chain Bridge that connects both sides of the river. U.S. Embassy Budapest is located on Liberty Square and has occupied the same building since 1935. Liberty Square is a site of many monuments memorializing significant events throughout Hungary's history; however, the combination of the monuments has been the cause of controversy over the years. There is a statue of Ronald Reagan in recognition of his work toward ending the Cold War and releasing Hungary from the Soviet Union, while there is also a large obelisk capped with the Soviet hammer and sickle to memorialize fallen Soviet Soldiers who contributed to Hungary's liberation from Nazi rule during WWII. And as of October 27, 2020, there is also a statue of George H.W. Bush commemorating his work to free Central and Eastern Europe from communist rule. Located on this square, the U.S. embassy is in a heavily trafficked and visible part of downtown Budapest and just a short walk to the Budapest Parliament building. The embassy itself is also historic, and two buildings were renovated to connect to one another as the post grew in size.

One of the most famous events involving the U.S. Embassy Budapest involves that of Catholic Cardinal Joseph Mindszenty. Cardinal Mindszenty was an active opponent of Nazi genocide during WWII and was imprisoned for about a year, until released in 1945 at the end of the war. Thereafter, he became a vocal opponent of communist rule and was sentenced to life imprisonment by the Soviets under false charges of attempting to overthrow the government. He was imprisoned for eight years beginning in 1948. In 1956, during the Hungarian uprising, he was broken out of prison and made good an escape to the U.S. embassy, where he sought asylum and was welcomed in. Unable to leave the premises without risk of being arrested again, he remained in the embassy for fifteen years.[125] He lived in what is today the Ambassador's office.[126] After negotiations with Pope Saint Paul IV, in 1971, Mindszenty was released into exile in Vienna, where he passed away in 1975. Aside from the history, culture, and beautiful architecture and scenery, visitors to Hungary can enjoy barrels of mulled wine, chimney rolls (a type of pastry), and the filming of major Hollywood movies. Unfortunately, I was not able to visit any other Seabee post in Southern Europe after Budapest due to COVID-19. The remaining accounts in this chapter of each city and what to expect come from the Seabees posted there or other personnel that have traveled through each location previously.

Another location in Southern Europe is Ankara, Turkey. It is a hidden gem and one of the most unique postings for a Seabee. Although there are two military installations in Turkey where the United States has a presence, none of the DOD members that serve at those installations are allowed to leave the post due to the security conditions posed by Turkey's border with Syria, Iraq, and Iran. Incirlik

Air Force base is in Adana, Turkey, and about a five-hour drive from Ankara but only a short distance to Syria. It is a full-size U.S. Air Force base with a U.S. commissary and other typical amenities you may find at any stateside base.

There is a second installation, Balgat. It is a Turkish base but only about a twenty-minute drive from the U.S. Embassy Ankara. The U.S. Air Force has a small presence on the Balgat installation, which includes a DOD Education Activity School and small commissary. For a Muslim country like Turkey, finding pork products is almost impossible; similar to finding beef in India. Conveniently, the small commissary specializes in importing pork products for many of the American citizens in the area that have access to the installation, including the Seabee and a few other U.S. diplomats and military personnel under Chief of Mission.

One of the most historic locations we have a Seabee posted in is Rome, Italy. Home to nearly 100 museums and countless ancient historical sites dating back to the Roman Empire. Living and working in the city offers an incredible range of food, people, and architecture. The U.S. embassy is located on the edge of the old city, where the Roman Colosseum is located and other ancient structures. It is also within a short distance of the Vatican City. U.S. Embassy Rome is a tri-mission. In addition to Mission Italy, there are missions to the Holy See and the United Nations. The Holy See is the governing body that oversees the Vatican, as well as the entire Catholic Church—as opposed to the Vatican City, which is only the geographic city-state itself.

The Chancery building on the embassy compound offers its own history. The Palazzo Margherita, formerly the Palazzo Piombino, was originally built for the Prince of Piombino; however, after a failed investment, it was purchased for the newly widowed Queen Margherita of Savoy, where she resided from 1900 until her death in 1926.[127] After her death, the building was taken over by the Mussolini government until it was purchased by the U.S. government in 1946 to house the embassy. An adjacent structure, the Mel Sembler Building, which used to house the National Insurance Institute of Italy, was purchased by the United States in 2003, when the tri-mission expanded into the additional space.[128]

As discussed earlier, it's fascinating to have an embassy reside in historic buildings, but construction or renovation work can get caught up in historic preservation codes. The embassy building in Rome is protected under the Italian law for cultural heritage and is listed on the DOS Register of Culturally Significant Properties.[129] Being an old building also means it has a lot of nooks and crannies that staff have turned into offices or storage areas. Despite the inefficiencies conducting work, the prestige of operating from the historical venue adjacent to the heart of Rome is valued, since many American tourists visit the area, and it creates an accessible venue for visa seekers. It, like many other locations, also showcases the length of diplomatic relations between Italy and the United States. The closer your facility is to the host nation's central government buildings often correlates to how close your countries are tied together. The strong ties between our two nations have considerably strengthened since WWII as Italy is also a member of NATO and a founding member of the EU.

Tucked away in the mountains of Southeastern Europe is Sofia, Bulgaria. Bulgaria is an old country and is still going through the process to become a full-fledged member of the EU by adopting the euro as its national currency. Despite its national currency, the lev, being fixed to the euro today, the exchange rate with their currency is still extremely favorable to the dollar. A small tight-knit embassy in a picturesque city situated at an elevation of 2,200 feet, the facility sits at the intersection of multiple mountains including Mount Vitosha, which is a significant tourist attraction. As the second oldest city in Europe, Sofia's aqueducts from the Roman and Ottoman empires are still visible across the city. Bulgaria is also the only European country to not change its names since 681AD, making it the oldest country in Europe. Today, the Statue of Holy Sofia (Sofia meaning wisdom) is in the middle of the city atop a pedestal that replaced a statue of Lenin in 2000.

There is estimated to be over 1,000 Thracian tombs in what is called the Valley of the Thracian Kings about two hours outside Sofia with only a small portion excavated. The entire area has been designated an archaeological region, and many of the tombs uncovered so far have been designated as UNESCO World Heritage Sites. Adding to the ancient history of Bulgaria is also the inception of the Cyrillic alphabet by what many believe to be two Bulgarian monks in the ninth century, Saints Cyril and Methodius, and the unique position it holds as the leading producer of rose oil in the world—nearly 1.6 tons per year. Rose oil is used in the cosmetic and perfume industry and rose oil from Bulgaria is considered the finest in the world.

In addition to the tombs and rose oil production, the country attracts Hollywood filmmakers. As the casting departments are always looking for extras, the diversity of the diplomatic community is always sought after for whatever type of movie is being filmed. A common goal of many posted in Sofia, including the Seabees, is to make it into a movie during their tour. Lastly, as Bulgaria was very much part of the Soviet Union prior to the breakup of the Communist Party, the Russian Oligarchy still has a presence in Sofia, and they can be seen roaming around town in their black SUVs and personal security details.

North of Bulgaria is Romania, where NSU has a Seabee posted in Bucharest. Romania was a communist country until after the Romanian Revolution in 1989. The more than 1,000 civilians killed during the revolution are memorialized with the Memorial of Rebirth located in Revolution Square. In 1991, Romania adopted a new constitution under a parliamentary democracy, and by 2007 they had joined the European Union. After Romania left communism behind, the United

States committed to building a new embassy behind the former Iron Curtain due to the now cordial relationship with Romania. A secure spot on the outskirts of Bucharest was identified to provide ample stand-off distance to meet physical security requirements.

The final location in Southern Europe with Seabees is the birthplace of democracy in Athens, Greece. It is home to our Southern European region's Chief Petty Officer in Charge and two additional Seabees. From Athens, the team travels extensively throughout Southern Europe and oversees many of the larger projects undertaken in the region. Greece's landscape is comprised of 80 percent mountains and its climate features mild winters and hot, dry summers. Snow in Athens is not out of the question despite the typical sunny Mediterranean climate. The ancient Parthenon and Temple of Zeus, famous around the world, are major tourist draws, but Athens is a modern city of approximately three million people. The National Archeological Museum is a must-see, and there is more to see than you could possibly cover in a single visit or even three-year tour in Athens.

The U.S. embassy is currently going through a complete renovation. In January 2007, a rocket propelled grenade was sent through the front embassy seal and landed in one of the bathrooms. After that, the post was considered high threat, and the threat level was only recently downgraded.[130]

Athens ESC is responsible for the U.S. diplomatic facilities in many countries, including Albania and Lebanon. Tirana, Albania, holds the title of oldest purposely constructed U.S. embassy in the world, built in 1920.[131] Every U.S. embassy prior to the one in Tirana was repurposed from an existing facility.

From oldest to newest. In Lebanon, one of the newest U.S. embassies is being built in Beirut. After years of abandonment following the 1983-84 bombings, the grounds and buildings that were previously bought by the U.S. government are now being reused. The new facility rises out of the mountainside. CE1 Drew Carlson, who was posted in Athens from 2017–2021, recalled his time he entered Lebanon for the first time. With Lebanon being a Muslim nation, the government doesn't recognize the State of Israel. Because of this, it is advised to not maintain an Israeli visa in the same passport as any of your visas for many Muslim countries to prevent any issues at customs and immigration. Since all NSU Seabees have multiple passports, although not as many as Couriers, who can have as many as six, this is achievable. However, CE1 wasn't aware of the issue and was caught up at immigration in Beirut. Fortunately, despite the delay, working with the expeditor who facilitates quick and efficient passage through airports, he was still able to enter the country. Similarly, Pakistan and India have a difficult relationship and border officials in one nation are often irritated if there is a visa from the opposite nation.

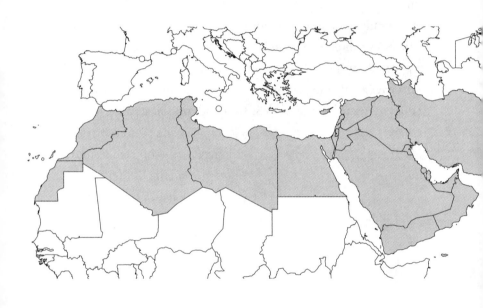

15

Near East Affairs

As a U.S. Navy Civil Engineer Corps Officer and Seabee serving after 9/11, there was a high likelihood of deploying to the Middle East, either in Iraq or Afghanistan during the Global War on Terrorism. However, I missed that opportunity due to the timing of assignments when I was in Naval Mobile Construction Battalion 133. I entered battalion following the last deployment to Afghanistan by an NMCB, which was in 2013. When I arrived at DOS, the prospect of visiting the Middle East, which mostly falls within the Near East Affairs region, was an opportunity that so many other officers before me had experienced. It was now time for me. Although, what I would soon learn and experience from visiting each country in North Africa and the Middle East would change my perspective of the region 180 degrees.

During my time with NSU, I was fortunate enough to visit Cairo, Egypt, on two occasions, and each time was a true adventure. The first time I visited Cairo, I was on a trip with my colleague, Branch Chief of the Overseas Support Branch Ralph Gaspard. Gaspard is an incredible individual as a SEO, physicist, an adjunct professor, and a die-hard fan of the New Orleans Saints. He has received the DOS Award for Heroism for his actions during an attack in Kabul, Afghanistan, in 2011 by members of the terrorist Haqqani network armed with "rocket-propelled grenades, 82mm recoilless rifles, AK-47s, and belt-fed machine guns." During the attack, Diplomatic Security personnel in the embassy's Regional Security Office moved several hundred people into secure locations on the compound, providing protection and coordinated support for employees as the attack continued throughout the night. Gaspard was relieved to report no embassy personnel were injured in the attack.[132]

As I was new to the job, it was good for both him and I to get better acquainted and there is no better way to do that than spend hours on planes together. Our plan was to visit Pretoria, South Africa; Dakar, Senegal; Cairo, Egypt; and Dubai, UAE. Midway through the trip, we had left Dakar on a Royal Air Maroc flight that stopped in Casablanca, Morocco, where we would then connect to an Egypt Air Flight into Cairo. Casablanca is the largest port in Morocco and one of the financial centers of Africa. About forty-five minutes from landing there, the plane was starting to make its descent. As a frequent flyer, it is noticeable when the descent begins. The thrust will be reduced and there is a short pause in the air that is shortly followed by the captain telling the passengers that the final descent has begun. However, this time was a little different. The moment the thrust reduced, the oxygen masks came down!

For many, this would be a time to start freaking out. For Gaspard, who was a few rows ahead of me and fast asleep, it was just another day. The guy next to me was trying to tell me this happened all the time: old planes and dated technologies. Therefore, at first, I thought that the oxygen masks coming down was part of the experience. However, when the flight attendant sprinted to the front of the plane and began knocking on the cockpit door, the experience turned more stressful. A moment later, she hurriedly announced that everyone must put on their oxygen masks. Finally, the innumerable pre-flight videos I'd seen of how to put a mask on were going to pay off. It is true the bags really don't inflate, but despite everything the videos tell you, I really questioned whether any oxygen was flowing into the mask. Panic about impending death led me straight to thoughts of what Maurissa, my wife, was going to do if I died on this flight. I prayed.

I started to get an incredible headache that started in my sinus and moved sharply into my forehead. This was because of oxygen deprivation, but I couldn't determine if it was because I wasn't breathing enough due to panic or there was no oxygen. The half-full plane of parents and children that had never flown before were all screaming at this point. I imagined the headlines of two American diplomats dying in a plane crash on the edge of the Sahara Desert. What followed was a very quick descent from 30,000 feet to 10,000 feet. The pilots managed to maintain control of the plane, and we made it to 10,000 feet, where we could remove our masks and breathe more normally. We flew at low altitude the last fifteen minutes all the way into Casablanca. We were met and surrounded by a squad of emergency vehicles on the runway. I didn't know if we were going to deplane on the runway or go down the emergency chute (that would have been fun). However, after several minutes of sitting on the plane with the emergency vehicles around us, the plane continued to taxi to our gate. The speakers chimed and someone said, "Thank you for flying Royal Air Maroc," as if nothing of interest had happened on the flight. The door opened, and we all got off. It was truly as if this was a regular occurrence. Nevertheless, I believe everyone walked off the plane thankful to be on the ground. It was at that point that I knew I was never going to fly Royal Air Maroc again.

I was extremely glad to be flying on Egypt Air next. After retelling this story to a few people, I learned that the U.S. government, in conjunction with the International Air Transport Association and the International Civil Aviation Organization, has a list of airlines that are "blacklisted" from flying based on their safety history. The U.S.

government is not supposed to ticket you on flights with blacklisted airlines. If you get stuck somewhere and the only flight is on one of those carriers, they'll ask you if you want to take it, but you are fully within your rights to refuse and to stay until the next available flight on a more reputable carrier. I discovered Royal Air Maroc was not on that list, but I added them to my personal blacklist. Coincidently, mentioning this to our Seabees in Dakar, it turned out that Royal Air Maroc is one of the "nicer" carriers to fly with, and they actually look forward to it. It must have been a fluke of a flight, but one of the most terrifying near-death experiences I've ever had. And this was only my second trip! I could only imagine what else I was going to experience in the next three years.

Later that evening, we finally made it into Cairo without any more issues. We had an expeditor meet us after we deplaned. If you've ever had an expeditor help you through the airport before, you'll know they really do "expedite." After hesitantly passing him both my passport and ticket, while Gaspard gave me a reassuring nod, we practically had to run to keep up. The expeditor asked if we already had visas, and because we did, he took us straight to the business-class immigration line. I wasn't sure what to think, since we hadn't flown business, but he seemed to know exactly what he was doing. When we got to the front, he had a quick exchange with the agent in Egyptian Arabic, and our passports were promptly stamped. I couldn't quite believe it. It had only cost 35 USD to hire an expeditor—money well spent! We picked up our bags and breezed through customs with another quick exchange. As I would learn, many countries honor diplomatic privileges, so border security will usually not inspect or x-ray your bags, even if the passport holder doesn't have true diplomatic immunity. In accordance with the Vienna Convention on Diplomatic Relations, it does allow diplomatic officials to pass through customs undisturbed if there is a bilateral agreement that both countries honor. In most cases, both countries want reciprocity when they travel to other countries, so they will allow those with diplomatic passports to bypass certain security, immigration, and customs requirements because no one wants an "international incident." I was beginning to get a taste of what it truly meant to travel as a diplomat and the responsibility I had to be a true representative of the United States while traveling abroad.

Arriving at the hotel late, we met up with the NEA Regional Director for Security Engineering (RDSE), Gharun Lacy, for a late dinner. Lacy was going to be traveling with us for the last two stops of this trip and had just flown in from Frankfurt, Germany. The next day was August 12, 2018. I remember this day clearly because when we arrived at U.S. Embassy Cairo, there was a bit of commotion. On the news that morning, there was a report of an explosion. The officials were saying it was only a car that caught fire only. But that car had caught fire and ignited two others, which sounded more like a car bomb, so the embassy recalled all personnel to ensure that we were all accounted for. The Engineering Services Office had accounted for everyone, but someone had reported they were near the explosion when it occurred. This individual was a Regional Security Technician—an Egyptian who had worked at the embassy for nearly twenty years and known by almost everyone there because of his great personality and character that brightened everyone's day. When the RST arrived at the embassy, we realized something wasn't right: the red pattern on his shirt was not a design but blood from his ear. He was in the vehicle right next to the car that exploded. He said it had to have been a car bomb. But he insisted he was fine and ready to work. The foreign nationals who work at the embassies are some of the smartest and hardest working people you may ever come across. The drive they have is driven by the idea of freedom because foreign nationals who work at a U.S. embassy overseas qualify for a green-card program, and after a certain number of years' service, they can apply for citizenship, which is almost always granted. This allows them to move to America and experience their own American Dream.

Not eligible for a security clearance to work inside the controlled-access areas of an embassy, RSTs work on the perimeter's physical security detail. Many of them are engineers and master electricians or mechanics—true tradesmen and masters of their craft, who can fix just about anything. We all emphatically encouraged the injured RST to go to medical and go home to rest after he'd gotten checked out. In twenty-four hours, I had begun experiencing firsthand what it was like to travel, work, and live abroad in some of the more challenging locations of the world.

Since the Arab Spring protests that rocked Egypt in 2011, a lot has changed. From being a somewhat friendly tourist destination to a high-threat country, where violence has become more prevalent each day. In 2014, ST moved the ESC operations to Dubai from Cairo because of the continued violence and unrest to better maintain operations in the region. Dubai today is much more of a transit hub like Cairo used to be.

The OIC in Egypt during the Arab Spring was Mark Graves. He vividly remembers that he was days from going back to Egypt after taking home leave when DOS ordered the departure of U.S. personnel. He was the OIC of the ESC and knew he was considered essential personnel, so he made his way back to Cairo, as ticketed, regardless. However, when he arrived, he was directed back to Washington, D.C., to wait until it was safe to return. It was six months later before DOS began to allow employees back in. However, if you were within sixty days of your rotation date, you weren't going to be allowed to return. Mark was in this exact situation, so he and his family ended up staying in a hotel for nearly nine months, quickly becoming a lifetime Marriott Gold Member. He did manage to return to Cairo for a couple days to clean things out and return his equipment that he had used while waiting in Washington, D.C. This is not an entirely uncommon experience for many in the foreign service, but it does demonstrate the volatility that can be experienced while serving overseas.

The rest of that August day was much calmer. We ate at a fantastic Lebanese restaurant called Taboula, around the corner from the embassy, where I would eat again on future visits. Hands down, the BEST hummus I've ever had. Honestly, I've been ruined by the world cuisine I've been fortunate enough to try while traveling! While food in the United States that is trying to imitate another country's cuisine can come close, it always pales in comparison to the real thing.

During this first visit, we only had a little spare time for sightseeing. We were able to visit the Egyptian Museum in Cairo, where King Tutankhamun's tomb was on display. I thought I had an idea of what the museum may look like from watching the 2003 movie *The Mummy*. To say the least, I was disappointed. Despite the museum being chockfull of mummies and artifacts from past millennia, it was in complete disarray with a barely working AC system, which made the visit a bit underwhelming and uncomfortable. Priceless items were on display that warranted much more prominence. The new Egyptian Museum has been a work in progress for nearly a decade. Unfortunately, when I went back in 2019, it was still unfinished. Ultimately, we did see King Tut in a twenty- by thirty-foot room with several guards who kept me from taking pictures. However, a quick slip of an Egyptian note into their hands and you were free to take as many pictures as you liked. This was the Egyptian culture of "tipping" to get things that weren't for sale.

On my second visit, we planned a full day excursion to the pyramids and other archaeological sites around Cairo. The great pyramids of Giza, the only remaining wonder of the ancient world and honorary member of the new seven wonders of the world, were truly incredible. How they built them still boggles the mind.

At the pyramids, we walked around and met up with a guide that our Seabee, BU1 Darcus Coleman, had gotten to know on the many times he had visited the site while hosting friends and family. Our Seabee took it upon himself to learn Arabic while posted there. For a single male in Egypt, it was the only way he was going to be able to talk to any women, and it also kept him from getting ripped off by local vendors. We hopped on some camels and headed into the desert a short distance to get a perfect perspective of the nine Great Pyramids of Giza. A visit to the Great Sphinx of Giza afterward, as well as the statue of Ramses and a few other notable pyramids, rounded out the day. All the while, we were wearing galabeyas, the traditional dress of male Egyptians. We garnered a lot of hoots and hollers from the locals by being foreigners in the garb, but they enjoyed that we were willing to adapt to their culture and experience it firsthand. To be honest, the galabeya was great. It kept me cool while preventing sunburn by minimizing exposed skin.

That evening, we were still feeling adventurous after visiting our Seabee's residence. We went to a South African restaurant that had recently opened and was known for its camel burgers. Yes, camel burgers. They were delicious. Throughout my travels, I have had the opportunity to eat many different meats, including camel in Egypt, zebra and kudu in South Africa, reindeer in Finland, and horse in Kazakhstan.

The Egyptian government has been building a new city in the desert called the New Administrative Capital, costing billions of dollars. It's about forty-five kilometers east of Cairo, in what is basically the middle of nowhere. This move will then lead every government that has an embassy in Cairo to build a new facility. This is believed to be due to the safety and security issues of Cairo; however, it is mostly being seen as a disconnect between the government and its people and an attempt to consolidate power to prevent another uprising to overthrow the government, like that of 2011.[133]

The NEA CPOIC billet has moved around over the years and, most recently, the billet moved from Abu Dhabi to Dubai, UAE. Many billets for DOS have moved due to various reasons. It could be political, it could be a shift in mission, it could be new missions, or most often, space limitations. As programs grow and workload increases, an organization often needs to hire more people. However, the process for moving and establishing new embassies and consulates takes years, if not decades, to provide enough space. Depending on the overall acreage of the site, there may be room for new buildings or annexes. However, it is often easier to build an entirely new and separate building than adding to an existing embassy. An embassy is a representation of the American Spirit, so the architecture of modern embassies in most countries is meant to evoke a desire to visit, work, or emigrate to America. Adding square footage to one side of an embassy doesn't often look as impressive. Today, embassies and consulates are designed with room for 10 percent growth in anticipation that, by the time it gets built, the additional space may already be taken up.

In the case of the CPOIC move from Abu Dhabi to Dubai, it was because of space. The U.S. Embassy Abu Dhabi, UAE, is meant to look like a sand dune. As the story goes, it was drawn on a napkin by the spouse of a former Ambassador, and that's where the design inspiration originated. Because of the architecture, there are few right angles in the building and the steep pitched exterior walls make every office just a little bit tighter. Abu Dhabi and Dubai both offer similar capabilities to travel to and from each constituent post of the ESC area of operations, so the move to the new consulate building in Dubai was of minimal impact in terms of logistics. The United Arab Emirates have multiple states, like the United States. While Abu Dhabi is the capital city of the UAE, Dubai is a major economic and financial hub, like New York or Frankfurt.

Dubai provides the ability to encounter cultures and people from all around the world. Emiratis bring experiences and influences back to the UAE from around the world, including fast food chains, indoor ski slopes, the largest indoor malls in the world (a boon, due to the extreme heat and humidity), or replicas of iconic structures around the world. I was not expecting to find a Five Guys, Hardees, Burger King, or California Pizza Kitchen, but I did. However, interestingly, due to the vast wealth of Emirates, you won't find Emiratis working in most stores. Foreign workers from all around the world perform most of the labor in the service and tourism industries, which make up most of the economy outside of oil. Citizens receive a distribution of the oil profits, like Alaskans in the United States, but the monthly amounts are nearly double the annual distribution paid to Alaskans. This makes working in everyday jobs minimally attractive. Dubai and a few other places around the world, such as Geneva, Switzerland, are the only locations where DOS hires non-local nationals from the host country for roles such as maintenance or the local security because, otherwise, the cost to hire locals, such as Emirati citizens, is extremely high.

While visiting the UAE, I was able to visit both Dubai and Abu Dhabi as they are only about one hour away from each other by car. In just twenty-four hours, we went to the famous tower of Burj Khalif and its adjoining mall; the Dubai Games, which were taking place; the Grand Mosque in Abu Dhabi (the world's largest); the Presidential Palace (a hotel where they used to have gold-bar vending machines); the "sail building"; the man-made islands, one depicting the countries of the world and the other a palm tree; and the Louvre in Abu Dhabi. To cap it all off, we also took an excursion into the desert, where we drove across sand dunes in Land Cruisers to an oasis, where we rode camels, sand boarded down dunes, held a hawk, and had a great feast while being entertained by fire artists and belly dancers under the starlit skies.

Despite the Las Vegas style glitz and glamour of the UAE, one of the most memorable visits I ever made was to Israel, one of the most strategic partners for the United States in the Middle East. As a Christian all my life, it was great having the opportunity to visit Jerusalem and Bethlehem. As I arrived at NSU, Israel had been in the news a lot because President Trump announced that the United States would move its embassy from Tel Aviv to Jerusalem to formally recognize Jerusalem as the capital of Israel, despite the fighting over the location for millennia between the Israelis and Palestinians. This was a controversial decision for the region that put the world on edge.

What made the move more unprecedented was the timeline to make it happen: three months. In Jerusalem, there was an existing U.S. consulate, but it was not ready to receive the U.S. Ambassador. Because the location of the office of the Ambassador dictates where the embassy is, this meant improving security and constructing an office space in the existing facility to officially "move the flag." This is where the Seabees were called in. Up to four Seabees from NSU were in Jerusalem at any one time to create an office space and install all technical security systems required for the communications, information, and material that would be transmitted within the office. Of course, the Seabees were successful in this mission. Recognizing their hard work, they were able to attend the ceremonial opening of the embassy and meet the numerous senior administration officials present, such as Prime Minister Benjamin Netanyahu.

After the move of the ambassador, the former Tel Aviv Embassy became known as the Tel Aviv Embassy Branch Office (EBO) because the construction project in Jerusalem was expected to take years to fully complete. As a result, most of the mission's workforce still work and live in Tel Aviv. The EBO is situated across the road from the Mediterranean Sea and is the result of two old hotels that were combined into one building. Between the salty air and the offset floors of the two buildings, the EBO is beyond renovation. The move to Jerusalem gives an opportunity for the United States to rebuild on a much greater scale aligned with the size of the mission. There are numerous offsite locations in Israel that the ESO is responsible for maintaining. To have a larger facility that can accommodate the office space inside the perimeter will be much better for security purposes, too.

When I traveled to Israel, it was in early December. I was fortunate enough to get a seat on a tour to Bethlehem, sponsored by the embassy, while a Christmas market was open. Because of the arrangement, we were easily able to pass through the gates into Bethlehem, which is situated in the contested West Bank, administered by the Palestinian Authority.

One of the locations that I was most surprised by was Amman, the capital of Jordan. Despite having the longest border with neighboring Israel, getting across the border into either country has required special permits and visas that were not always easy to come by. Unless you are a foreigner or diplomat, passage is even more difficult, but possible. For a long period, there were no direct flights. Prior to the most recent conflict between Palestine and Israel that began on October 7, 2023, passage between Israel and the rest of the Middle East had been steadily improving. There were a handful of direct flights between Tel Aviv and Amman since the 1994 Israel-Jordan Peace Treaty.[134] Previous to this treaty, Israel had made peace with Egypt in 1979 following the Camp David Accords in 1978, when the Egypt-Israel Peace Treaty was signed.[135] Flights to other Arab countries, including the UAE and Bahrain, have only begun since the Abraham Accords were signed in August of 2020.[136] To get to any other Arab countries before the various agreements have been signed, a traveler from Israel would need to pass through a friendly country to continue on to their destination. This would mean the country would need to recognize the State of Israel, which many Arab countries do not. Istanbul, Turkey, was often a thoroughfare, as Turkey was the first Muslim-majority country to have recognized the State of Israel in 1949.[137] Diplomatic relations between the United States and Israel began in 1948 and with Jordan in 1949.[138]

Jordan's proximity, commitment, and support to a peaceful solution between Israel and Palestine has earned it significant bilateral assistance from the United States, as well as the first Free Trade Agreement with any Arab nation that was established in 2000.[139]

I landed in Amman, after traveling through Istanbul, in the early evening as it was getting dark. I found a taxi for the ride into the city. It was on this journey that my idea of what to expect was turned upside down. First, I saw an Ikea and then a Starbucks. I hadn't realized how westernized Jordan was as a result of the Free Trade Agreement. I originally imagined Jordan would have been more like Egypt than Israel.

Jordan has a robust tourism industry with the Dead Sea and the ancient city of Petra in the south. The journey to Petra is about three and a half hours south of Amman. It is well worth the trip. By leaving early in the morning to get there before noon, you can beat the heat and make the hike from the Petra Visitor Center all the way up to the monastery at the top of 800 rocky steps. For the Hollywood fan, there is an Indiana Jones-inspired souvenir shop that refers to Petra's involvement in the production of *Indiana Jones and the Last Crusade*. Tourism to Petra has been booming ever since the movie's release. In addition to Petra and the Dead Sea, there are Roman ruins scattered throughout the city of Amman.

Traveling into and out of Baghdad also requires a government flight from Amman into the Baghdad Diplomatic Support Center (BDSC). This center is where the U.S. government conducts air transportation from within the fence line of the Baghdad International Airport. From here, a short helicopter ride will take you to the largest U.S. government diplomatic compound in the world. Laid out over 100 acres, it takes up a large portion of the international zone and many old palaces of Saddam Hussein. It has been built to withstand artillery fire, that it takes quite often, and the facility looks much like a college campus. It is similar to the compounds in Kabul and Islamabad, where personnel are posted for about twelve months unaccompanied and live and work much like a military deployment. However, for civilians, the security and amenities are much better than many military servicemembers may recall from their deployments. Unfortunately, due to the resurgence of the Taliban, Afghanistan's diplomatic facilities have been abandoned since 2021.

A country I never thought I would visit was Algeria. Algiers, its capital, is mostly known for its coastal fishing villages and the Saharan desert that covers four-fifths of the country. Algeria was also home to some naval battles between French and British forces in colonial times. The great admirals of the day made their names in these battles, and the course of history was heavily influenced by the outcomes. Algiers was part of the Roman Empire and is home to a few Roman ruins. Making the journey to these ruins can be rough, as the roads are heavily worn, but if you're adventurous enough to make the journey, it should not be missed. The ruins are relatively unprotected, allowing visitors to walk over two-thousand-year-old mosaics and touch artifacts in situ.

On the opposite end of the Near East Affairs region is Kuwait City, Kuwait. Kuwait has been closely connected with the United States since Saddam Hussein invaded Kuwait in 1990, which was soon followed by the Gulf War and the liberation of Kuwait on February 28, 1991. The United States has been a welcome presence in Kuwait ever since. Today, there are still a number of U.S. military outposts in Kuwait that train and provide a ready force for Middle East affairs. One of the closest active bases to Kuwait City is Camp Arifjan, about an hour away by car. Our Seabee posted in Kuwait for my entire tenure had to have a thick skin as an unmarried white woman. A force to be reckoned with, she reported to have staved off repeated advances by local Kuwaitis who had difficulty accepting no for an answer. Nevertheless, she comfortably settled into Kuwait, which sits right on the Persian Gulf where it's always hot.

Kuwait's Emir (head of state) resides in Bayan Palace. The former residence was Mishref Palace, but it was abandoned after the Iraqi invasion in 1990. The U.S. embassy is located immediately adjacent to the Mishref Palace grounds and close to Bayan Palace. The U.S. Embassy Kuwait City is built like a fortress and is one of few U.S. embassies with a true 100-meter standoff distance from each side. This was a product of the 1983 Kuwait embassy bombing discussed earlier. Despite the friendly relationship with the Kuwaitis, there was a large demonstration when it was announced that the United States was moving its embassy in Israel to Jerusalem. From our Seabee's rooftop, she watched the peaceful protestors move down the street toward the embassy before later dispersing.

There are a lot of things to do in Kuwait, despite the hot temperatures. Kuwait is home to some of the largest malls in the world—so large that it's like walking into a city in a bubble that's air conditioned. The Avenues is the largest mall, and it has twelve districts. The shops are set up along pedestrianized streets as long as half a mile.[140] The different sections of the mall are made to look like outdoor shopping spaces, and one section is a close replica of a nearby outdoor trading market. If you are willing to take on the heat and are in town at the weekend, try to catch robot monkey camel racing. I thought they were making it up when they mentioned it to me, but it's a robot that will race a camel, in lieu of a person, around a track. What makes it even more heart-pounding is that you can drive a vehicle along the track on either the inside or outside to follow along.[141] Finally, Kuwaitis love American vehicles, especially American pickup trucks. However, only Kuwaitis are allowed to drive personal trucks. The only way a foreigner can have a truck is for it to be a commercial truck. Everyone else is only allowed to drive cars or SUVs.[142] Most Kuwaitis drive luxury cars during the day, but at night the exotic and supercars come out. The Bugatti, McLaren, Ferrari, Lamborghini, and Bentley are extremely common, and can all be seen in a single night rolling up and down the streets of Kuwait City.

One of the last stops I made in the Middle East was Muscat, Oman. Oman has similar characteristics to Kuwait, and the population is mostly confined to the coast due to terrain. The steppe plateau leaves less than a mile of habitable land along the coast. The old palace did not please the Sultan, so he built a new one, and the old one was converted into a Ritz-Carlton property. When traveling overseas as part of the U.S. government, personnel are required to stay in hotels that meet certain security standards but stay under a set per diem. Unbelievably, this palace met those conditions. We made the most of our stay, in addition to touring post. We kayaked on the Gulf of Oman and went to the old fort that overlooks Port Sultan Qaboos, also called Mutrah Fort. From there, we had an incredible view of the Sultan's 200-foot yacht.

The Omani Empire used to reach along the coast of East Africa as far south as Tanzania. Today, Oman is contained within Southwest Asia, situated on the Arabian Sea, and is bordered by the UAE, Saudi Arabia, and Yemen. Despite the much smaller area of influence, from what was once an expansive empire, it still retains a critical strip of land in the narrowest section of the Strait of Hormuz. Of the many things to see and do in Oman, venturing to various wadis is a refreshing recreational activity. Wadis are valleys, oases, or streambeds that turn lush during rainy season and will provide incredible greenery in stark contrast to the surrounding desert during and shortly after rainy season.

16

Africa

On my first trip outside of the Western Hemisphere as OIC, and only my third trip overall, I traveled with Ralph Gaspard to Africa and the Middle East. Gaspard was the Branch Chief of the Overseas Support Branch with whom NSU staff worked closely for operation and support planning. On this specific trip we planned to visit Pretoria and Johannesburg, South Africa; Dakar, Senegal; Cairo, Egypt; and Dubai, UAE. The trip was meant to allow us to grow our working relationship and perform office visits at specific posts that warranted our presence. While on this trip, I got a chance to meet with my Seabees in between several other meetings with post officials as I learned some of the "ropes."

Our first stop in South Africa was to visit the relatively new U.S. Consulate General Johannesburg and observe some of the new technologies and ongoing upgrade projects. The two posts are just an hour's drive from each other, so it was easy to visit both locations. Traveling to South Africa for the first time, I had my first experience of remaining on a plane for twenty-four hours, learning the difference between a direct flight and a non-stop flight. A non-stop flight takes you to your destination without touching down anywhere on route. A direct flight takes you from your origin to your destination but may stop on the way. This flight was a direct flight to Johannesburg, South Africa from Dulles International Airport via Dakar, Senegal. Each leg of the flight was approximately eight hours, plus a fifty-minute stopover in Dakar for refueling, letting some passengers on or off. On a direct flight you are not required to deplane if you are ticketed through to the destination. However, it does mean that no matter what class you are in, you have to be prepared to land, which makes sleep, even in business class, an interrupted affair.

When we finally made it to Johannesburg twenty-five hours later (five-hour time difference plus twenty hours of flying), we still had an hour's drive to Pretoria. The majority of countries have a major international airport in their capital city. However, Pretoria does not. Instead, Johannesburg and Cape Town are home to South Africa's largest airports. While in Pretoria for a short while, we still had time to visit a lion park, where we got to see male and female lions from the backseat of our own vehicle. All they told us to do was not roll the windows down! If not asleep in the shade, the lions would come out and circle the car whenever they were getting close to their next meal. The remainder of this visit to South Africa was uneventful. My second visit to Pretoria was a different story.

Master Chief and I had figured out a way to see all our Seabees once per year—at least in theory. The goal was to improve face-to-face meetings from once every two years to once every year. We found the benefit of meeting everyone face to face, for even a day, provided incredible awareness of issues and reassured all personnel that they were not forgotten. This second trip was a regional training event. We conducted the same training as we provided in Frankfurt a month before and provided the personnel time to network and build their work relationships, which was also a means to address mental health concerns stirred up by a suicide in the command the year prior. If our personnel had time to connect in person, it provided opportunity to spot personnel issues earlier because they may later be more able to catch a subtle change in that individual's demeanor or speech when talking on the phone or communicating by email. Had they never met in person, they may not have been able to develop a bond of understanding and learn what each other's baseline personality was like.

During the regional training week, we would also physically train together. This time, we played the Marine Security Guard Detachment in ultimate frisbee. Seabees and CEC officers are incredibly good at ultimate frisbee: it is our game of choice. We crushed the Marines in the friendly game. However, earlier that day, when I woke up, I was feeling unwell. The night before we had a team dinner at a restaurant called Carnivores. There, they serve meat of many types of African game, such as kudu (an antelope), zebra, antelope, wildebeest, and, if you weren't feeling adventurous, chicken. Unfortunately, something I ate was not well cooked. By early afternoon, having had little appetite all morning and exhausting myself during ultimate, I was feeling a bit lightheaded. Trying to tough it out, I attempted hydrating but was getting increasingly woozy. Someone noticed I looked pale, even going past white to yellow. As my legs were a little wobbly, they helped me over to the medical unit. Just in time, too. I made it to the medical unit, but when they asked me if I was okay, I passed out and hit the deck. I came to after a brief period, and they moved me to their treatment room. Fortunately, Pretoria is a medical hub and has a full medical suite to treat minor medical issues beyond what most embassies can support. I got hooked up to an IV, and they checked my vitals. To be safe, they called TRICARE, the military's health insurance, for pre-authorization for me to go to the hospital in town. They wanted me to receive a full check up to get me back on my feet and antibiotics for what we all assumed was food poisoning. I was also supposed to fly out the next night and really did not want to delay another day.

After about six hours in the hospital Emergency Room, I was released, and Chief Long took me back to my hotel, where I recuperated until late the next morning. I returned to the embassy in the afternoon and continued, mostly sitting, to carry out the remaining training with the region. Although this would be awful for anyone to experience once, this was the second time I'd had food poisoning while on travel abroad. The first time I was in Seoul, Republic of Korea, with my wife, Maurissa. We were shopping downtown the day after an anniversary dinner. Maybe the meat wasn't cooked enough because I passed out in the street. A helpful tourist got me on my feet and to the nearby police station, where an ambulance was called, and I ended up in my first overseas hospital.

After departing Pretoria on my trip with Gaspard, we headed back on the direct flight to Washington, D.C., but instead of going non-stop, we disembarked for our second stop in Dakar, Senegal. Dakar is located on the westernmost tip of Africa with the powerful Atlantic Ocean crashing along its shores. A French-speaking country, due to its previous colonization by France, its weather is very tropical. The climate reminded me a lot of Guam's, where I served for three years. We arrived in Dakar at around 1:00 AM. We took a taxi from the airport to our hotel, near where our Seabees resided to make it easier for logistics. After checking in, we were led to the elevator. Given the hotel only had about twenty rooms, the elevator was small and could barely fit two people with their luggage. The hotel didn't have a lot of the amenities we were used to seeing while traveling with the DOS, but it gave us a chance to get a few hours of sleep before our visit to the embassy that same morning.

U.S. Embassy Dakar closes at 1:00 PM on Fridays because much of the population attend afternoon prayers. This resulted in our visit during working hours being very short; however, we carried on with our visit through meetings on Saturday. That weekend began with lunch at a restaurant overlooking the Atlantic, and it was a great getting to know our Seabees and other ST personnel while eating fresh fish caught earlier that day. The next day, we went to the local markets where we experienced the many smells of a wet market and the act of bartering to buy locally made items. Following here, we went to the African Renaissance Monument that was built to commemorate the fiftieth anniversary of Senegal's independence from France. This monument was enormous, approximately one and a half times the size of the Statue of Liberty in New York City. Interestingly, the African Renaissance Monument was constructed by North Korea.[143]

That afternoon, Gaspard was feeling a bit hungry and got some chicken shawarma. Bad choice. He ended up with food poisoning and was out for the count for the rest of the time we were in Dakar.

On my last trip with DOS before COVID-19 hit, my wife, Maurissa, had elected to accompany me on my swing through Africa in March 2020. We started in Frankfurt and realized nearly every conference or major event had been canceled in the previous few days. As our Seabees were already there, we proceeded with our events until we received direction to do otherwise. Everyone was able to head back or proceed to their follow-on locations, not yet knowing what was to come. In Frankfurt, we held our annual training event for most of our command personnel posted overseas, as well as our Seabee Ball. Following the conclusion of training, we headed to Addis Ababa, Ethiopia. Leaving Frankfurt, we knew that there was an outbreak of a virus that had started in China and was showing up in pockets around the world. We arrived in Addis Ababa after a red-eye flight to discover Ethiopia had implemented temperature screenings that day, so we were a little delayed getting out of the airport. We got to the hotel, and Maurissa went to sleep while I went to work.

We first toured U.S. Embassy Addis Ababa, which is also home to the U.S. Mission to the African Union, which is headquartered in the city. After a full day of work, we still hadn't heard any updates regarding the coronavirus and whether to keep going or return to our posts. We returned to the hotel and got cleaned up before we headed out again for dinner. We were in for a treat of another Ethiopian meal served over a fire at our table. We ate like kings again and enjoyed a show of traditional song and dance. Chief Long, who was the CPOIC for the Africa region, and Maurissa were both invited up on stage to try traditional dance skills to the delight of the crowd. It was hard to imagine that these shared meals and gatherings would not be possible in just a couple days' time due to the looming lockdowns.

The next day, CM1 Brian Parsam had arranged for a driver to take five of us around the city to explore. We first stopped at one of the oldest churches in Addis: Holy Trinity Cathedral. Although Addis was never colonized by another country, the city was heavily influenced by the Coptic Orthodox Church of Alexandria, Egypt in the fourth century and is currently home to thirty-six million Orthodox Christians.[144] We next went up the highest peak in Addis Ababa, Mount Entonto, and got an incredible view of the city from a new overlook that was still under construction. Continuing up the mountain, we arrived at one of the oldest churches, St. Mary Church of Entonto. The church's extremely vibrant colors were an incredible sight, as was the palace of Emperor Menelik II. After taking in the church and palace, we walked back down the road a little way and grabbed lunch that was made from scratch in front of us. We also had some freshly ground coffee, which is a major export of Ethiopia. We later got to try our hand at making injera, an Ethiopian flatbread, which is used to scoop up other food as utensils aren't used in the traditional Ethiopian settings. It all was amazing.

Stuffed to the brim, we headed back to our van and back down into the city. The next stop was the National Museum of Ethiopia, where we got to see "Lucy," one of the oldest hominin fossils in the world. The last place we drove by was the Addis Mercato—the largest outdoor market in Africa—but we weren't able to walk around it due to restrictions, but what we saw while driving by appeared to be miles of stalls and piles of old containers that are recovered and reused. Vehicles and people could be seen carrying loads that seemed way too large, but somehow everything was magnificently balanced.

Although we didn't make it to Nairobi, Kenya, I first learned about Kenya in first grade. My elementary school had a sister school in Nairobi that a few of my teachers would travel to in the summer with multiple suitcases of school supplies that we had collected for the children there. I also learned some Swahili phrases, but the only one that stuck was "jambo," which is a greeting of "hello" when you first meet someone.

As mentioned earlier, the post was one of two bombed in 1998. Today, the post remains one of the larger U.S. missions around the world with approximately 2,000 U.S. government personnel and local staff. Kenya is home to the Big Five animals, which include rhinoceros, African elephant, lion, leopard, and African buffalo. The Big Five are often seen on safaris that take place not too far from the city, attracting tourists from all around the world. Kenya is also home to the Kalenjin tribe, known as the "running tribe" due to how many world-class runners the tribe produces.

There are plenty of NSU stories from Nairobi. One of NSU's First Class Petty Officers posted to Nairobi, BU1 Marc Pacheco, saved a girl suffering from dehydration by carrying her off a mountain during a hike in 2018. He carried her three miles down the mountain to the end of the road where a vehicle was waiting for her. Pacheco also recalled sitting in traffic one day and, out of the blue, two men came up to his vehicle, tore off both of his side mirrors, and ran off. He was stunned more than upset; were his mirrors the only things they wanted? Another one of our Seabees posted there, UT2 Brandon Ingalsbe, was sitting outside a gas station in his vehicle waiting for some of his local friends to meet up. However, while waiting, a man walked up and claimed that Ingalsbe had hit the car parked next to him. The man asked for 5,000 Kenyan shillings (50 USD) or he was going to get the owner of the damaged car. The man left and returned with another man. At this point, Ingalsbe got out of his vehicle and saw where there was a scratch under some dirt the man first had to brush off to show them. The man then asked for 8,000 Kenyan shillings. At this point, Ingalsbe mentioned he was going to call embassy security, but as he turned, the man punched him three times in the gut. Many of our Seabees have a lot of skills in their toolbox. Whether they are Marine Corps Martial Arts Program (MCMAP) certified by the Marines or amateur weightlifters, you simply don't want to ever get into a fight with a Seabee for any number of reasons. UT2 Ingalsbe was no exception. Skilled in jiu-jitsu, he quickly gained the upper hand and put the man in a choke hold. Immediately the first man stepped back, realizing that his friend was in trouble and had picked the wrong target that night. The next day, UT2 Ingalsbe reported the incident to the RSO and made a police report. In Nairobi, it is common to find that the first to report any incident is usually the story the authorities tend to side with. His attacker was probably too humiliated to try to claim he was attacked by a foreigner.

Just south of Kenya is Tanzania. The country is beautiful and home to Mt. Kilimanjaro, the highest peak on the African continent, and Lake Tanganyika, the deepest lake in Africa and second deepest in the world. NSU's history is incomplete without mention of U.S. Embassy Dar es Salaam. Today, "Dar" has rebuilt a new embassy about five minutes from the old embassy that was bombed in 1998 on the peninsula of the city, where many embassies and government buildings are located. Across the narrow waterway from Dar es Salaam, via a short ferry or flight is the island of Zanzibar, known for growing spices.

USAID and the U.S. peace corps have a large presence in Tanzania and at the embassy compound. The ESO has two constituents, including Harare in Zimbabwe and Malawi, Mozambique. When Master Chief Joe Maioriello visited Dar in 2019, he felt extremely safe. The hotel where he was staying employed Maasai warriors, who are native to the Kenyan and Tanzanian region of Africa and speak Swahili. They are also extremely tall. Dressed in traditional clothes, with a spear and club, they have a commanding presence and are not to be messed with. Maioriello needed to get to the ATM one evening, which was located across the street from the front of the hotel. As it was about 11:00 PM, the concierge was hesitant to let him go alone. The concierge signaled to a Maasai warrior and told him to accompany the guest to the ATM across the street. With two thuds of his spear, the warrior ensured NSU's AOIC came back safely with his money. Maioriello noted that he never felt safer in his life.

The capital of Nigeria is Abuja; however, the NSU Seabee is posted in Lagos, Nigeria, which is the most populated city and the country's former capital. The consulate in Lagos was the former embassy of Nigeria and is located on a peninsula on the southern coast. Home to twenty-one million people and the second largest city in Africa, second to Cairo, the country was a former colony of Britain and English is the official language. However, there are five other major languages and about 520 other languages spoken within Nigeria.

Due to traffic conditions in Lagos, there are shuttles from each of the main compounds where most U.S. personnel live. These shuttles drop the employees at a dock, where a boat takes them across the waterway to the consulate to avoid the downtown traffic. It is a tough post to live at, due to the overwhelming population and climate, so not many families accompany personnel to post. Nevertheless, the Seabee stays busy at post with two constituent posts in N'Djamena in Chad and Cotonou, Benin Republic. Like Algiers, travel for U.S.

government personnel outside of the city's green zone requires armored car transport.

Before the pandemic hit, I was able to visit Accra, Ghana, for a site survey. Accra was one of the new posts that was identified for a resident Seabee as part of NSU's growth in 2019. My flight to Accra from Dulles happened to also be the inaugural direct flight to Johannesburg via Accra. Accra is an up-and-coming tourist destination for Americans, due to the United States' amicable ties with Ghana. Arriving at post, I was surprised to find a large DOD presence. They had their own plane to facilitate military coordination throughout West Africa. Country to country flights are not always convenient, depending on who colonized which country. Often, a flight to an adjacent country would take you in the opposite direction to catch a connecting flight that would take you to your actual destination. This is similar to the situation of traveling to Israel from other parts of the Middle East.

One TDY location that is extra difficult for Seabees and civilians to travel to is Angola. Due to the exchange rate of 1 USD to about 600 Angolan kwanza, as well as concerns over food safety, NSU Seabees have learned to bring all their own food for the week while performing maintenance at the post. Due to food safety protocols in Angola for U.S. personnel, it is highly recommended they only eat at the hotel. However, the hotel is extremely expensive, and the per diem alone would not be enough to cover all meals.

Fortunately, Seabee ingenuity will take them far. While with NSU, their trade skills also come in handy both on and off the job. Retired SEO George Herrmann remembered one TDY trip out of ESO Abidjan, Cote d'Ivoire, in 1981 to Brazzaville, Republic of Congo. A team of four were sent to enlarge a restricted office space. The story is not about the work they did at the embassy, but that at their hotel. Electricity in Brazzaville circa 1981 was less than stellar. At the hotel where they stayed, they learned in their first two nights that you either got hot water and lights with no AC, or cold water, no lights, and AC. The outgoing personality of the Seabee, who Herrmann recalled was a construction electrician named Pete, was about to make their stay for the rest of the trip a whole lot more comfortable. "Before work on their third day, Pete checked out the hotel's wiring system. He discovered that the hotel was wired with two power phases, one that supported the lights and the hotel water, and the other kept the AC running; however, there was only one single phase source." Herrmann and Pete then asked the management if they would allow them to adjust the wiring each evening, so the guests would have the benefit of all these services. The hotel agreed. So, at the hotel each evening, Pete would move the single wire with power onto the terminal for lights and hot water. They would wash up, change clothes, and go out somewhere. Then each night at about 8:00 PM, the wiring would be switched so that the AC worked and hotel guests would get a good night's sleep.[145] All in a day's work for a Seabee.

17

South Central Asia

South Central Asia is an incredible part of the world, rich with history and bustling cities. It is also the meeting point of once large empires: the British Empire in India and Russia in Kazakhstan. Both attempted to create influence in Afghanistan, to no avail. A part of the world I never thought I'd travel to except for a war time deployment, Afghanistan and Pakistan (an independent nation after the partition of the British Indian Empire in 1947) are two of the top three high-threat locations for DOS. Another high-threat area, Baghdad, Iraq, falls under NEA.

One of the strangest things I have ever done is flown commercially into a war zone as a member of the U.S. military. The anxiety of getting onto a flight full of Afghans was a moment of extraordinary disbelief. After nearly twenty years at war, my fellow Americans and I stuck out like a sore thumb. None of us knew each other, but we knew we were all going to the U.S. embassy. They may have been contractors or diplomats themselves, too, but almost certainly not all active military. Active military personnel don't fly commercial airlines into an active war zone, or do they? As previously mentioned, while attached to DOS, we are given diplomatic status and advised to not make it brazenly apparent that we are military. We travel and lodge like diplomats and carry out business unarmed. However, if we are asked directly whether we are military personnel, we are required to answer yes.

I didn't sleep on that flight, even though it was an 11:30 PM flight landing in Kabul at 5:00 AM. It was a Fly Dubai flight, which is owned by Emirates, from Dubai into Kabul. Landing at Kabul International Airport brought a sigh of relief, but we still had to deplane. Our instruction was to not enter the airport because our life quite literally depended on it. We deplaned on the tarmac and were immediately escorted into an armored vehicle. From there, we transited to the other side of the airfield to catch our helicopter flight to the embassy. We returned the same way.

The embassy in Kabul was originally one building. That building still exists; however, the new part of the embassy was built around three of the four sides to the building, which still has bullet holes in it from previous attacks as a daily reminder of where you are. I received a tour of the impressive compound. The way to improve security on the compound after nearly twenty years at war and non-stop construction is to make each building survivable from indirect fire and by acquiring as many high-rise buildings as possible within sniper range of the compound. Downtown Kabul is never quiet at night, just like Baghdad. The sound of AK-47s being shot in the distance, either as celebration or in combat, is a regular occurrence. Despite the ongoing war, I met many incredible Afghans and was fortunate enough to acquire a genuine Afghan rug from the market on compound. I managed to fit it into my suitcase for the journey home and have proudly displayed it ever since.

On December 31, 2019, a protest destroyed three compound access controls and fifty-six security cameras on the Baghdad embassy compound perimeter. The U.S. military responded by killing Iranian military officer Qasem Soleimani by missile strike on January 3, 2020, after he landed at the Baghdad International Airport. Given Iraq is a war zone, carrying out a strike there as opposed to anything in Iran, was determined to be less of an issue. Due to alarm that the Iranians may retaliate, U.S. Embassy Kabul went into lockdown in their safe haven for more than twenty-four hours. It was possible that missiles would fly over Kabul as they crossed Afghanistan on their way to Iraq from Iran. It was a very tense time for U.S. government personnel and Seabees on the ground waiting for whatever may happen.

I also flew into Pakistan commercially, but since it wasn't a war zone, it was a little less stressful. The most stressful part of flying to Pakistan was the fact I was entering from India. Due to their strained relationship, there are no direct flights, so I was required to fly through Istanbul. Boarding my flight on Turkish Airlines in New Delhi, I gave border control my passport with my Indian visa but no Pakistani visa. They knew I was traveling to Pakistan, but one of the main rules is to not show anyone that you have more than one passport to the best of your ability. Compared to traveling to an Islamic nation with an Israeli visa, traveling between India and Pakistan is less problematic, but not by much. As a diplomat, you do not need to show a visa to go to the country you are flying to. If asked, however, you should only say you have it separately and hold firm. The Vienna Convention is something to be familiar with in these types of situations.

I didn't know what to expect in Islamabad, Pakistan. Islamabad used to be a Seabee Office (CBO). This means that a Seabee was the only technical security representative at the post. Of course, this was prior to November 1979, when the embassy was destroyed by a hostile mob. Since then, the office has been much more robust. When I finally landed, I was met by an expeditor as I walked into the terminal from the gate. We moved along, and he got me to my ride at 1:00 AM with my Seabee and driver, who took me to the compound, forty minutes away. All temporary duty personnel stay at the IslamAbode "hotel" on the compound, which is really a DOS-run housing block. The compound had been going through a significant rebuild to improve the quality of life and expand on-compound housing for the diplomats to reduce the need for off-compound housing. Off-compound housing in Islamabad at that time required a high level of security to be provided by the landlords leasing the properties, which results in monthly rents of between 5,000 and 10,000 USD for each residence and around-the-clock security guards, as well. Our Seabee still lived off-compound at the time, but follow-on Seabees now reside on-compound in the State Department Apartments (SDA). What was different for Americans than any other country's personnel were that Americans could not travel outside the compound perimeter of their house or the embassy compound without motor pool driving them. Even leaving your yard and walking next door was not allowed; a motor pool driver in an up armored vehicle would need to pick you up and drive you next door! Perhaps a little over the top but, based on the threat conditions, understandable. I remember driving by a white woman out for run along the edge of the compound as we drove out one day. I was told she was Canadian or British and they don't have anywhere near the restrictions that the Americans have.

However, despite what appeared to be strict limits, DOS allowed you to be dropped off without a security team at a restaurant or shop to be picked up later if motor pool couldn't wait there the entire time. We went to a hotel for dinner that, by all accounts, was a five-star hotel for Islamabad, and the service was incredible. However, after all the security, it felt incredibly weird to be sitting at a hotel where just about anyone could walk in. Today, nearly everyone has been moved onto the compound into the SDAs. The environment in Pakistan, however, has slowly improved, so DOS is beginning to allow two-year assignments and some accompanied tours. It was here I picked up a cricket ball with the U.S. Embassy Islamabad seal because where else are you going to find that!

There are three constituent posts in Pakistan: Peshawar, Karachi, and Lahore. Karachi, on the coast, used to be a big tourist destination and is relatively safe. Although in June 2002, it was significantly damaged by a fertilizer bomb driven by a suicide bomber to the post in a truck. Following this attack, Seabees were sent in to rebuild the portion of the consulate that was damaged. Ron Stuart remembered that one of the Seabees brought an entire suitcase of canned tuna because he thought food would be in short supply. Food, in fact, was plentiful; however, the security situation was dire. The team sent there decided to sleep at the site to avoid leaving the compound. Due to this, the entire suitcase of canned tuna did end up being eaten by the team before they wrapped up repairs.[29] Peshawar is in the middle of territory influenced by ISIL (formerly ISIS), Al Qaeda, and the Taliban. The foreign service officers who live there don't really "live," but exist. They live in their offices for however long they are assigned there and rarely, if ever, leave the building. It takes an extremely committed and strong-minded professional to survive the constant terrorist threat right outside the gate. When motorcading from Islamabad, you'll drive by any number of ISIL flags: a numbing reminder of how important the mission is to support the oppressed and gather intelligence to prevent the next 9/11.

India borders Pakistan to the east. India is home to over a billion people, and arriving in New Delhi was like walking into a mob. Thankfully, I found my driver, and we were soon off to the hotel near the embassy quarter. Despite the location and beautiful surroundings, it was ill-advised to walk around alone after dark. Not leaving the hotel property, I found a rooftop Italian restaurant where I gorged myself on delicious bread and pasta. The day at the embassy was hot, but it also wasn't a bad day for air quality. One of the hard truths about India is the pollution. The Air Quality Index (AQI) for most of the world normally remains in the range of 0 to 100. However, in some countries, like India, the AQI can read up to 1500 or 1600. Of course, that means you should wear a mask approximately eight out of twelve months of the year. This is mostly due to the number of combustible engines on the road whether scooters, tuk-tuks, motorcycles, or automobiles. At times, the amount of honking you'll also experience when driving in India is deafening. Most people didn't have four wheeled vehicles a few decades ago. As individuality and driving became more mainstream in India, some families today are still experiencing buying their first car. I was told that honking was announcing, "Look at me, I am driving a car" just as much as saying, "Get out of my way," or "Let me go first." India takes the crown for the worst driving conditions I've ever experienced and that includes Thailand, Vietnam, and the Philippines.

One of my Seabees, CE1 Valencia Biggs, told me a story of the first week she was in New Delhi. She was riding with a colleague to the embassy one morning when they came to a stoplight. A man approached to attempt to sell them something, which is common at intersections throughout India. He was holding a canvas bag. The man did not appear to be threatening, and she didn't give it a second thought. However, the man was persistent and insisted that she buy whatever he had. CE1 cracked the window enough to ask what he was selling. How could someone buy something if they didn't know what it was? Immediately, the man casually pulled out an adult cobra and exclaimed "Buy, you buy!" This was at 8:15 AM, and just another morning in New Delhi.

My introduction with the RSO was quick, but what struck me was the real threat in the country: disease. Americans were more at risk of disease than terrorism. Drinking untreated water or eating improperly prepared food is more likely to kill you. Unfortunately, there are regular medical evacuations of personnel with unknown diseases or viruses, and these claim the lives of one or two personnel, on average, each year. Master Chief and I both understood the dangers, and we have essentially limited anyone of our Seabees with small children from getting posted in New Delhi, as it is hard for infants and toddlers to wear face masks to protect them from the poor air quality. Despite the AQI not being terrible when I was there, it was still evident in the constant haze over the city. My CPOIC in New Delhi told me how during Diwali, the festival of lights, involving fireworks and fires, it can be difficult to see twenty feet in front of you. While still trying to heed the information and warnings, I still was hopeful to get some real local food. We set out at lunchtime in a tuk-tuk and found a local establishment with a good reputation. A plate with a multitude of slots for different sauces and spicy concoctions was loaded up, which cleared out my sinuses immediately.

On our cultural day, we made the journey to the Taj Mahal—about a three-hour drive from New Delhi. My CPOIC and his family were pumped to be able to make the trip. Unfortunately, only one of my other Seabees was available to go, due to a scheduling conflict (our other Seabee was TDY). The three-hour drive took us through the vast city of New Delhi, which took almost ninety minutes to get out of, and then it was open fields and a six-lane highway with almost no traffic. The road was almost exclusively built for people to travel to the Taj Mahal, which was completed in 1648AD and is located in the district of Agra. We arrived at the Taj Mahal at mid-morning before the heat was too overwhelming and most of the tourists from New Delhi would arrive. I like to compare the Taj Mahal to the Grand Canyon. Taking a picture of the Taj Mahal cannot do it justice. The building itself was built in memory of the wife of Mughal Emperor Shah Jahan. What I found most incredible was that it was built nearly 500 years ago. The craftmanship and perfect symmetry are amazing, and it is built on a scale that takes your breath away.

India has an incredible beauty and is filled with a colorful culture and history. However, there is overwhelming poverty everywhere you look. Trying to make an impact among those less fortunate, both Seabees in New Delhi took it upon themselves to collect and distribute hotel shampoos and other hygiene items from the multiple hotels they stayed at during their numerous TDY trips to constituent posts. This small gesture of giving was always met with smiles and gratitude. Every time CE1 Biggs or SW2 Smith came around on Friday evening to deliver the supplies, the children would come running from each alleyway in anticipation of what they may have brought for them this time. The humanitarian assistance mission, even when unofficial, is deeply ingrained in many Seabees' characters, and to see them in action without the desire for recognition serves as a stark reminder of why many love serving with the Seabees.

One place that I had trouble finding on the map before visiting was Kazakhstan. The country was formally established after the fall of the USSR and was the first such country to be recognized as its own sovereign state by the United States in 1989. Kazakhstan is located south of the heart of Russia, to the west of China and Mongolia, and north of India. The country is rather large but mostly barren. Known for its long cold winters, Almaty is the main tourist destination due to skiing. However, the capital Astana, previously known as Nur-Sultan, was built out of a small village. The first president, Nursultan Nazarbayev, was elected at the time the country was reestablished in 1990. President Nazarbayev only stepped down in March 2019 after his fifth term as president. He retains the constitutional title of "Leader of the Nation," chair of the security council, and has other critical policy-making decision abilities. During his tenure, he led changes to the constitution that allowed him to be an advisor into perpetuity for the remainder of his life.

Astana is a city designed for the future. It has seen an onslaught of non-stop construction for nearly twenty years, utilizing the country's vast oil and mineral profits. A town that began as a small city of

325,000 is now home to over a million people. It hosts museums, world energy expo facilities, and some of the most interesting and large-scale art pieces and monuments you may ever see. Due to the extreme cold during ten months of the year (it is essentially a frozen tundra), you can find plenty of things to do indoors. There are massive malls that even include an indoor beach. The scale of the construction and the buildings completed over the last two to three decades will leave you bewildered. The House of Ministries at the heart of the city, and serving as a gateway to the presidential palace, is nearly three-quarters of a mile long. Despite the futuristic look of the city, Kazakhstan's people were originally nomadic. One of the unique experiences is to go for a dinner feast in a yurt, which is a tent of the kind that the population would have mostly lived in at one time. Kazakhs also have a meat-rich diet, including horse, since growing vegetables in the tundra isn't easy.

18

East Asia Pacific

East Asia and the Pacific have seen many significant historical events. One of the most historic locations in the EAP region for the United States is Manilla, Philippines, a nation of approximately 7,000 islands. Its people and governments are forever grateful for what General Douglas MacArthur promised and followed through on during WWII. The relationship between the two nations began in 1898, when the United States received the Philippines as a territory after defeating Spain in the Spanish American War. The Philippines eventually received their independence from the United States in 1946, following the end of WWII. However, in December 1941, the Japanese invaded the Philippines, just hours after the attack on Pearl Harbor and, at the same time, Guam and Singapore. General MacArthur famously told the Filipinos, "I shall return!" after he departed Corregidor Island for Australia in March 1942.[146] Despite some animosity between the Philippines and the United States prior to WWII, General MacArthur kept his word, and when he landed at Leyte Gulf in 1944, he stated:

"People of the Philippines: I have returned. By the grace of Almighty God our forces stand again on Philippine soil—soil consecrated in the blood of our two peoples. We have come dedicated and committed to

the task of destroying every vestige of enemy control over your daily lives, and of restoring upon a foundation of indestructible strength, the liberties of your people."[146]

After successful battles on the island of Luzon that pushed the Japanese to the north and eventually forced them to depart from the islands, General MacArthur raised the Stars and Stripes at U.S. Embassy Manila in 1945, following the Battle of Manila Bay.[147] The embassy was spared significant damage, even with the Japanese occupation and the U.S. military's air and naval bombardment. Of course, this was not just coincidence, the United States didn't want to have to rebuild its embassy, so they avoided bombing it as best they could. The flagpole used to raise the flag in 1945 remains, still flying the American flag. If you look closely enough, you can see that the foundation of the flagpole has bullet holes in it from the war.

During my visit to Manila, the ESC took a tour of Corregidor Island on our cultural day. Corregidor Island was where the U.S. military forces in the Philippines were headquartered prior to the war and Japanese invasion. It was surrendered to the Japanese in May 1942 but later retaken by the United States in 1944. Much of the infrastructure, old barracks, and other facilities are still there as reminders of the past. While some have been overtaken by jungle, others are well preserved. The rest of my time in Manila was filled with lumpia (spring rolls) and other delicious Filipino food.

After being stationed in Guam for three years prior to joining NSU as the OIC, I had traveled in East Asia quite a lot with my wife; however, traveling for a vacation is different than traveling officially. I had last traveled to Bangkok, Thailand, in February of 2017, when they were still mourning the loss of their longtime monarch, King Adulyadej, in 2016. Returning to Bangkok in the summer of 2019, I had gained new perspective and found the city to be more pleasant than New Delhi (India), Jakarta (Indonesia), and Hanoi (Vietnam), but it remains in the top five places for worst traffic I've visited.

Bangkok is a major transit hub, much like Frankfurt, Germany, and DOS has a presence there to match. The embassy sits right in the heart of downtown, on a beautiful compound with its own iguana population. One of the few "short" buildings on the block, the embassy has the feel of a sanctuary right in the middle of the city. As the mission has grown over the years, there are several offsite locations, including a second small compound across the street. In the opposite direction, the Ambassador's compound plays host to VIP visitors and special events in addition to being home to the Chief of Mission Residence (CMR).

About half of the U.S. community that works at the embassy lives within walking distance in a few high-rise blocks. Nearly everyone else lives about forty-five minutes away in a U.S. expatriate "golf cart" community in houses or apartments with a little more room to spread out. Much of the community used to be where a lot of Chevron employees resided when the oil company had a larger presence in the region. It is rare to hear complaints from personnel posted in Bangkok. The cost of living is relatively inexpensive, and you can find just about everything that's available in the states. When I visited, I unknowingly coincided with a visit by then Secretary of State Mike Pompeo as he attended the Post Ministerial Conferences during the ASEAN (Association of Southeast Asian Nations) Foreign Ministers Meeting. This offered a unique opportunity to hear him speak and potentially meet him in a small gathering at the CMR. Chief Arnie Pineda, my CPOIC, was able to get us on the invite list, and we went to the gathering. After some brief remarks, the Secretary took some questions and then came down from the platform to greet everyone and pose for photographs. Before he was about to depart, I finally got his attention and, after a short exchange, I was able to give him one of the NSU challenge coins to thank DOS for their continued support of the Seabees.

For our cultural day, we hired a driver to take us out to the former capital city of Ayutthaya, founded in 1350, about a ninety-minute drive north of Bangkok. It is a UNESCO world heritage site and one of the handful of things Maurissa and I hadn't gotten to see during our previous visit. I ended up taking an extra day in Bangkok, as this was the midpoint of a thirty-one-day trip that included business in ten locations and fifteen flights. The first two weeks of the trip, I made stops in San Diego, Port Hueneme, Honolulu, and Guam to conduct recruiting and command briefs for NSU to wardrooms within NAVFAC, the NCF, and the Naval Beach Group. It was an exhausting trip and the longest one during my time with NSU. Taking a break midway was needed to do laundry and recover before making the push through the second half of the itinerary.

After leaving Bangkok, I flew into Jakarta, Indonesia, in the early evening. Jakarta took the cake for some of the worst traffic, behind New Delhi. Driving to the hotel from the airport was only supposed to be about forty minutes. Instead, we sat for half an hour at a toll booth that wasn't accepting cash for some reason. After that debacle, I made it to the hotel just in time to grab a bite to eat in the lounge. We only spent one full day on the ground because the flight departing was a red-eye.

After our first day checking out the recently opened embassy, we explored the old downtown of Jakarta on the morning of day two. Jakarta has a heavy Dutch influence and historic buildings, including Café Batavia, completed in the 1850s. After an excellent lunch, we visited our Seabee's residence and went to a few shops in the mall next door before heading back to the airport to continue south to Canberra, Australia. However, a week after I returned home, the government of Indonesia announced that they would be moving their capital city to the province of East Kalimantan on the island of Borneo due to rising sea levels, pollution, and general overpopulation in Jakarta.[148] Many countries have moved their capitals throughout history. Indonesia and Egypt are two countries that have most recently announced plans to do so. Over the first twenty-five years of the United States' existence, the capital moved multiple times. It began in New York City, then Philadelphia, and, finally, Washington, D.C., in 1800, where it has stayed ever since. However, consideration to move the capital to St. Louis, Missouri, was floated following the American Civil War in 1867, given its central location within the lower forty-eight states and to distance itself from Richmond, VA, which was considered the capital of the Confederacy.[149]

We arrived in Canberra, Australia, after a brief layover in Sydney. Canberra is a planned city and the largest inland city in Australia. Beginning construction in 1913, Canberra is about a three-hour drive from Sydney and was built inland far enough to be safe from a seaborne attack.[150] The new parliament building, which began operation in 1988, sits atop Capital Hill (not "Capitol Hill," as in the United States) in Canberra.[151] When we visited in August 2019, it was the middle of winter in Australia. We were able to visit the Australian War Memorial that sits at the north end of the city at the foot of the Mount Ainslie Nature Reserve, as well as the Tidbinbilla Nature Reserve about forty-five minutes outside Canberra, home to wild koalas, kangaroos, and platypuses. While exploring Canberra and the nature reserves, it began snowing! Originally from Wisconsin, I experienced snowfall every month from October through May. Seeing snow in August was my first. Unfortunately, the nature reserve was not spared during the horrific wildfires that came in January 2020, and nearly a quarter of the land burned. Our Seabee stationed there at the time, SW1 Kyrah Cantu, remained at post and helped prepare air purifiers for use in the embassy due to the thick smoke covering the territory.

While Canberra is the farthest south post that NSU has Seabees permanently posted, it has fourteen constituent posts throughout the South Pacific that keep the Seabees and the rest of the office on the road a significant portion of the year. For example, traveling all the way to out to Fiji or Tonga can take twelve to forty-eight hours of island-hopping on planes. Part of the reason for this is that nearly all their international flights connect through Sydney. There have been discussions about moving the ESC to Sydney; however, the consulate doesn't have the space. Unique to Canberra, there is a diplomatic zone where over seventy-five embassies are located, each nation was encouraged to build facilities to replicate designs common to their own countries and homelands. The United States has a red brick façade that embraces the style of Thomas Jefferson's Monticello.

Settling in for the twelve-hour flight from Sydney to Beijing, you realize how far it is from the Southern Hemisphere to the Northern Hemisphere; it takes about the same amount of time as crossing the Pacific east to west. In the announcements at the beginning of the Air China flight, the airline nonchalantly informs passengers that passengers are under video monitoring. Video monitoring and photo surveillance in China is evident everywhere you go. On every street and building you enter, cameras are everywhere, recording everything. China has one of the most expansive and advanced video surveillance systems on the planet. Even driving on the interstate, your photo is taken about every 200 meters.

From the moment you get on the plane, there is uninterrupted surveillance. China is discreet about it, but if you know what to look for, you'll realize how apparent it really is. Whether it be trees of cameras, random light flashes, way too many smoke detectors for a single room, or mirrors that don't fog. You are being watched. Privacy in China is nearly impossible, and surveillance is simply an accepted part of life. For tourists, logging into a Wi-Fi network will almost certainly mean malware has been downloaded onto your phone and everything you do will be tracked. If you log in, you may as well throw away your device when you leave the country because all your passwords and personally identifiable information will have been compromised. Never leave your devices unattended, either. Hotel safes are not going to prevent your items from being tampered with, whether you notice it or not. The best thing you can do is leave your good electronics at home, bring throwaway devices, or never leave your items unmonitored. It is also best to never use the internet while in the country, unless on a device that you plan to throw away and do not access any of your personal information.

The U.S. Embassy Beijing is large, due to the size of the mission and the number of U.S. visitors to China each year. Our Seabees there are some of our most agile and well-trained. On the embassy grounds is situated a version of an extremely recognizable piece of art by Jeff Koons called "Tulips," that originally debuted in Paris, in addition to several incredible art pieces in the chancery. The embassy's construction used innovative techniques (classified information) and was completed by cleared Americans, despite being in the heart of downtown Beijing.

One of the Seven Wonders of the World is the Great Wall of China. Over 3,000 miles long, the most common spot to walk upon and experience the wall is Mutianyu. We went there and hiked the wall for a few hours. The scale of it is truly incredible. If seeing the Great Wall wasn't enough, we also visited Tiananmen Square and the Forbidden City. The Olympic village was also not too far out of town, but we ran out of time to see the Beijing National Stadium, known as the Bird's Nest, and other facilities built for the 2008 Summer Olympics and later used in the 2022 Winter Olympics. We did eat some incredible Chinese food. Dumplings and hot pot were on the menu, and they did not disappoint. We also visited a local shopping center. The local shopping center was next to a regular mall but home to many fine goods at significantly reduced prices to those in the United States. Of course, they are all made in China, so there are no importing costs. Because it's the local shopping center, there are certain black markets that with the right knock behind a certain landmark will open the doors to all the fake purses that you can imagine. I skipped the purses but found a souvenir magnet and postcard and was happy to be on my way.

Traveling to Hanoi, Vietnam, was the tenth stop on this four-week adventure. Learning about the Vietnam War throughout various points in my life left me very curious as to what Vietnam was like today. My first observation when arriving in a new city or country is the driving. In Hanoi, drivers are erratic. Jakarta, Indonesia, was busy, but Hanoi took traffic to the next level. Small-engine motorcycles created intense emission pollution, but the vibrant city shone brightly through the smog.

U.S. Embassy Hanoi is in desperate need of replacement. In an old, low-level building, its numerous renovations to make things fit mean that it is barely useable today. The United States is in the process of breaking ground on the new embassy compound in a nearby location within the city in a land-swap and building deal that will simultaneously give the Vietnamese a new embassy in Washington, D.C.

In nearby Laos, Cambodia, Steve Romero recalled a story from a former NSU Seabee that had been sent TDY to U.S. Embassy Laos to rewire a post communication center in 1993. On this TDY, the construction electrician got into a predicament that would have caused an international incident had his high-voltage technical expertise not been able to save the day. Working on rewiring the center, he had nearly completed his work. He had only to push in the breakers to reenergize his work, but the breakers were getting increasingly difficult to push in. He should have stopped and checked his work instead of trying to, literally, push through to the finish line. As he pushed in the last breaker, within a few moments, it sounded like a bomb blast went off outside the embassy, and all the power went out, not just in the embassy but also the few blocks surrounding it! His faulty wiring had blown the transformer of the Laotian utilities when resetting the breakers. This was not good.

The police, firefighters, and utility service provider made it to the scene, trying to keep everyone away. When a transformer blows, the cause is often unknown, despite there only being a few potential sources. They wouldn't be able to tell where the overload or short circuiting occurred, but they knew it wasn't due to a lightning strike. Also, the condition of the Laotian utilities may not have been the best at the time, so the age and degradation of the transformer could have also factored in. Only those in the embassy would have any idea that it was caused by the Seabee. Thankfully, no one got hurt from the explosion, but there was still no power within a few blocks' radius. The Laotians did have a spare transformer on hand, so the enterprising Seabee offered his services in what was likely a means to recover power sooner and prevent anyone from identifying it was he who overloaded the circuit and caused the explosion. Naval Construction Force Seabees are trained on high-voltage electricity, whereas NSU Seabees only work on low-voltage systems. This is how the NSU Seabee on TDY to Laos was able to both expertly repair the transformer; the low-voltage rewiring of the PCC would need to be revisited the next day to see what he had mis-wired. When all was said and done, the Seabee helped repair the transformer and found his mistake in the embassy before pushing the breakers in one final time.[102]

One of my last places to visit in EAP was also a place I had visited and transited multiple times before: Tokyo, Japan. With the fish market selling the freshest raw tuna, you'll find it is a foodie paradise. I was finally able to visit the Imperial Palace and had my full share of udon noodles, too. The U.S. Embassy Tokyo is downtown, amid several high-rise buildings on what would be a property valued in the billions. After WWII, the United States was able to secure a large footprint in the downtown for its mission that it never intends to give up. Japan has seven constituent posts all within the country. ESO personnel fly to about half of them and take a train to the other half, enjoying Japan's vast highspeed rail network. One thing we didn't do during our visit was the Mario Kart tour. Only in Japan can you dress up like your favorite Mario Kart character and tour the city by go-kart. While on our visit, there were a lot of discussions to ensure our Seabee made it to Tokyo before the 2020 Summer Olympics took place in July (at least that's what they thought at the time), to avoid the high cost of hotels before moving into his residence. This visit to Tokyo coincided with the emergency of COVID-19 from Wuhan, China. Little did we know that everything was going to change in just a few weeks.

After traveling throughout all of these countries around the world, I'm not alone in the belief and hope that more Americans would get a chance to see some of the incredible countries we were fortunate to visit with NSU, "to see how the rest of the world lives" as past NSU OIC Adam Gerlach put it.[19] The experience really produces a different perspective to look at the world and how policies of the "developed" world have impacted those of the "developing" world—not always for the better.

19

A Global Pandemic

During my time as OIC of NSU, we experienced travel stoppages for a couple reasons. We first experienced a hard stop in 2019 after a significant government shutdown caused a lapse in funding that started on December 22, 2018, and didn't end until January 25, 2019. However, nothing would prepare us for COVID-19 between March 2020 and August 2020. As I was writing this book, the world was still in the midst of it, nearly two years later. As the virus spread from Wuhan, China went into lockdown and authorized departures for non-essential mission personnel began. As of February 4, 2020, our three Seabees remained behind to maintain physical and technical security systems at U.S. Embassy Beijing. It would be more than five months before their family members would be able to return. Although they were beginning lockdown, the rest of NSU and the world were still able to carry on for the time being, and NSU convened their annual command training event in Frankfurt, Germany.

Although we made it to Frankfurt, the dominos began to fall throughout the rest of Asia and beyond. We realized countless events in Frankfurt had been canceled prior to our arrival that left NSU as the main occupants of a 600-room hotel. We were able to hold our largest Seabee Ball on March 7, 2020, with 225 people. Despite the gatherings, there were no reported positive COVID-19 cases from our event. We all took off from Frankfurt on either March 9 or 10. Some of us continued to carry out TDY missions from Frankfurt, including both Master Chief Joe Maioriello and me. We also happened to each have our dependents with us. His wife and son and my wife. Maioriello's family were staying in Europe and traveling by train, whereas my wife and I were catching up with the Africa Region CPOIC and our two Seabees in Addis Ababa, Ethiopia.

Arriving in Addis after a red-eye flight from Frankfurt, we were hit with the first day of temperature screenings for arriving international passengers. It was near chaos. As crazy as it was, we made it out and safely to our arrival party and off to our hotel to change before heading into the embassy for a full day. We did as much as we could on the first day, and then did our cultural day the second day. But by that time, the situation was growing ever more uncertain. We were receiving reports from around the world about things shutting down. We had a decision to make. Do we continue our trip to Nairobi, do we go straight to Dar Es Salaam, or do we go home and avoid getting stuck in Africa? Nairobi told us not to come, and Dar es Salaam said we could come but they were not recommending it.

After we found out that Nairobi was denying our entry, due to the developing international pandemic. We had planned to take leave to the island of Zanzibar and Durban, South Africa, after the regional training scheduled for Cape Town was completed; however, that was up in the air now, too. Nairobi closed, but Dar es Salaam was still open, although it was also going to be harder to get back stateside if we got stuck there. From Addis, there was a non-stop flight to D.C., as well as from Cape Town. After a couple calls on March 11, late in the evening, we decided that we needed to head back to the United States as soon as possible. I made the appropriate itinerary changes and canceled the rest of our hotel and flight reservations for the remainder of the trip.

We got a flight out on the evening of March 12, just as SECDEF issued a stop movement order for DOD. On March 13, the World Health Organization declared COVID-19 a pandemic. Taking the flight allowed us to get back to the United States, but we needed to quarantine upon our return for fourteen days. Had we not made it back before the order was issued, getting tickets to get back would have been much more difficult and more expensive because, suddenly, thousands of ex-pats from all around the world were trying to get back to the United States.

In the weeks following, while quarantined inside our apartment in D.C., we listened to reports of countries across Africa shutting down their borders and canceling all inbound and outbound international flights. We did get sick when we were back, but to this day we don't know if it was the roadside food we ate in Addis Ababa or COVID-19, most likely it was both. It was a rough couple of weeks, to say the least. I lost my sense of smell for four months, which, as health specialists and scientists later determined, was a symptom for positive COVID-19 patients. An issue with having that symptom is that you don't know when you are no longer positive unless you get a negative COVID-19 test.

It wasn't until July that we would have our first positive COVID-19 case at NSU. No one was traveling except for mission-critical support. However, we did have one Seabee who went TDY to Lisbon, Portugal, on January 4, 2020, for what was originally a three-month TDY to provide gap support. This means he was covering a personnel gap while people relocated. Given COVID-19 and no one able to move to Lisbon, he agreed to stay, and we kept him there. He continued to Madrid, Spain, for another month. Prior to returning to the United States on August 12, he had spent over seven months TDY to Portugal and Spain. From the time he left the United States to the time he returned, the whole world was in a completely different state than it was when he left.

After a time, travel began again slowly for NSU in support of projects; however, CUCM and I were not able to get back on the road to do the other 50 percent of our job performing resident inspections. It was not until May 2022 that the OIC and AOIC were given the green light to travel freely internationally. If we had finally gotten back out on the road before then, we planned to stay on the road to make up for lost time and to check on all our personnel, especially those without families. It's one thing to be posted independently under normal circumstances; it is something completely different to be unable to move around due to a pandemic.

One of the most striking stories from the field during the initial outbreak was from SW1 Barker and CE1 Krause who were in Phnom Penh, Cambodia, returning from a TDY the week after Frankfurt. They had received a COVID-19 test from the Navy Medical Research Unit in Bangkok prior to going on the trip. The day they were leaving Cambodia, they were scheduled on the last flight out. This flight to Bangkok had nearly 300 people on board, and many tourists were catching connecting flights back to Europe. Bangkok was requiring paperwork to enter the country, but the airline interpreted that as needing paperwork to transit as well. Because of that, SW1 and CE1 were the only two people allowed on the aircraft, and the other passengers were left stranded. They flew back to Bangkok on an empty plane, knowing they were two of the last individuals to get out of Cambodia before it went into complete lockdown.

As the pandemic took hold around the globe, maintenance and repair on mission-critical assets still had to be completed. These missions were limited, and the personnel who went had to jump over many hurdles. One of the most difficult locations we sent personnel at that time was Ulaanbaatar, Mongolia. It had been nearly a year since any technical security personnel had been able to visit the post. Praise from both the Ambassador and RSO reflected on the incredible work of the two Seabees we sent. Despite having undergone the world's longest institutional quarantine and state-administered testing regimen, they maintained solid bearing and remained true to task. The Seabees, CE2 Solomon Garbadass and UT1 Robyn Cantu, performed their tasks and completed their mission with professionalism and proficiency synonymous with NSU. Their tireless efforts and assistance over and above the call of duty were desperately needed and most appreciated.

In South America, CE1 Appelhanz was sent with a team to Asuncion, Paraguay. This was their first trip since the onset of COVID-19. Only a shortlist of people could leave the airport. Then, if cleared, had to undergo a two-week quarantine. The quarantine was in a hotel. The hallways had plastic tapped up to make it easier to clean. Those in quarantine would be delivered food. They would hear a knock on the door when food was placed outside. They could open the door for food but not for any other reason. When they finished eating, they placed the remains in a bag, sprayed disinfectant into it and, only then, placed it back outside. They could also not open the windows and the HVAC was shut off to prevent air circulation, making it incredible stuffy and hot. To make things worse, CE1 also got sick from the food. Conditions were so bad that one person jumped out of their third-floor window to escape quarantine. Unfortunately, the individual survived the initial jump but not the injuries. When the mission was complete, and they were trying to get back to Montevideo, Uruguay, their flights were continuously being canceled. Due to this, the group booked a private six-seater plane to fly back. This worked; however, they still had to quarantine two more weeks when they arrived.

We all encountered incredible difficulties throughout the COVID-19 pandemic. For those living overseas, such as the NSU Seabees and thousands of other U.S. government personnel, life was extremely difficult, and the hardship could never quite fully be realized by those back home in the United States.

20

Havana Syndrome

Although I never was able to travel to Havana, Cuba, a lot happened with our two Seabees we had posted there during my time as the OIC. Shortly after taking charge of the command, our first Seabee was posted to Havana. Within fourteen days, they encountered an anomaly that soon became a recurring national headline.

The Mystery of the Havana Syndrome
—The New Yorker, 09NOV2018

Another Diplomat was Diagnosed with 'Havana Syndrome.'
Here's what we know.
—The Washington Post, 03DEC2018

'Havana Syndrome' Likely Caused by Directed Waves
—BBC, 06DEC2020

During the period November 2016 to May 2018, there were twenty-four reported recurrences of an anomaly causing medical complications. Our Seabees were aware of the risk because others had reported that they were experiencing dizziness, migraines, and nausea.

In the case of our Seabee, while on a video call with their fiancé from their apartment in Havana, they heard a sound much like a cicada; however, it was excruciatingly loud and menacing. Since they were already on the phone and aware that this sound was like those reported from the briefs they received upon arrival, they started recording with their phone. Their recording captured audio and video while moving around their apartment and outside as they tried to identify the source. By opening the door and closing it, the sound would stop and start. They continued to record and provided the first piece of material evidence to one of the most perplexing and still unresolved investigations by the U.S. government.

Due to the number of other cases, our Seabee was medically evacuated and sent to the Hospital of the University of Pennsylvania in Philadelphia to undergo tests and observation. The patient was able to recover within a few months, but whatever happened caused brain trauma comparable to a victim of an Improvised Explosive Device (IED) blast in Iraq and Afghanistan. Despite the right to privacy, the Seabee wanted to help solve this problem, so they allowed world renowned scientists and physicians to interview them repeatedly. They were the first and only U.S. military service member to be hit by one of these attacks. Many speculate these attacks were being caused by nefarious foreign-actor activity, although some reports find this unlikely while a recent investigation may indicate otherwise. Our Seabee was courageously intent on pushing back against whoever or whatever was causing the so-called Havana Syndrome. None of the other victims were willing to participate in the investigation to the same extent. Our Seabee was able to help a plethora of three-letter agencies determine what didn't happen in Cuba, which was just as significant as determining what the cause was.

About a month after our Seabee was released from the Hospital of the University of Pennsylvania and was back in Washington, D.C., they were asked by the JASON group in Palo Alto, CA, for an interview. JASON comprises elite scientists, physicians, psychologists, and other experts from various research fields that are contracted by the U.S. government to jointly solve some of the United States' most perplexing problems when the government doesn't know where to even start looking.[152,153] The name of the group, JASON, comes from the Greek mythological figure Jason, leader of the heroic band of Argonauts.[154]

When we were debriefed on the study by JASON, they cited our Seabee's interviews and audio video recording for roughly 70 percent of the report. The Seabee's awareness and wherewithal to stay in the area of their dwelling where they were being attacked to gather the information also earned them the Secretary of State's Award. This award is the highest honor that can be bestowed upon any member of the Department of State by the Secretary.

I hope that one day the story will be finished when the U.S. government is able to figure out what happened in Havana, but at the time I left the unit in 2021, DOS was still trying to resolve these incidents and officially determine the source and/or foreign actor that was causing the occurrences. Since the first incidents in fall 2016, there have been dozens of reported incidents throughout Asia and Europe causing side effects and medical evacuations similar to those widely reported in Havana.

We were able to get another Seabee into Havana to support the mission about seven months later. Since the attack in May 2018, the embassy began downsizing the number of personnel it had on the ground in Cuba to mitigate the risk until they could figure out what was going on. As stated earlier, the investigation is still ongoing to determine what caused the numerous cases of mysterious medical maladies. In Cuba, following the attacks, foreign relations became further strained, even though the mission had only been reopened in 2015 under President Obama.

Aside from the attacks, the embassy had also been struck by a hurricane that caused more damage to an already aged and crumbling facility. NSU was asked to send in a Seabee with skills to not only perform the DS mission but work on HVAC systems and other utilities. Our answer was another Second Class Petty Officer, but a Utilitiesman this time. They were poised for anything but none of us could have prepared them for the level of responsibility they would soon undertake.

As personnel continued to dwindle, the Engineering Service Office—normally comprised of three people—was reduced to one, our Seabee, for more than eighteen months out of their thirty months at post. They held duties for every position in the Regional Security Office, except the RSO during their tenure. They also were the Seabee who most applied their Seabee Combat Warfare Specialist training while with NSU. They inventoried supplies, did security sweeps, filed reports, and attended every level of meeting which regularly included senior staff and the Chief of Mission, Deputy Chief of Mission, Chargé d'Affaires, and Principal Officer (all one person at this time). Let me remind you this was a Second Class Petty Officer who makes approximately 40,000 USD a year, in a room with Senior Foreign Service Officers making nearly four times what they do. Regardless, the senior leaders were looking to them to solve all their technical and physical security issues, as well as pick up the slack in facility maintenance and cover any number of other jobs. Never deterred by pressure, the can-do spirit of our Seabee was beyond comparison with anyone else in their rate and rank. They continued to perform at the most remarkable level to keep the facility secure and running. Nearing the end of their posting, and most well deserved, they were meritoriously advanced to First Class Petty Officer.

Conclusion

Naval Support Unit has served through decades of conflict and uncertainty. Continuously evolving and building upon its foundation to provide critical support to the Department of State and Diplomatic Security, NSU is poised to be anywhere in the world at a moment's notice. The impact the Seabees of the unit have made has often been profound and historic. NSU will remain in support of DOS as long as this partnership for national security remains beneficial for both DOS and the U.S. Navy.

Today, the relationship between DOS and NAVFAC has grown beyond NSU. The relationship is being leveraged to remove red-tape and breakdown stove piped organizations to improve secure-space construction worldwide in the face of strategic competition to be faster, smarter, and more efficient. The Naval Construction Force and Seabees continue to adapt to new and more focused operational requirements, such as airfield and waterfront damage repair in anticipation of needs in the Pacific, and less focused on the Global War on Terrorism mission requirements of the last two decades. As infrastructure investment from the U.S. government increases to a level not seen since the post-WW II era, the Civil Engineer Corps and Seabees face the challenge of recruitment and retention of engineers and skilled tradespeople that are in high demand.

Since serving with NSU, I have grown evermore aware of the challenges in our world and nation that require partnership and engagement between industry and government to overcome. I look forward to following the future accomplishments of NSU, the Seabees, and the outcomes of NAVFAC's strategic partnerships with outside agencies, like DOS and industry.

Acknowledgments

When I first set out to write this book, I didn't know what it would take to complete. I most certainly could not have done it myself without the encouragement and direct support of family and friends, as well as the many new people I would meet while investigating, researching, and seeking to publish *Detachment November.*

As I set out writing this book during the COVID-19 pandemic, the excitement and encouragement from my wife, Maurissa, and Ariel and Spencer Aaltonen, our two friends who moved in with us while they moved to Washington, D.C., was invaluable. I am forever grateful for your support and for caring about what I set out to do. Also, without the support of my parents, Paul and Mary Jo Dahms, none of this would have been possible. I was blessed with the opportunities to pursue my interests growing up and eventually become an engineer that led me into the Navy and the production of this book!

To the countless current and former Seabees, Civil Engineer Corps Officers, and Foreign Service Officers, Security Engineering Officers, and Security Technology Specialists, this would not have been possible without your willingness to share your stories and expertise. I would specifically like to thank Joe Maioriello, Stephan Haycook, Carmelo Melendez, Ron Stuart, Tamika Abbott, and Ralph Gaspard for your insight, support, and assistance in connecting me to countless individuals and resources to complete this story.

As I finished the manuscript and was trying to figure out what to do next, I was blessed to have the mentorship of RDML Michael Giorgione to help guide me through the entire process, as well as Mary Kate Soliva, Jean Cannon, Susan Brook, and Sharon Disher who helped open doors and expand my network. I could also have not done this without my long-time mentor, Mitch Weber, and long-time friend, Andy Gesior, two individuals who took the time to read the initial manuscript and provide incredible constructive criticism and recommendations. Finally, Lorna Partington Walsh who was my fantastic copy editor, who took my Navy shorthand and made it understandable for anyone to read. Lorna also connected me with Amplify Publishing Group (APG). APG gave me the opportunity to reach a larger audience and achieve the best quality print I could've ever imagined.

History of Unit Commendations

Period of Action	Award
07JAN67-31DEC74	Meritorious Unit Commendation
26AUG77-30JUN78	Meritorious Unit Commendation
01JAN79-30JUN82	Meritorious Unit Commendation
01JAN83-30JUN84	Navy Unit Commendation
01JAN88-31DEC89	Meritorious Unit Commendation
01JAN90-31DEC92	SECNAV Letter of Commendation
01APR96-30JUN99	Navy Unit Commendation

List of OICs

1964 DET November	LT Gail Pickart
1966-1967	LT Robert Parker
1967-1970	LT Richard Laurence
1970-1974	LT James Stark
1974-1976	LT Michael Hoff
1976-1979	LT George Roussos
1979-1981	LT Joseph Dean
1981-1982	LT Thomas Wisehart
1982-1985	LT James McConnell, Jr.
1985-1987	LT Craig Savant
1987-1990	LT Michael Peek
1990-1993	LCDR Francis Luttazi
1993-1996	LT Richard Schnabel
1996-1999	LT Carmelo Melendez
1999-2001	LT Tarey Isbell
2001-2003	LT Scott Kosnick
2003-2006	LT Marc Doran
2006-2010	LT Patrick Connor
2010-2012	LT Jessica Streiter
2012-2015	LT James Galloway
2015-2018	LT Adam Gerlach
2018-2021	LT Timothy Dahms
2021-2024	LT Michael Hamilton
2024-Present	LT Aaron Ignacio

List of AOICs

1966-1967	CUCM Joseph DeFranco
1967-1970	CUCM Johnson
1970-1972	BUCS McFarland
1972-1974	CUCM Richard Day
1974-1979	CUCM Raymond Nowakowski
1979-1982	UTCM Neil Goulette
1982-1985	Master Chief Robert Lee
1985-1988	EQCM Glen Kellerman
1988-1991	EQCM Rutherford
1991-1992	EQCM Cecil Howard
1992-1995	CUCM Jack Lancour
1995-1999	CUCM Rick DeBolt
1999-2003	CUCM Stephan Haycook
2003-2006	CUCM Joe Diaz
2006-2008	UCCM Glen Mummert
2008-2011	UTCS Kevin Hartford
2011-2015	CECS Alan Reyes
2015-2017	UCCM James Petty
2017-2020	CUCM Joseph Maioriello
2020-2023	CBCM Louie Alvarez
2023-Present	CBCM Michael Bonifer

Endnotes

1. U.S. Department of State, "A Short History of the Department of State," Office of the Historian. Last accessed September 09, 2020. https://history. state.gov/departmenthistory/short-history.

2. U.S. Department of State, "Principal Officer and Chiefs of Mission," Office of the Historian. Last accessed September 29, 2020. https://history.state.gov/ departmenthistory/people/principals-chiefs.

3. U.S. Mission to International Organizations in Vienna, "The U.S. Mission and our History," U.S. Mission to International Organizations in Vienna. Last accessed September 30, 2020. https://vienna.usmission.gov/a-history-of-unvie/.

4. U.S. Department of State. *Diplomatic Security Service: Then and Now: The First Century of the Diplomatic Security Service.* U.S. Department of State, Diplomatic Security Service, 2019.

5. U.S. Department of State, Diplomatic Security. *History of the Bureau of Diplomatic Security of the United States Department of State.* 1st Edition. Global Publishing Solutions, 2011.

6. Bainbridge, John, "Upward Mobility for Security Engineers," *ST Remembrances*, August 29, 2018. *Diplopedia.*

7. Roosevelt, Franklin Delano. "The Infamy Speech." U.S. Congress, Washington, D.C., December 8, 1941.

8. Naval History and Heritage Command, "ADM Ben Moreell," U.S. Navy. Last modified January 27, 2020. https://www.history.navy.mil/content/history/museums/seabee/explore/civil-engineer-corps-history/adm-ben-moreell.html.

9. Cragg, Jenn, "10 Things You Need to Know About Your Seabees," *The Sextant,* March 3, 2017. https://usnhistory.navylive.dodlive.mil/Recent/Article-View/Article/2686682/10-things-you-need-to-know-about-your-seabees/.

10. Naval Facilities Engineering Command. *History of the Seabees.* Command Historian, 1997. Naval Facilities Engineering Command.

11. Naval Facilities Engineering Systems Command Expeditionary Warfare Center, "Mobile Utilities Support Equipment," Naval Facilities Engineering Systems Command. Last accessed November 8, 2020. https://exwc.navfac.navy.mil/Products-and-Services/Shore-Technical-Department/Mobile-Utilities-Support-Equipment/Program-Information/.

12. Joint Staff Director for Joint Force Development (J-7). *Joint Operations.* Joint Publication 3-0, October 22, 2018. U.S. Department of Defense, Washington, D.C.

13. Safire, William. "On Language; Up the Down Ladder." *The New York Times.* November 15, 1998. https://www.nytimes.com/1998/11/15/magazine/on-language-up-the-down-ladder.html

14. Office of the Director of National Intelligence, "Members of the Intelligence Community," Office of the Director of National Intelligence. Last accessed December 27, 2020. https://www.dni.gov/index.php/what-we-do/members-of-the-ic.

15. United Nations. *Vienna Convention on Diplomatic Relations 1961.* United Nations, April 18, 1961. Vienna, Austria.

16. Bainbridge, John, "My First Inspection Trip in the Foreign Service," *ST Remembrances,* September 7, 2018. *Diplopedia.*

17. Wellman, James. "Official Visitor Security Guidelines," memorandum, Consulate General of the United States of America, undated.

18. Schwartz, Louis, "Privileges and Immunities," memorandum, United States Department of State, September 25, 1987.

19. Gerlach, Adam. Interviewed by the author, February 26, 2021.

20. Federation of American Scientists, "A Counterintelligence Reader, Volume 4 Chapter 2: Russia," Last accessed on March 09, 2024. https://irp.fas.org/ops/ci/docs/ci4/ch2.pdf.

21. U.S. Navy War College, "Counterintelligence: Chi Mak," U.S. Navy War College. Last accessed on January 22, 2021. https://usnwc.libguides.com/c.php?g=661096&p=6633118.

22. "Marine who Served in Moscow Embassy Held in Spy Inquiry," *New York Times*, January 11, 1987, https://www.nytimes.com/1987/01/11/us/marine-who-served-in-moscow-embassy-held-in-spy-inquiry.html.

23. Simpkins, Joe. Interviewed by the author, October 17, 2022.

24. U.S. Department of State, "Estimate of Damage to U.S. Foreign Policy Interests," Foreign Relations of the United States, 1964-1968, Volume XIV, Soviet Union. Last accessed on February 28, 2022. https://web.archive.org/web/20160316205538/http:/fas.org/irp/news/2001/03/moscowbugs.html.

25. Goudy, Robert, "Letter of Appreciation and Commendation for Project DEMO Crew," memorandum, Naval Support Unit State Department, October 27, 1967.

26. Hoff, Michael, "Letter to Deputy Assistant Secretary of State for Security Mr. Victor H. Dikeos," February 12, 1976.

27. Herrmann, George, "The Fastest Car in All Bolivia," *ST Remembrances*, January 4, 2018. *Diplopedia*.

28. Herrmann, George, "The Frankfurt PX Limo Service," *ST Remembrances*, March 26, 2020. *Diplopedia*.

29. Stuart, Ron. Interviewed by the author, July 7, 2021.

30. Bainbridge, John, "The STS 2560 Skill Code," *ST Remembrances*, August 28, 2018. *Diplopedia*.

31. Peek, Michael, "DS Progress Report: The First Three Years," memorandum, Naval Support Unit State Department, July 21, 1988.

32. Bluejacket.com, "U.S. Navy Enlisted Rating Structure," last accessed on March 8, 2021. https://www.bluejacket.com/usn_ratings.html.

33. Blazich, Jr. Frank, "This Week in Seabee History: Aug 26-Sept1," Navy History and Heritage Command, last accessed on September 21, 2021. https://web.archive.org/web/20200211164859/ https:/seabeemagazine.navylive.dodlive.mil/2018/08/26/ this-week-in-seabee-history-august-26-september-1/.

34. Dikeos, Victor, "Letter to Secretary of the Navy J. William Middendorf, II," December 13, 1974.

35. Langer, C.J., Hopper, M.G., Algermissen, S.T., and Dewey, J.W. "Aftershocks of the Managua, Nicaragua Earthquake of December 23, 1972." *Bulletin of the Seismological Society of America,* Vol 64, No. 4, pp 1005-1016. August 1974.

36. U.S. Embassy China, "History of the U.S. and China," U.S. Department of State. Last accessed on March 9, 2021. https://china.usembassy-china.org.cn/ history-of-the-u-s-and-china/.

37. U.S. Department of State, "The Seizure of the Saudi Arabian Embassy," summary, U.S. Department of State, declassified May 4, 2006.

38. U.S. Department of State, "$21.8M Sought to Combat Terrorism," *Department of State Newsletter*, No. 148, p 18, August/September 1973.

39. U.S. Embassy in Cuba, "Brief Diplomatic History," U.S. Department of State, last accessed on March 11, 2021. https://cu.usembassy.gov/ our-relationship/policy-history/.

40. Haycook, Stephan. Interviewed by the author, May 12, 2021.

41. Wren, Christopher, "Classified Material Believed Safe in U.S. Embassy Fire in Moscow," *New York Times,* August 28, 1977, https://www.nytimes. com/1977/08/28/archives/classified-material-believed-safe-in-us-embassy-fire-in-moscow.html.

42. Officer in Charge, Naval Support Unit State Department. *Standard Operating Procedures.* NSUSTATEINST 1320.1B p. B-4, undated. Naval Support Unit State Department, Washington, D.C.

43. Grier, Peter, "Cleaning the Bug House," *Air Force Magazine*, September 2012, p. 98-102. last accessed on February 28, 2022, https://www. airforcemag.com/PDF/MagazineArchive/Documents/2012/September 2012/0912embassy.pdf.

44. Tubbs, Paul, "Changing times 1977-1979," *ST Remembrances*, January 9, 2018. *Diplopedia.*

45. Tracy, Thomas, "Letter to Secretary of the Navy Edward Hidalgo," March 18, 1980.

46. U.S. Virtual Embassy Itan, "Policy and History," U.S. Department of State, last accessed on March 11, 2021. https://ir.usembassy.gov/policy-and-history/.

47. Office of the President of the United States. *Executive Order 10631: Code of Conduct for members of the Armed Forces of the United States*, dated August 15, 1977 (with amendments from 1966-1970, 1977, and 1988). The White House, Washington, D.C.

48. Haynes, H. H., "Peacetime Conduct of Military Personnel in a Hostage or Terrorist Situation," memorandum, Naval Facilities Engineering Command, June 17, 1980.

49. Roach, J. A. "Code of Conduct, Applicability to Peacetime Hostages," memorandum, Office of Judge Advocate General, Department of the Navy, May 22, 1980.

50. Bainbridge, John, "Beirut," *ST Remembrances*, September 6, 2018. *Diplopedia*.

51. McConnell, James. Interviewed by the author, November 5, 2021.

52. Bainbridge, John, "The Bugs and Bombs Tour," *ST Remembrances*, January 9, 2018. *Diplopedia*.

53. Haycook, Stephan. Memorandum for the record. 1983

54. Congressional Budget Office. *Building a 600-Ship Navy; Costs, Timing, and Alternative Approaches*, dated March 1982. U.S. Congress, Washington, D.C.

55. Lamb, Robert. "Letter to Assistant Secretary of Defense Lawrence Korb," November 5, 1984.

56. U.S. Department of State, "Law Enforcement," Bureau of Diplomatic Security, U.S. Department of State. Last accessed March 18, 2021. https://www.state.gov/law-enforcement/.

57. Federal Bureau of Investigation, "International Operations," Federal Bureau of Investigation. Last accessed on March 18, 2021. https://www.fbi.gov/about/leadership-and-structure/international-operations.

58. United States Secret Service, "Our Protective Mission," United States Secret Service. Last accessed on March 18, 2021. https://www.secretservice.gov/protection.

59. "Rebel Aircraft Attack Managua, Bombing Airport and Residences," *New York Times*, September 9, 1983. https://www.nytimes.com/1983/09/09/world/rebel-aircraft-attack-managua-bombing-airport-and-residences.html.

60. Herrmann, George, "Sorry, We've Got to Work Late Tonight," *ST Rememberances*, January 5, 2018. *Diplopedia*.

61. Christian, Shirley, "4 Marines Slain in A Rebel Raid in San Salvador," *New York Times*, June 21, 1985. https://www.nytimes.com/1985/06/21/world/4-amrines-slain-in-a-rebel-raid-in-san-salvador.html

62. Assistant Secretary of The Navy Manpower and Reserve Affairs, *Navy and Marine Corps Award Manual*. SECNAVINST 1650.1H, August 22, 2006. Department of the Navy, Washington, D.C.

63. Military Intelligence Hall of Fame, "Honorable Vernon A. Walters," U.S. Army Intelligence Knowledge Network, last accessed on December 11, 2021. https://www.ikn.army.mil/apps/MIHOF/biographies/Walters, Vernon.pdf

64. 99th U.S. Congress, *H.R. 4418: Omnibus Diplomatic Security and Antiterrorism Act of 1986*, U.S. Congress, Washington, D.C. https://www.congress.gov/bill/99th-congress/house-bill/4418.

65. Savant, Craig, "Concern About the Direction of NSU," discussion paper, April 16, 1987.

66. Stethem, Patrick, "Robert Stethem Legacy Lives on for 31 Years," *Navy Seabee Foundation*. Last accessed on March 18, 2021. https://seabeehf.org/robert-stethem/.

67. Peek, Michael, "Off-duty Contract Work by NSU Personnel," memorandum, October 6, 1988.

68. Guerrero, Eileen, "Mount Pinatubo Produces Biggest Eruption Yet," *AP News*, June 14, 1991. https://apnews.com/article/1eddb394c82be348ac10fa0034bec143

69. National Centers for Environmental Information, "Significant Earthquake: Cairo 10 October 1992," National Oceanic and Atmospheric Administration, last accessed on March 28, 2021. https://www.ngdc.noaa.gov/nndc/struts/results?eq_0=5339&t=101650&s=13&d=22,26,13,12&nd=display.

70. National Hurricane Center, "Hurricane Andrew, 16-28 August, 1992," National Oceanic and Atmospheric Administration, last accessed on March 28, 2021. https://www.nhc.noaa.gov/1992andrew.html.

71. Luttazi, Francis, "Nomination of the Naval Support Unit, State Department for the Navy Unit Commendation," memorandum, June 11, 1993.

72. Lawson, Timothy, "Communications Behind the Iron Curtain," *The Foreign Service Journal,* last accessed on March 28, 2021. https://www.afsa.org/communications-behind-iron-curtain.

73. U.S. Embassy Moscow, "U.S. Embassy and Consulates in Russia," U.S. Department of State, last accessed on March 28, 2021. https://ru.usembassy.gov/embassy-consulates/moscow/.

74. Bainbridge, John, "You Want Me to do What Where," *ST Remembrances,* August 28, 2018. *Diplopedia.*

75. Bainbridge, John, "Establishment of the MEBCO Seabee Team Standard Operating Procedures," memorandum, February 1, 1998.

76. Luttazi, Francis, "Nomination of the Naval Support Unit, State Department for the Navy Unit Commendation," memorandum, February 18, 1993.

77. Dalton, John, "Letter of Commendation," citation, 1993.

78. Flowers, Clifton, "Seabee Program," memorandum, October 6, 1998.

79. Milligan, Shawn. Interviewed by the author, May 4, 2021.

80. Melendez, Carmelo, "Nomination of Naval Support Unit for the Navy Unit Commendation for the period of April 1996 through June 1999," memorandum, 1999.

81. Clinton Digital Library, "Haiti: Restoring a Democracy," National Archives, last accessed on April 15, 2021. https://clinton.presidentiallibraries.us/haiti-topic-guide.

82. Melendez, Carmelo, "Summary of Action ICO CUCM Debolt, Ricky," memorandum, 1999.

83. Melendez, Carmelo. Interviewed by the author, April 26, 2021.

84. Renken, James. *Navy Seabees Mission Tanzania.* Amazon, 2018.

85. Fox, Steve. Interviewed by the author, May 27, 2021.

86. Isbell, Tarey, "Priority Manning for NSU Shore Duty Component (UIC: 65498)," point paper, January 24, 2001.

87. Office of the Press Secretary (Moscow, Russia), "Expanded Threat Reduction Initiative Fact Sheet," The White House. June 4, 2000. Last accessed on April 8, 2021. https://clintonwhitehouse4.archives.gov/WH/New/Europe-0005/factsheets/fs--expanded-threat-reduction-initiative.html.

88. 106th Congress, *S.1234: Foreign Operations, Export Financing, and Related Programs Appropriations Act, 2000*, U.S. Congress, Washington, D.C. last accessed on April 8, 2021. https://www.congress.gov/bill/106th-congress/senate-bill/1234.

89. Kosnick, Scott. Interviewed by the author, November 2, 2021.

90. U.S. Embassy in Afghanistan, "History of the U.S. and Afghanistan," U.S. Department of State, last accessed on April 20, 2021. https://af.usembassy.gov/our-relationship/policy-history/history-of-the-u-s-and-afghanistan/.

91. "History of Arg," last accessed on April 15, 2021. https://president.gov.af/en/history-of-arg-presidential-palace/

92. Beck, Chris, "Karzai Protective Detail Summary," memorandum for the record, 2002.

93. Torres-Torres, Luis. Interviewed by the author, May 10, 2021.

94. Dynda, Lyle. Interviewed by the author, August 13, 2021.

95. Doran, Marc, "Specific Accomplishments: January 1, 2001-January 1, 2004," memorandum, 2004.

96. "USS Blue Ridge LLC 19 History," USCarriers.net, last accessed on December 11, 2021. http://www.uscarriers.net/lcc19history.htm.

97. "Giant U.S. Embassy Rising in Baghdad," *USA Today*, last accessed on April 29, 2021. https://usatoday30.usatoday.com/news/world/iraq/2006-04-19-us-embassy_x.htm.

98. Dobbins, J., Jones, S., Runkle, B., and Mohandas, S., "Occupying Iraq: A History of the Coalition Provisional Authority." *RAND National Security Research Division*. 2009.

99. Doran, Marc, "NSU General Overview and Accomplishments," memorandum, March 5, 2005.

100. U.S. Embassy and Consulates in China, "New Embassy Complex," U.S. Department of State. Last accessed on May 2, 2021. https://china.usembassy-china.org.cn/embassy-consulates/beijing/new-embassy-complex/.

101. Walsh, Susan. "Rice Orders Monitoring of Blackwater in Iraq," *NBC News*, October 6, 2007. https://www.nbcnews.com/id/wbna21162150.

102. Romero, Steve. Interviewed by the author, July 13, 2021.

103. U.S. Senate, "Report on the Terrorist Attack at Benghazi," Congressional Record Volume 158, Number 170, December 30, 2012. https://fas.org/irp/congress/2012_cr/benghazi.html.

104. "Ex-Russian Spy Skirpal Poisoned by Nerve Agent on Door of Home," *Reuters*, March 29, 2018. https://www.cnbc.com/2018/03/29/ex-russian-spy-skripal-poisoned-by-nerve-agent-on-door-of-home.html.

105. "Russia to Close U.S. Consulate in St. Petersburg, Foreign Minister Says," *Associated Press*, last accessed on 10MAY2021. https://www.pbs.org/newshour/world/russia-to-close-u-s-consulate-in-st-petersburg-foreign-minister-says.

106. U.S. Department of State, "Ministerial Meetings," U.S. Department of State, last accessed on May 2, 2021. https://oaarchive.arctic-council.org/handle/11374/373.

107. Wong, E., Jakes, L., and Myers, S., "U.S. Orders China to Close Houston Consulate, Citing Efforts to Steal Trade Secrets," *New York Times*, July 22, 2020. https://www.nytimes.com/2020/07/22/world/asia/us-china-houston-consulate.html.

108. Richardson, John, "The Charge of Command," memorandum, 06APR2018.

109. Debolt, Rick. Interviewed by the author, November 6, 2021.

110. Maioriello, Joe. Interviewed by the author, May 19, 2021.

111. Herrmann, George, "The Caracas Taco Stand," *ST Remembrances*, January 3, 2018. *Diplopedia*.

112. Wallace, Dustin. Interviewed by the author, June 23, 2021.

113. LaGrone, Sam, "Cuba Restores Memorial to USS Maine," *USNI News*, February 15, 2013. https://news.usni.org/2013/02/15/cuba-restores-memorial-to-uss-maine.

114. Trotta, Daniel, "Mansion Where Obama to Stay in Havana "Built to Impress," *Reuters*, March 18, 2016. https://www.reuters.com/article/us-usa-cuba-residence/mansion-where-obama-to-stay-in-havana-built-to-impress-idUSKCN0WK2MU.

115. Walter Elkins, "U.S. Army Hospital Frankfurt History," last accessed on August, 1, 2021. https://www.usarmygermany.com/Sont. htm?https&&&www.usarmygermany.com/units/Medical/USAREUR_ USAHFrankfurt.htm.

116. Bradley Parker Architects, "U.S. Consulate Frankfurt, Germany," last accessed on August 1, 2021. http://www.bradleyparker.com/ portfolios/u-s-consulate-frankfurt-germany/.

117. U.S. Embassy & Consulates in Germany, "History of the America House," U.S. Department of State, last accessed on August 1, 2021. https:// de.usembassy.gov/history-of-the-amerika-haus/.

118. U.S Department of State, "FY20 Report of the Visa Office," U.S. Department of State, last accessed on August 1, 2021. https://travel.state.gov/content/ travel/en/legal/visa-law0/visa-statistics/annual-reports/report-of-the-visa- office-2020.html.

119. U.S. Embassy United Kingdom, "New U.S. Embassy in Nine Elms, London," U.S. Department of State, last accessed on August 2, 2021. https://uk.usembassy.gov/our-relationship/policy-history/new-embassy/ new-london-embassy-in-nine-elms/.

120. McGinnis, Chris, "Former U.S. Embassy in London to Become Luxury Rosewood Hotel," *SFGate*, last accessed on 02AUG2021. https://www. sfgate.com/travel/article/Former-US-Embassy-in-London-to-become- luxury-12496894.php.

121. North Atlantic Treaty Organization, "What is NATO," North Atlantic Treaty Organization, last accessed on August 2, 2021. https://www.nato.int/ nato-welcome/index.html.

122. U.S. Embassy France, "Embassy Location and Building," U.S. Department of State, last accessed on August 2, 2021. https://fr.usembassy.gov/ embassy-consulates/paris/embassy-location-building/.

123. U.S. Embassy Germany, "History of the Embassy in Berlin," U.S. Department of State, last accessed on August 3, 2021. https://de.usembassy.gov/ history-of-the-embassy-on-pariser-platz/.

124. Mascaro, L., Jalonick, M., and Tucker, E. "Trump Directed Quid Pro Quo, Top Witness Says," *AP News*, November 20, 2019. https://apnews.com/ article/donald-trump-ap-top-news-politics-russia-impeachments-6486944b07 6b4df99a583a3a7c85574d.

125. U.S. Embassy in Hungary, "Cardinal Mindszenty," U.S. Department of State, last accessed on September 7, 2021. https://hu.usembassy.gov/embassy/budapest/embassy-history/cardinal-mindszenty/.

126. Catholic News Service, "Diplomat Recalls Friendship with Hungarian Cardinal Who's Up for Sainthood," *Catholic Review*, last accessed on September 7, 2021. https://catholicreview.org/diplomat-recalls-friendship-with-hungarian-cardinal-whos-up-for-sainthood/.

127. Hedquist, Valerie, "Il Palazzo and La Pizza Margherita," *Smithsonian Journeys*, December 24, 2014. https://www.smithsonianjourneys.org/blog/il-palazzo-and-la-pizza-margherita-180953729/.

128. U.S. Embassy to the Holy See, "U.S. Embassy to the Holy See," U.S. Department of State, last accessed on September 9, 2021. https://va.usembassy.gov/u-s-embassy-to-the-holy-see/.

129. Bureau of the Comptroller and Global Financial Services, "Register of Culturally Significant Properties," U.S. Department of State, last accessed on September 9, 2021. https://2009-2017.state.gov/s/d/rm/rls/perfrpt/2014/html/235106.htm.

130. Fisher, I. and Carassava, A." U.S. Embassy in Athens is Attacked," *New York Times*, January 12, 2007. https://www.nytimes.com/2007/01/12/world/europe/12cnd-greece.html.

131. U.S. Embassy in Tirana, "U.S. Embassy Tirana," U.S. Department of State, last accessed on September 9, 2021. https://al.usembassy.gov/embassy/tirana/.

132. U.S. Department of State, "U.S. Department of State Awards," U.S. Department of State, last accessed on September 9, 2021. https://2009-2017.state.gov/m/ds/c32817.htm.

133. Menshawy, Mustafa, "Why is Egypt Building a New Capital," *Al Jazeera*, July 5, 2021. https://www.aljazeera.com/opinions/2021/7/5/why-is-egypt-building-a-new-capital.

134. Ministry of Foreign Affairs, "The Washington Declaration," Government of Israel, last accessed on September 16, 2021. https://www.mfa.gov.il/mfa/foreignpolicy/peace/guide/pages/the washington declaration.aspx.

135. Ministry of Foreign Affairs, "Camp David Accords," Government of Israel, last accessed on September 16, 2021. https://www.mfa.gov.il/mfa/foreignpolicy/peace/guide/pages/camp david accords.aspx.

136. Reichmann, D., Lee, M., and Lemire, J., "Israel Signs Pacts with Two Arab States: A "New" Mideast?" *AP News*, September 15, 2020. https://apnews.com/article/bahrain-israel-united-arab-emirates-middle-east-elections-7544b322a254ebea1693e387d83d9d8b.

137. Dahl, B. and Slutzky, D., "Timeline of Turkish-Israeli Relations 1949-2006," The Washington Institute for Near East Policy, 2006.

138. Bureau of Near Eastern Affairs, "U.S. Relations with Israel," U.S. Department of State, last accessed on September 16, 2021. https://www.state.gov/u-s-relations-with-israel/.

139. Bureau of Near Eastern Affairs, "U.S. Relations with Jordan," U.S. Department of State, last accessed on September 16, 2021. https://www.state.gov/u-s-relations-with-jordan/.

140. The Avenues, "About Us," The Avenues, last accessed on September 16, 2021. https://www.the-avenues.com/about-us.

141. Lowey, Mark, "The Camel Races of Kuwait - A Photo Essay," *Aramco Expats*, January 13, 2021. https://www.aramcoexpats.com/articles/the-camel-races-of-kuwait-a-photo-essay.

142. Fattahova, Narawa, "Why You Can't Drive a Pickup Truck in Kuwait," *Kuwait Times*, April 25, 2014. http://news.kuwaittimes.net/pdf/2014/apr/25/p02.pdf.

143. "Senegal Inaugurates Controversial $27M Monument," *BBC News*, date. last accessed on September 22, 2021. http://news.bbc.co.uk/2/hi/africa/8601382.stm.

144. Author, "Orthodox Christianity in the 21st Century," *Pew Forum*, August 11, 2017. https://www.pewforum.org/2017/11/08/orthodox-christianity-in-the-21st-century/.

145. Herrmann, George, "Chez Le Petite Logis," *ST Remembrances*, January 4, 2018, *Diplopedia*.

146. MacArthur, Douglas. "The I Shall Return Speech." Radio Address, Leyte Gulf, Philippines, October 20, 1944. https://teachingamericanhistory.org/document/radio-address-upon-returning-to-the-philippines/.

147. U.S. Embassy in the Philippines, "U.S. Embassy Commemorates 75th Anniversary of U.S. Flag Raising after Battle of Manila," U.S. Department of State, February 20, 2020. https://ph.usembassy.gov/u-s-embassy-commemorates-75th-anniversary-of-u-s-flag-raising-after-battle-of-manila/.

148. Chappell, Bill, "Indonesia Plans to Move Its Capital to Borneo from Jakarta," *NPR*, August 26, 2019. https://www.npr.org/2019/08/26/754291131/indonesia-plans-to-move-capital-to-borneo-from-jakarta.

149. Gershon, Livia, "The Ill-fated Idea to Move the Nation's Capital to St. Louis," *Smithsonian Magazine*, April 22, 2021. https://www.smithsonianmag.com/history/ill-fated-idea-move-nations-capital-st-louis-180977569/.

150. National Museum of Australia, "Founding of Canberra," National Museum of Canberra, last accessed on October 24, 2021. https://www.nma.gov.au/defining-moments/resources/founding-of-canberra.

151. Parliamentary Education Office, "Australia's Parliament House," Australian Parliament, Canberra, Australia, last accessed on October 24, 2021. https://peo.gov.au/understand-our-parliament/parliament-house/australias-parliament-house/.

152. Federation of American Scientists, "JASON Defense Advisory Panel," Federation of American Scientists, last accessed on October 27, 2021. https://irp.fas.org/agency/dod/jason/.

153. Federation of American Scientists, "Acoustic Signals and Physiological Effects on U.S. Diplomats in Cuba," Federation of American Scientists, last accessed on October 27, 2021. https://irp.fas.org/agency/dod/jason/titles.pdf.

154. Finkbeiner, Ann, "Jason – A Secretive Group of Cold War science Advisors- is Fighting to Survive in the 21st Century," *Science*, June 27, 2019. https://www.science.org/content/article/jason-secretive-group-cold-war-science-advisers-fighting-survive-21st-century

Index

A

Abidjan, Cote d'Ivoire, 226

Abuja, Nigeria , 225

Accra, Ghana, 226

Acts

    Diplomatic Security and Anti-
        Terrorism Act of 1986, 91

    Foreign Assistance Act of 1961,
        108

    Foreign Operations, Export
        Financing, and Related
        Programs
            Appropriation Act of 2000,
            107

    Foreign Relations Authorization
        Act of 1986, 10, 85

    Freedom Support Act of 1992,
        108

    Immigration Act of 1924, 4

Adams, John, 5, 175

Adams, John Quincy, 3, 175

Addis Ababa, Ethiopia, 221, 222, 223,
    250, 251

Advantage at Sea, Dec 2020, 36

Afghanistan, 58, 110, 111, 113, 114,
    199, 229, 231, 256

    Arg (Afghanistan Presidential
        Palace Compound), 111, 113

    Herat, 126

    Kabul, 110, 111, 112, 114, 126,
        130, 131, 145, 199, 211, 230,
        231

African Union (AU), 6, 221

Albania, 117, 119, 196

Albright, Madeleine, 102, 103, 104,
    105

Algiers, Algeria, 212, 225

Al-Qaddafi, Muammar, 125

Ames, Aldrich, 31

Amman, Jordan, 210, 211

Amphibious Construction Battalion
    (ACB), 50, 136, 165

Angola, 226

Ankara, Turkey, 192, 193

Appelhanz, CE1, 253

Aristide, Jean Claude, 100

Association of Southeast Asian
    Nations (ASEAN), 6, 241

Asuncion, Paraguay, 253

Athens, Greece, 80, 196, 197

Australia, 239

    Canberra, Australia, 145, 242, 243, 244

    Sydney, Australia, 243, 244

Austria, 5, 184, 185

    Vienna, 145, 183, 184, 185, 188, 192

        Convention on Diplomatic Relations of 1961, 25, 28, 75, 126, 231, 282

        State Opera, 185

B

Bainbridge, John, 11, 26, 61, 80, 96, 97

Barker, Cody, 252

Battalion Artist, The, xxv

Beirut, Lebanon, 10, 64, 79, 80, 81, 82, 84, 85, 86, 91, 92, 96, 100, 196, 197

    Baaklini Annex, 80, 82

Belgrade, Serbia, 99

Benghazi, Libya, 125, 126, 127

Bermuda, 166, 167

Biggs, Valencia, 234, 236

Bin Laden, Osama, 100

Bonn Agreement, 110

Boone, David, 31

Borneo, 242

Bosnia, 99

    Bosnian War, 99

    Sarajevo, 99

Brazzaville, Republic of Congo, 226

Brussels, Belgium, 178, 179

Bryan, Bob, 69

Bucharest, Romania, 195, 196

Budapest, Hungary, 191, 192

Buenos Aires, Argentina, 170

Bureau of Diplomatic Security (DS), 10, 11, 12, 13, 25, 28, 41, 44, 53, 85, 100, 111, 112, 114, 258

Bureau of Overseas Building Office (OBO), 70, 105

Bureau of Yards and Docks , 15, 16, 20, 39, 40, 136,

Bush, George H.W., 191

Bush, George W., 116

C

Cairo, Egypt, 94, 102, 105, 124, 145, 199, 200, 202, 203, 204, 205, 206, 217, 225

Cambodia, 252

    Laos, 246, 247

    Phnom Penh, 252

Camp David, xxiv, xxv, 20, 50, 56, 136, 139

    Camp David Accords 1978, 210

    Inside Camp David, xxv, 136

Canada, 170

    Montreal, 183

    Ottawa, 170, 181

Cantu, Kyrah, 243

Cantu, Robyn, 253

Caracas, Venezuela, 167

Carlson, Drew, 197

Carter, Jimmy, 68

Casablanca, Morocco, 117, 200, 201

Castro, Fidel, 68, 168

Centers for Disease Control and Prevention (CDC), 5

Central Intelligence Agency (CIA), 23, 24, 88, 96, 102, 117, 119

China, 27, 29, 31, 36, 66, 221, 236, 244, 245
    Beijing, 123
        Great Wall of China, 245
        Tiananmen Square, 245
        Wuhan, 248, 249
Coastal Riverine Group (CRG), xxv, 50
Code of Conduct, 72, 73, 74
Cold War, 23, 36, 54, 63, 69, 84, 93, 96, 186, 191
Coleman, Darcus, 206
Committee for State Security (KGB), 23, 24, 26
Construction Battalion Maintenance Unit (CBMU), 47, 50
Cotonou, Benin Republic, 225
Cuba
    Guantanamo Bay (GTMO), 168
    Havana, 30, 68, 106, 166, 168, 169, 255, 256, 257
    Havana Syndrome, 150, 255, 256
Curtis, George, 67
Cusco, Peru, 172
Czechoslovakia, 66
    Prague Spring 1968, 66

D

Dakar, Senegal, 200, 202, 217, 218, 220, 221
Dar es Salaam, Tanzania, 61, 100, 101, 102, 103, 104, 105, 224, 250
Darrah, William B., 66
Debolt, Rick, 140
Defense Attache Office (DATT), 44, 45, 82, 102
Democratic Republic of Congo, 99

Department of Defense (DOD), xxiv, 5, 21, 24, 34, 35, 39, 56, 73, 102, 107, 109, 111, 114, 121, 122, 123, 127, 129, 130, 131, 135, 144, 192, 193, 226, 251
Department of Homeland Security (DHS), 5, 24
Department of State (DOS), xxiii, xxiv, 3, 5, 6, 7, 10, 11, 12, 13, 14, 25, 27, 29, 33, 34, 36, 39, 41, 44, 46, 48, 51, 52, 53, 54, 56, 57, 58, 61, 63, 65, 66, 67, 72, 76, 77, 78, 85, 91, 92, 94, 95, 96, 97, 98, 100, 101, 102, 104, 109, 110, 111, 114, 116, 117, 119, 120, 121, 123, 124, 127, 128, 129, 130, 131, 136, 137, 138, 139, 140, 141, 142, 144, 145, 152, 153, 154, 162, 170, 171, 176, 179, 183, 186, 187, 188, 194, 199, 204, 207, 208, 220, 221, 229, 231, 232, 241, 257, 259, 260
Desert Shield, 21
Desert Storm, 21
Dickey, Mark, 185
Diego Garcia, 19
Dikeos, Vicktor, 51, 67
Diplomatic Security Service (DSS), 6, 7, 10, 11, 28, 65, 68, 85, 86, 131
Director of National Intelligence (DNI), 24
Division of Technical Security, 10
Division of Technical Services, 8
Dobbins, James, 110, 111
Doran, Walter, 120
Drug Enforcement Administration (DEA), 5, 24
Dynda, Lyle, 115, 117, 118, 119, 120

E

England, Gordon, 120
European Union (EU), 5, 195
Expanded Threat Reduction Initiative (ETRI), 107
Explosive Ordnance Disposal (EOD), xxv, 18, 50

F

Federal Bureau of Investigation (FBI), 5, 24, 85, 101, 102, 103, 189
Federal Emergency Management Agency (FEMA), 106
Federal Security Service (FSB), 24, 186, 187
Fighting Seabees, The, xxv
Florida , 94
    Florida Regional Center, 94, 165
    Tampa Bay, Florida, 11
Foreign Building Operations (FBO), 33, 55, 69, 80, 82, 98, 99
Foreign Intelligence Service, 24, 186
Fox, Steve, 102, 103, 104, 105, 107
France, 3, 5, 175, 179, 180, 185, 220, 221
    Normandy, 18
    Paris, 179, 245
Franklin, Benjamin, 5, 175, 179

G

Garbadass, Solomon, 253
Gerlach, Adam, xxv, 30, 145, 248
Germany, 5, 7, 92, 118, 180, 184
    Berlin, Germany, 179
    Frankfurt, Germany, 31, 59, 64, 96, 117, 175, 203, 241, 249
    Republic of, 88

Giorgione, Mike, xxv, 136, 262
Global War on Terrorism, 21, 121, 199, 259
Goldsmith, Marshall, 154
Gorbachev, Mikhail, 93, 98
Goudy, Robert, 36
Graves, Mark, 204
Grenada, 123
Guam, 15, 16, 19, 104, 169, 172, 239, 240, 242, 283
Gulf War, 94, 100, 212

H

Hagan, John , 140
Hanssen, Robert, 31
Harare, Zimbabwe, 225
Harry S. Truman Building, 87, 88, 189
Haycook, Stephan, 82, 83, 84, 86, 88, 89, 90, 100, 107, 109, 119, 121, 122, 152, 261
Helsinki, Finland, 181
Herrmann, George, 59, 60, 87, 167, 226, 227
Herzegovina, 99
Hidalgo, Edward, 72
Hiss, Alger, 31
Hoff, Michael, 51, 55
Honduras, 86
Hong Kong, British Colony, 67
Houston, Texas, 130
Hussein, Saddam, 122, 211, 212

I

Ingalsbe, Brandon, 223, 224
Inman, Bobby, 10
    Inman Panel, 10

International Atomic Energy Agency
(IAEA), 6, 184
International Monetary Fund (IMF),
6
International Narcotics Control
Board, 6, 184
Iran, 36, 70, 71, 72, 192, 231
Iran Hostage Crisis (November
1979), 72, 92
Tehran, 70, 72, 73, 74
U.S. Embassy Tehran Overrun
(February 1979), 9, 70
Iraq, 58, 70, 122, 123, 192, 199, 230,
231, 256
Al Hilah, 123
Baghdad, 140, 229
Basra, 123
Kirkuk, 123
Mosul, 123
Multi-National Force- Iraq
(MNF-I), 122, 123
Isbell, Tarey, 119, 121
Israel, 197, 208, 209, 210, 211, 213,
226
Abraham Accords (2020), 210
Egypt-Israel Peace Treaty (1979),
210
Israel-Jordan Peace Treaty
(1994), 210
Jerusalem, 209, 213
Tel Aviv, 209, 210
Istanbul, Turkey, 210, 211, 231
Italy, 172
Rome, 6, 179, 183, 193, 194
Sigonella, Sicily, 19

J

Jackson, Jesse, 117

Jakarta, Indonesia, 33, 241, 242, 246
Japan, xxiii, 5, 16, 247, 248
Hiroshima, Japan, 18
Nagasaki, Japan, 18
Tokyo, Japan, 247
JASON Defense Advisory Panel, 257
Jefferson, Thomas, 3, 175
Jones, Jr., John Paul, 88

K

Karzai, Hamid, 111, 113, 114
Kazakhstan, 206, 229, 236
Astana, 148, 181, 236
Nur-Sultan, 236
Keflavik, Iceland, 19
Kennedy, John F., 23, 145
Khartoum, Sudan, 65
Kinshasa, Zaire, 99
Kissinger, Henry, 95
Koons, Jeff, 245
Korb, Lawrence, 85
Korean War, 19
Kosnick, Scott, 109, 137
Krause, CE1, 252
Kuwait City, Kuwait, 81, 95, 212,
213, 214
Kyiv, Ukraine, 185

L

Lacy, Gharun, 203
Lagos, Nigeria, 225
Lamb, Robert, 85
Lansing, Robert, 7
La Paz, Bolivia, 58, 59, 171
Lima, Peru, 81, 99, 115, 116, 171
Lisbon, Portugal, 123, 251
Livingston, Robert, 5

London, United Kingdom, 177
Lonetree, Clayton, 31
Long, Bryan, 220, 222

Munich, Germany
    1972 Olympics, 9
Muscat, Oman, 214

M

MacArthur, Douglas, 239, 240
Machu Picchu, 172
Madison, James, 3
Maioriello, Joseph, 143, 144, 145, 147, 149, 150, 225, 250, 261
Mak, Chi, 31
Malawi, Mozambique, 225
Managua, Nicaragua, 66
Marshall, John, 3
McConnell, James, 81, 88
McCullough, David, xxvi
Melendez, Carmelo, 100, 102, 103, 105, 138, 143, 187, 188, 261
Memorandum of Agreement, 51, 141
Mexico, 5
    Mexico City, 170, 171
    Mexican Plateau, 171
    Mexican War of Independence, 171
Milligan, Shawn, 117, 118, 119, 188, 189
Mindszenty, Joseph, 192
Mobile Utilities Support Equipment (MUSE), 20, 40, 50
Monroe, James, 3, 175
Montevideo, Uruguay, 170, 171, 172, 253
Moreell, Ben, xxvi, 16, 17
Moscow Embassy Building Control Office (MEBCO), 97, 106
Mount Weather Emergency Operations Center, 106
Mummy, The, 205

N

Nairobi, Kenya, 61, 67, 100, 101, 102, 104, 105, 106, 183, 223, 224, 250
National Defense Strategy, 2018, 36
National Geospatial-Intelligence Agency (NGA), 24
National Reconnaissance Office (NRO), 24
National Security Agency (NSA), 10, 24
Naval Air Systems Command (NAVAIR), 135
Naval Construction Force (NCF), 39, 81, 91, 104, 121, 136, 138, 154, 242, 247, 259
Naval Construction Group (NCG), 40, 50
Naval Construction Regiment (NCR), 50, 120
Naval Construction Training Center (NCTC), 50
Naval Facilities Engineering and Expeditionary Warfare Center (EXWC)...40, 41, 136
Naval Facilities Engineering Systems Command (NAVFAC)...xxv, 15, 20, 39, 40, 41, 42, 49, 72, 73, 91, 92, 104, 107, 119, 122, 135, 136, 137, 149, 154, 155, 162, 242, 259
Naval Information Warfare Systems Command (NAVWAR)...135

Naval Mobile Construction Battalion
(NMCB), 43, 48, 49, 50, 53, 54, 65,
69, 106, 119, 138, 139, 143, 199
ONE (NMCB 1), 81
THREE (NMCB 3), 104, 105
ELEVEN (NMCB 11), 33
FOUR (NMCB 4), 34
ONE THREE THREE (NMCB
133), 199
Naval Sea Systems Command
(NAVSEA), 135
Naval Special Warfare, 60
Navy Crane Center (NCC), 41, 136
Navy Seabees: Mission Tanzania, xxvi,
104
N'Djamena, Chad, 225
Nea Makri, Greece, 19
Netanyahu, Benjamin, 209
New Delhi, India, 110, 231, 233, 234,
235, 236, 241, 242
New York City, New York, 109, 145,
183, 207, 221, 243
Nimitz, Chester, 16
Noel, Cleo, 67
North Atlantic Treaty Organization
(NATO), 5
North Korea, 36, 221
Nursultan, Nazarbayev, 236

O
Obama, Barack, 169, 257
Obama, Michelle, 169
Office of Security (SY), 7, 8, 9, 26,
33, 57
Office of Security Technology (ST),
8, 10, 11, 12, 13, 14 54, 61, 68, 96,
101, 111, 122, 124, 127, 128, 129,
137, 165, 166, 204, 221

Operations
Operation Enduring Freedom,
21
Operation Iraqi Freedom, 21,
117
Project DEMO, 36
TOPHAT, 96
UPHOLD DEMOCRACY, 100

P
Pacheco, Mark, 223
Pakistan, 197, 229, 231, 232, 233
Islamabad, 77, 231
Karachi, 233
Lahore, 233
Peshawar, 233
Palau, 21
Palo Alto, California, 257
Panama, 71
Panama City, 58, 64, 86
Parsam, Brian, 222
Pearl Harbor, 7, 16, 239
Philippines, 15, 169, 234, 239, 240
Corregidor Island, 239, 240
Leyte Gulf, 239
Manila, 64, 94
Manila Bay, Battle of, 240
Pickering, Timothy, 3
Pinckney, Thomas, 5
Pineda, Arnold, 241
Pompeo, Mike, 128, 241
Port au Prince, Haiti, 100
Powell, Colin, 93
Preparatory Commission of the
Comprehensive Nuclear-Test-Ban
Treaty Organization...6, 184
Prime Base Engineer Emergency Force
(BEEF), 35

Pristina, Kosovo, 99
Puerto Rico, 15, 169
    Roosevelt Roads, 19

Q
Quito, Ecuador, 171

R
Rapid Engineer Deployable Heavy
    Operational Repair Squadron,
    Engineer (RED HORSE)...35
Reagan, Ronald, 79, 84, 88, 93, 191
Renken, James, xxvi, 104
Revolutionary War, 3, 24
Rice, Condoleezza, 124
Romero, Steve, 124, 125, 166, 246
Rosslyn, Virginia, 11, 110
Rovaniemi, Finland, 129
Rumsfeld, Donald, 109, 121
Russia, 7, 8, 27, 29, 31, 36, 70, 85, 98,
    107, 128, 129, 185, 187, 229, 236
    Desk, 189
    Leningrad, 186
    Moscow, 25, 31, 35, 63, 66, 68,
        69, 77, 93, 95, 97, 98, 106,
        107, 108, 116, 128, 129, 181,
        185, 186, 187, 188
    Spaso House, 93
    St. Petersburg, 27, 69, 128, 130,
        186
    Vladivostok, 120
    Yekaterinburg, 115
Ryan, Jack, 28

S
San Francisco, California, 130

San Salvador, El Salvador, 76, 86, 87
    Salvadoran Civil War, 76, 86, 87
Saudi Arabia, 214
    Saudi Arabian Embassy Attack
        1973, 67
Schaufelberger, Albert, 86
Sea, Air, and Land (SEAL) Teams,
    xxv, 18
Seattle, Washington, 128
Secret Intelligence Bureau, 7
Shevlin, BU2, 129
Shields, Marvin, 19
Shultz, George, 10, 87, 88, 93
Simpkins, Joe , 31, 96, 186, 187
Smith, Sheldon, 236
Sofia, Bulgaria, 194, 195
South Africa, 206, 217, 218
    Durban, 250
    Pretoria, 200
    Johannesburg, 176, 217, 218
Spain, 171, 239, 251
    Madrid, 251
    Rota, 81, 83
    Spanish American War, 239
Stethem, Robert D., 91, 92
Stevens, Christopher, 125
Stuart, Gilbert, 179
Stuart, Ron, 60, 61, 126, 233, 261
Suggs, Clinton, 91
Switzerland, 5, 68, 183, 184
    Bern, 183
    Davos, 184
    Geneva, 182, 183, 208

T
Thailand, 5, 234
    Ayutthaya, 242
    Bangkok, 88, 176, 240

Thurmont, Maryland, 20, 56, 136
Tillerson, Rex, 127
Tinian, 18
Tirana, Albania, 118, 119, 196
Title 5 USC section 5536, 92
Torres-Torres, Luis, 112, 113
Tracy, Thomas, 71
Transportation Security
    Administration (TSA), 5
Tripoli, Libya, 123, 124, 125, 126
Trump, Donald, 127, 185, 209
Tubbs, Paul, 70, 71

U

Ulaanbaatar, Mongolia, 252
Underwater Construction Team
    (UCT), 18, 47, 50, 91, 139
United Arab Emirates(UAE), 207
    Abu Dhabi, 94, 108, 145, 207,
        208
    Dubai, 56, 200, 204, 207, 208,
        217, 230
United Nations (UN), 5, 6, 59, 79, 88,
    183, 184, 193
    Commission on International
        Trade Law, 6, 184
    Industrial Development
        Organization, 6
    Office of Outer Space Affairs,
        6, 184
    Office on Drugs and Crime, 6,
        184
U.S. Agency for International
    Development (USAID), 5, 225
U.S. Army Corps of Engineers, 169
U.S. Congressional Budget 1974, 67
U.S. Department of Agriculture
    (USDA), 5

U.S. Marine Corps Embassy Security
    Group (MCESG), 44, 145
U.S. Mission to International
    Organizations in Vienna
    (UNVIE)...6, 184
U.S.S. Cole (DDG-67), 108
U.S.S. Maine (ACR-1), 169
U.S.S. Shreveport (LPD-12), 83
U.S.S. Stethem (DDG-63), 92
U.S. Secret Service, 85, 86

V

Valletta, Malta, 126
Vehicle Armoring Program, 57, 58, 65,
    86, 100
    Fully Armored Vehicle (FAV), 58
    Light Armoring Vehicle (LAV),
    58
Vietnam, 19, 27, 34, 63, 81, 88, 234,
    246
    Hanoi, 241, 246
    Vietnam War, 39, 78, 84, 88,
        120, 246

W

Walker, C.C., 58
Wallace, Dustin, 169, 170
Walters, Vernon, 88
War of 1812, 3
Washington, D.C., 7, 44, 46, 50, 65,
    67, 90, 101, 106, 109, 110, 118,
    121, 124, 128, 129, 140, 145, 148,
    152, 162, 165, 166, 176, 180, 204,
    205, 220, 243, 246, 256, 261
Washington, George, 24
White House Communications
    Agency (WHCA), 50

White House Military Office
(WHMO), 20, 50, 136,
World Bank, 6
World Health Organization, 251
World War I (WWI), 4, 6, 7, 15, 16,
184
World War II (WWII), xxiii, xxiv, xxv,
xxvi, 7, 15, 16, 18, 19, 21, 23, 88,
94, 170, 175, 180, 185, 191, 192,
194, 239, 247, 259

Y
Yeltsin, Boris, 94, 98
Yugoslavia, 99
Yugoslav Wars, 117

About the Author

Timothy Dahms is an active-duty U.S. Navy Civil Engineer Corps Officer and former Officer in Charge (OIC) of the Naval Support Unit (NSU), Department of State. Raised in Waukesha, Wisconsin, he received his commission in 2011. He earned a B.S. in Civil Engineering from the University of Wisconsin-Platteville in 2010, obtained his Professional Engineer license in 2016, and earned a M.S. in Civil Engineering from Stanford University in 2022. Throughout his Navy career, Timothy has held assignments worldwide in Jacksonville, North Carolina; Gulfport, Mississippi; Guam; Washington, D.C.; and Palo Alto, Ridgecrest, and San Diego, California. An active member of the Society of American Military Engineers, Timothy regularly presents technical and leadership topics at national conferences. Leading up to his first book *Detachment November*, he has written articles about NSU for *State Magazine* and *The Military Engineer*. Timothy currently resides in San Diego with his wife Maurissa.